If we have not succeeded in changing mankind, who can ever succeed? Tell me, son: Who will change man? Who will save him from himself? Tell me, son: Who will speak on his behalf? Who will speak for me?

—Elie Wiesel,
A Jew Today

SUNY Series on Modern Jewish Literature and Culture

Sarah Blacher Cohen, Editor

Legacy of Night

THE LITERARY UNIVERSE OF ELIE WIESEL

Ellen S. Fine

WITH A FOREWORD BY TERRENCE DES PRES

STATE UNIVERSITY OF NEW YORK PRESS

ALBANY

An earlier version of Chapter 3 appeared in *Responses to Elie Wiesel: Critical Essays by Major Jewish and Christian Scholars*, ed. Harry James Cargas. © 1978. Reprinted by permission of Persea Books, New York.

Published by
State University of New York Press, Albany

© 1982 State University of New York

For information, address State University of New York
Press, State University Plaza, Albany, N.Y., 12246

Library of Congress Cataloging in Publication Data

Fine, Ellen S.
  Legacy of night, the literary universe of Elie Wiesel.

(SUNY series on modern Jewish literature and culture)
Bibliography
Includes index.
1. Wiesel, Elie, 1928-   —Criticism and interpretation. 2. Holocaust, Jewish (1939-
1945), in literature. I. Title. II. Series.
PQ2683.I32Z68   813'.54   81-14601
ISBN 0-87395-589-7   AACR2
ISBN 0-87395-590-0 (pbk.)

To the memory of my father
BENJAMIN FINE
whose humanity and wisdom
have shaped the pages of this book

Contents

List of Abbreviations

The following are abbreviations of the English translations of Elie Wiesel's works used in this study. The translations are from the French.

A　　The Accident. Trans. Anne Borchardt (1962). In Night, Dawn, The Accident: Three Tales. New York: Hill & Wang, 1972.

BJ　　A Beggar in Jerusalem. Trans. Lily Edelman and Elie Wiesel. New York: Random House, 1970.

D　　Dawn. Trans. Frances Frenayne (1961). In Night, Dawn, The Accident: Three Tales, New York: Hill & Wang, 1972.

GF　　The Gates of the Forest. Trans. Frances Frenayne. New York: Holt Rinehart and Winston, 1966.

JT　　A Jew Today. Trans. Marion Wiesel. New York: Random House, 1978.

LT　　Legends of Our Time. Trans. Steven Donadio. New York: Holt, Rinehart and Winston, 1968.

MG　　Messengers of God: Biblical Portraits and Legends. Trans. Marion Wiesel. New York: Random House, 1976.

N　　Night. Trans. Stella Rodway (1960); foreword by François Mauriac. In Night, Dawn, The Accident: Three Tales. New York: Hill & Wang, 1972.

O　　The Oath. Trans. Marion Wiesel. New York: Random House, 1973.

OGA   *One Generation After.* Trans. Lily Edelman and Elie Wiesel. New York: Random House, 1970.

SF   *Souls on Fire: Portraits and Legends of Hasidic Masters.* Trans. Marion Wiesel. New York: Random House, 1972.

T   *The Testament.* Trans. Marion Wiesel. New York: Summit Books, 1981.

TBW   *The Town Beyond the Wall.* Trans. Stephen Becker. New York: Holt, Rinehart and Winston, 1964.

Foreword

THE HOLOCAUST would seem to have no end. The destruction of Europe's Jews stopped in 1945, but the spectacle of the death camps continues to haunt us, and not merely as a fading memory or as a bad dream that lingers. This memory does not fade, this nightmare goes on and on. The Holocaust *happened*. That in itself is the intractable fact we can neither erase nor evade. And the more we think of it, the more it intrudes to occupy our minds, until *l'univers concentrationnaire* becomes a demonic anti-world that undermines our own. After Auschwitz, nothing seems stable or unstained—not the values we live by, not our sense of self-worth, not existence itself. We dwell in aftermath, and I do not think I exaggerate to say that the Holocaust has forced upon us a radical rethinking of everything we are and do. Where this enterprise will lead I cannot say. Terminal despair is a real possibility. So is nuclear holocaust; what did happen can happen, and historical precedent tends to influence options for the future. The stakes, in other words, are very high. But exactly for these reasons we have turned with new determination to the study of Holocaust matters, hoping thereby to alert understanding, to reveal the enormity of our present predicament, and most of all, to transform our expanding awareness of man's capacity for destruction into a kind of consciousness identical with conscience.

Every age produces the event which defines it, and in our time the Holocaust is *ours*. It demands that we face the kind of limitless horror our technological and bureaucratic civilization makes possible, and also—if we are to recover the benefit of hope—that we give an account of goodness commensurate with the facts of the Final Solution. The exterminating angel has arisen before us, blocking all light, demanding battle in a night without promise of dawn. Where shall it come from, the strength to face this encounter?

Forty years after the event, many books have been written. Conferences proliferate, the number of courses offered by our schools and universities are increasing. This is all to the good, a necessary step in our collective effort to establish genuine forms of response. The facts, at least, are being recognized. Denial is no longer possible. But the more we know, the less we feel assured of understanding. The darkness does not dissipate; it seems, on the contrary, to deepen. We need guidance. But from whom can it come? Not from our political leadership, certainly, busy trading blood for oil. And not from the institutions of a discredited culture which made possible—in thought, and then in deed—the death of the six million. It shall have to come from the victims, as moral knowledge always has. What we need is a voice, a voice arising from the darkness it survives. To hear this voice and heed it becomes the beginning of wisdom. That, at least, is Ellen Fine's belief, and on its basis she has written a remarkable study. The voice of the witness is the source of conscience, and therefore of guidance, in the post-Auschwitz world.

There are many such voices, many survivors of the camps whose mission has been "to tell the world." And every word given in testimony becomes part of a message—a new language of the human soul— earned at infinite cost. But as Ellen Fine reminds us in *Legacy of Night*, one voice above others has repeatedly called to us to receive and attend it. Without respite, rooted in memory's pain, Elie Wiesel's voice has borne patient witness for more than twenty years—since the publication of *Night* in 1958—and has addressed us with such steadfast care that by now it speaks not only to us and for us but also *in* us. Here, then, is our starting point. Here, amid this unspeakable darkness, is a voice—and a vision—we can trust.

At first he was ignored. Then his work was said to be limited to Jewish themes, Jewish problems. But if the Holocaust was a catastrophe for the Jews, it was a tragedy for the Christians, a product of Christian culture, a disaster encompassing the whole of Western civilization. Wiesel therefore bears witness to an event which touches us all. His voice carries the survivor's special authority, his reputation has become international, and by now the man himself is deeply reverenced. Fame, however, can be a doubtful blessing. It can obscure as much as it reveals, and Wiesel has not escaped this paradox. As he has said of himself, if in the beginning he spoke in order to change the world, he continues to speak so that the world shall not change him. Indeed, the world changes slowly if at all, partly because, having paid respect to the man, we assume that we know his meaning. As if, perhaps, the survivor's message were but a disturbing cliché. That is often the fate of men and women who become our moral heroes. We end up taking them for granted. Or we make them into symbols whose meaning *we* assign. And then, of course, we are no longer listening.

Yet we do honor Wiesel, and we know instinctively that his task is central to ethical enlightenment. But that is only the beginning, for what does bearing witness entail? How did Wiesel *become* the voice we now know? After all, the distance between Auschwitz and a lecture hall in New York is impossibly far. The condition of survivorship and the profession of writing are not necessarily one. And between the boy clinging to his father as they saw small children dumped living into pits of flame, and the man at his desk writing books which are the resonance of that first indelible sight—what passages of mind and soul conjoin that past and this present? Does the survivor simply have a voice, or as Ellen Fine suggests, must some struggle between the "dead" self and the "surviving" self be won before his voice may truly speak? And if, finally, the act of bearing witness has its own logic and is not merely a mode of static repetition, what is its inner dynamic, its spiritual history or, as it appears in Wiesel's novels, its own specific "story"?

If we read Wiesel's fiction as Ellen Fine has read it, we shall know that bearing witness does have its own life and function. It is a special case of conscience in action, a form of vigilance that cannot cease. And like all behavior that is essential to our humanness, it has a definite structure. Its origin was the impact of the death camps. Its medium is the terribly painful drama of memory. And its intended end is a second beginning in ourselves, we who must live in the Holocaust's shadow. The witness re-establishes human continuity, speaking for the dead and to the living, preserving the past in order to guard the future. This is a complicated process, darkly empowered; but Ellen Fine sums it up in a brilliant formulation by restating Wiesel's notion that *to listen to the witness is to become a witness.*

This means, first of all, that having crossed a threshold of moral being by our reception of the survivor's voice, we are moved by a sense of obligation to pass it on, to transmit the survivor's testimony so that others may likewise be inspired and transformed. But there is more. We become participants, we share in an active bond between the survivor and ourselves—and here especially we receive a truly remarkable gift. For by coming to understand the survivor's experience as a witness, we come in our lesser way to comprehend the condition of aftermath. The capacity to speak and mobilize conscience is *not* given; it comes through precarious struggle. Little by little, after many obstacles, the survivor's voice begins to exist. Only slowly, after passing through a realm where death and life contend, does the survivor arrive at his identity as witness.

The psychic depth at which this experience occurs cannot be reached by normal modes of analytic discourse. How then shall we know it? We shall require a mode of perception as profound as the spiritual ordeal it presumes to reveal, and this vehicle can only be the arts—in Elie Wiesel's case his fiction. Here is a witness who is also an artist, and what he gives us through imaginative re-creation is the spiritual "story" of survivorship establishing its identity, then creating its voice, and then, out of darkness and against the counter-weight of silence, beginning to speak. To approach the mystery of the survivor's voice through Wiesel's fiction is to assume two principles which Dr. Fine soundly justifies: first, that we shall learn more from artistic representation than from discursive statement; and then, that if Wiesel's novels are read in the order in which they are written, they reveal themselves to be integral units of a larger revelation, a spiritual narrative in serial form, a faithful symbolization of the journey that began in *Night* and has come full-circle—the older themes summed up and re-opened at a higher level—in *The Testament*.

This has been Ellen Fine's aim and method, and with extreme sensitivity she has examined Wiesel's novels to uncover the "story" in terms of which the individual books, read in sequence, are essential episodes. Dr. Fine has discovered that the plot of Wiesel's larger story is *the becoming of the witness,* and that in each book the protagonist embodies conditions to be engaged and overcome if the survivor-as-witness is to fulfill his destiny. There is, to begin with, the "Lazarene" figure who dominates the initial struggle between the "dead" and the "surviving" parts of the self, along with the need of the son to conclude or at least carry on "the unfinished story of the father." There is then the motion of return, back to the "dead town," to the inevitable encounter with the indifferent spectator, to homecoming as perpetual exile, and likewise the emergence of "the double" with whom the surviving self must finally merge. Gradually the self re-enters life and community and assumes the burden of bearing witness despite the strong claims of silence, after which the survivor's "voice" is ready to command our attention. To speak is then to live. What remains is the re-establishment of severed connections, between fathers and sons, generation unto generation, and especially between the dead and those who remain and come after. The emblem of this last task is "the Book," which in turn affirms anew the sacred power of words to recover human communion and, against the usurpation of silence, the redemption of language as the medium through which silence is preserved and transcended.

Elie Wiesel is not an ordinary writer. We cannot read him without the desire to change, to lead better lives. His books are of the kind that save souls, and for this reason Ellen Fine's *Legacy of Night* is not an ordinary exercise in literary criticism. If to listen to the witness is to become one, then to approach Wiesel's fiction with sympathy and rigor, as Dr. Fine does, is to grow, to gather power and move with cumulative force toward a vision which may be terrible in its torment but which greatly enlightens and uplifts. No living writer knows our predicament better than Elie Wiesel, and his novels touch us to the quick, bearing directly upon our deepest problems. How *shall* we live in the latter days of this awful century? We are like peasants divining reality by the rumors we happen to hear, but who also, when the wind turns, scent fearful secrets and at night detect a faint infernal glare above the horizon of our local world. And so we listen, no longer fooled by rumor and official reports, listen for a voice as steady as the unseen stars. Thanks to Wiesel it is there. To read his fiction is to partake of a sorrow that shall perhaps never subside but which gives hope the character of a cause. The victims have perished. The future is uncertain. The cause, meanwhile, is ourselves.

TERRENCE DES PRES
Colgate University

Acknowledgments

I WISH TO express my deepest appreciation to the following scholars and writers who contributed to the preparation of this book through their invaluable insights as well as their intellectual and moral support: Terrence Des Pres, Daniel Stern, Rosette Lamont, Lawrence Langer, Irving Halperin, Harry James Cargas and Erika Ostrovsky.

I feel especially grateful to Elie Wiesel, not only for his literary universe which has profoundly enriched my life, but also for his continuing and warm encouragement.

My thanks also go to the staff of Les Editions du Seuil in Paris for graciously granting me access to their extensive archives.

Finally, a special note of gratitude to my family, friends, and colleagues whose understanding and dedication helped me to persevere.

New York 1981

Introduction

Ce que les gens désirent tous—quelques-uns à leur insu—c'est d'être témoins de leur temps, témoins de leur vie, c'est d'être, devant tous, leurs propres témoins.

—Jean-Paul Sartre

Survivors of the Holocaust, a term designating the planned mass murder of the Jews by the Nazis during World War II,[1] are confronted with a difficult task. They have experienced the total collapse of the world in which they lived, the shattering of a civilized society, and the dissolution of its moral values. They have encountered evil in its most extreme form. Pushed beyond human limits, they endured a catastrophe that resists all rational modes of interpretation. Some survivors have chosen silence as a way of commemorating their losses, while others are compelled to speak out—to bear witness. The act of bearing witness is often perceived as a sacred mission, a responsibility, and a command—the means of paying tribute to the dead and of reestablishing a connection to life.

The imperative to testify characterizes the life and literature of Holocaust survivor Elie Wiesel. Obsessed with the need to remember and to transmit the story and history of the six million Jews annihilated by the Nazis, Wiesel has committed himself to the role of witness (or what is called in French *témoin*) as the justification for his existence. He considers writing "not a profession, but an occupation, a duty,"[2] and his primary function as a writer is to give testimony. His *témoignages*, novels, plays, legends, essays, dialogues, and speeches form concentric circles around the dark event of the Holocaust and the identity of the Jew in its aftermath.

Essentially a messenger deeply concerned with informing and warning the world of the horrors of genocide, Wiesel tells his own tale—that of a young Orthodox Jewish boy growing up in a small Eastern European town destined to be destroyed by the Nazi invaders. He describes the odyssey that led from his native town of Sighet, nestled in the Carpathian mountains of Transylvania, to the macabre *univers concentrationnaire* of Auschwitz and Buchenwald, and finally to postwar France, Israel, and the United States. His works retrace this journey, recollecting and chronicling the personal and historical circumstances that have structured his life before, during, and after the Holocaust.

Wiesel writes from the perspective of a witness-storyteller who knows that the essence of his story—filled with unanswered political, philosophical, and theological questions—is impossible to communicate. Nevertheless he has chosen the vocation of writer, with the objective of using written language as a vehicle of communion. In his literary universe, he seeks to assimilate the multiple levels of his encounter with history, to form legends and myth out of memory. His response to the voyage into Night takes the form of artistic creation, which, as Albert Camus has noted, does not remove us from the drama of our time, but instead brings us closer.[3] Elie Wiesel's books represent a mode of survival, an attempt to come to terms with existence in a post-Holocaust epoch. At the same time, they demonstrate a survivor's ability to fictionalize the raw material and transmute it into works of art.

The purpose of this study is a close reading of Wiesel's creative testimony as literature. The network of recurring and interlacing themes, leitmotifs and images will be explored as they first appear in the memoir, *Night*—foundation of the author's entire oeuvre—and subsequently unfold in the novels bound to its legacy: *Dawn, The Accident, The Town Beyond the Wall, The Gates of the Forest, A Beggar in Jerusalem, The Oath,* and *The Testament,* written from 1958 to 1980. Wiesel's other collections of tales, essays, and portraits will be used to clarify and expand the motifs found in the fiction. Critical analyses have already treated the theological references in Wiesel's work.[4] My focus is on the structure and fabric of his fictional landscape as seen through the texts themselves. The central motif of *the witness* will serve as the organizing principle around which themes and subthemes emerge, evolve, and are transformed.

The witness can be defined as the person who sees or knows by his or her presence and perception; and the one who testifies in words and deeds. In the first case, he or she is an observer, a spectator; in the second, an active participant who chooses to give testimony. One must distinguish therefore between witnessing an event and bearing witness to it, between observing a phenomenon and taking the responsibility for speaking about it.

In Wiesel's novels there is a general progression from witnessing to bearing witness. The survivor-protagonist, whose voice has been silenced by nocturnal flames, struggles to express himself and to recover the faculty of speech. He slowly learns to reach out to others and to reaffirm his identity as a member of the human community. The assertion of the voice is linked to the vocation of witness and is at the core of the thematic development. In their quest for a voice, the Wieselean characters pass through various stages, reflecting the author's own spiritual-intellectual itinerary. Their story is basically his, for he is very much a part of many of his protagonists. Yet, transposed into a fictional mode, Wiesel's story exposes the reader to the intensely problematic nature of the witness. The contradictions inherent in the act of testifying are revealed in both conscious and unconscious forms. A close study of the texts discloses an underlying tension between the compulsion to tell the tale and the fear of betraying the sanctity of the subject. The author has created characters who allow him to confront himself, and a new kind of protagonist—emblem of our times—issues forth from the literary mind after Auschwitz: *the protagonist as witness.*

Wiesel's novels lend themselves to a chronological investigation. They follow a logical sequence, each exploring a particular option open to the survivor after the journey to the end of night: killing, suicide, madness, faith and friendship, return from exile, silence, and involvement in revolutionary movements, in history itself. "The books came one after the other to answer the questions I was asking myself," Wiesel tells us. "Each time a gate closed, the possibilities diminished, and one hope after another was stripped away."[5] But if each text shuts a door, it also points the way to the volume that follows. The continuity and cumulative force of his oeuvre are sustained by the repetition of themes and the reappearance of characters who resemble one other. The author even joins one work to the next by a deliberately chosen phrase. "I always smuggle into every book one sentence which is the substance of the next books—a Jewish tradition," he declares.[6]

This study will discuss the novels in chronological order, not for the purpose of interpreting the manifest theme around which each book revolves, but rather to trace the course of the protagonist as witness: his sharpened consciousness as bearer of memory, the mythification and demythification of his role, as the act of speaking—and of writing—becomes more difficult. To gain insight into Wiesel's

treatment of the theme and its impact on his function as a writer is my
objective. In order to understand the struggles of the fictional witnesses, let us first consider what personally motivated Wiesel to become
an author. Two major factors influenced his dedication to the written
word: his religious background as an Orthodox Jew and the event of
the Holocaust.

Elie Wiesel was born on September 30, 1928 in Sighet, a border
town with a long and complicated political history. Once a part of the
Austrian Empire, the town was given up to Hungary, handed over to
Rumania and then taken back by Hungary at the beginning of World
War II. During the war, Germany incorporated Sighet into the Third
Reich. The Soviet Union took over at the end of the war, finally
rendering the town to Rumania. Presently located about a kilometer
from the Soviet frontier, Sighet has approximately 120,000 inhabitants.

Wiesel grew up in the town's *shtetl*, or Jewish section. His father,
Shlomo, was a middle-class shopkeeper who spent much of his time
working for the community. In the early years of the war he helped
save Polish Jews who had escaped to Hungary. Because of his efforts he
spent a few months in jail. Shlomo instilled humanist values in his only
son (Wiesel had three sisters) and encouraged him to learn modern
Hebrew and to read its literature. His father, Wiesel tells us, represented "reason" and his mother "faith."[7] The daughter of Dodye Feig, a
fervent Hasid and a farmer who lived in a village near Sighet, Sarah
Feig was a highly cultured woman who insisted that her son study the
Torah, Talmud, mystical doctrines of the Kabbala, and the teachings of
Hasidic masters. She wanted him to be both a rabbi and a Ph.D.

Immersed in religious texts, the young Wiesel learned to venerate
the Book and to regard everything connected to the word as sacred.
"Jewish theology made a writer of me," he states.[8] At the age of twelve
he wrote a long commentary on the Bible, which he found some twenty
years later under a pile of discarded volumes in the only synagogue left
in Sighet. Had it not been for the war, he probably would have
continued to write commentaries on the Bible and Talmud. If anyone
had told the pious youth pouring over the same page of the same book
of the Torah for days on end that some day he would become a
novelist—and a French novelist at that—he would have turned his
back, convinced that he was being mistaken for someone else.

To an Orthodox Jew in the *shtetl*, novels were puerile, a waste of
time. How could the fictional universe invented by man compare to the
transcendent mystery of holy scripture? In the Orthodox tradition the

scribe or *sofer* is highly respected in contrast to the writer of fiction, who is considered a *batlan,* someone who has nothing better to do. Several years after the war Wiesel returned to his grandfather's town to see the old Hasidic rabbi, who at once recognized him as "the grandson of Dodye Feig." Asked how he earned his living, Wiesel replied that he wrote. "You write?" the rabbi responded in disbelief. "That's your work? Are you serious? You do nothing else? No other profession? You spend your life writing, that's all?"[9]

The Holocaust was to radically change Wiesel's destiny and take him far from the kingdom of Dodye Feig. In March 1944 the Germans came to Hungary; one month later they began the mass deportations from Transylvania, including fifteen thousand Jews from Sighet and approximately eighteen thousand from neighboring villages. At the age of fifteen, Wiesel was plunged from the stability of small-town life into the grotesque universe of Night. Along with his parents and three sisters, he was deported to Auschwitz, where his mother and younger sister were immediately sent to the gas chambers; his two older sisters managed to survive. Wiesel and his father stayed together as they were shunted from Auschwitz to Buchenwald where the youth watched his father slowly die. This was to mark him for the rest of his life, and his vow to bear witness to his father's murder is reflected throughout his writing. Indeed, Wiesel's entire literary structure appears to be founded on the need to transmit his father's legacy and to reaffirm the paternal authority by telling the story.[10]

After his liberation from Buchenwald, Wiesel wanted to go to Palestine but was prevented by British immigration restrictions. Refusing to be repatriated to Sighet, he was put on a train with four hundred other child refugees who had been in Buchenwald. Originally destined to go to Belgium, the train was rerouted to France by De Gaulle. At the border the young passengers were asked if they wanted to become French citizens, and Wiesel, unable to understand, failed to respond. Consequently, he remained stateless until 1963, when he was granted American citizenship.

At first, Wiesel spent time in Normandy, France, under the auspices of the children's aid organization, Oeuvres du Secours aux Enfants, and then went to Paris where he studied the Talmud and earned a living as a tutor in Yiddish, Hebrew, and the Bible. A young French philosopher, François Wahl, helped him to learn French by introducing him to the great classical authors, beginning with Racine.[11] Wiesel learned the language by listening in silence. He took courses at the Sorbonne in philosophy and literature and, although he never officially completed his studies, he wrote a long dissertation on comparative ascetism. In postwar France he was exposed to intellectual movements such as existentialism and to the thinking of such men of letters as Albert Camus,[12] Jean-Paul Sartre, and André Malraux, whose philosophical and moral explorations of the human condition and whose notion of the writer as witness to his times were to influence his own work. Wiesel also seems to have incorporated into his writing the later stylistic techniques of the French *Nouveau Roman* which interrogate reality and question systems of time and causality found in established narrative forms.

Learning French for Wiesel was like entering a house that welcomed him; it offered him a haven, a refuge, a home, and meant a "new beginning, a new possibility, a new world."[13] The adoption of French as his written language marked a significant change in consciousness—the death of one era and the initiation into another. It was the expression of a certain faith in the ability to start again, a distancing from the brutal experience of the Holocaust, a rejection of the past. Yiddish, his mother tongue, and Hebrew, the language of his early educational training, evoked painful emotions, while the Hungarian and German languages were those of the oppressors. Wiesel therefore chose French as the foundation for rebuilding his new house and for reconstructing his intellectual life. Although he eventually published newspaper articles in Hebrew, Yiddish, and even in English (which he learned on a trip to India in 1952), his books have always been written in French, a language that he says "lends itself to narrative."[14]

Adapting to an unfamiliar linguistic framework demands discipline and a shift in orientation. For the young survivor of the Holocaust, French represented a Cartesian language, dominated by reason, logic, and clarity. To introduce Midrashic tales and mystical notions of the Kabbala into a nonmystical language was a challenge and form of defiance. "It is a question of plunging into a language that is foreign to me and expressing ideas not made for it," Wiesel observes.[15] Piotr Rawicz, a survivor from the Ukraine who also writes in French, confirms this notion: "Elie Wiesel enriches the French domain with philosophical matters and emotional states that would have made their entrance into the letters of Descartes' land with difficulty if it had not been for him."[16] Indeed, Wiesel's style is unique because of the way it fuses aspects of the French novel with Jewish lore. His narrative structure is often fragmented: characterized by shifts in points of view, disjointed images, contradictory statements, and a blending of fact and fiction, of history and imagination. The effect produced is similar to the mode of the *Nouveau Roman* and, at the same time, is in keeping with the tradition of the Jewish storyteller who weaves folktales, anecdotes, and parables into the fabric of his texts, transmitting messages that are highly ambiguous. This peculiar combination of French stylistics and Jewish legends has caused some critics to view Wiesel's works as collections of short sketches rather than completely developed novels,[17] although in his most recent novel, *The Testament*, the main character and plot are more fully elaborated than in any of the previous books. Many commentators in France have called Wiesel a poet and a visionary rather than a novelist in the conventional sense.[18]

It is not the intention of this study, however, to establish whether Wiesel's works are great novels. The thrust of his writing does not lie in his literary techniques and he has openly rejected the notion of art for art's sake. He is basically a storyteller with something to say. If the French language has provided the edifice for Wiesel's creative endeavors, his motivation to become a writer and the subject matter of his publications are clearly not to be found in the French heritage. He first realized that he was going to write when he looked at his face after the liberation of Buchenwald and knew that he had to speak about "*that* face and *that* mirror and *that* change"; "I knew that anyone who remained alive had to become a storyteller, a messenger, had to speak up."[19] The Holocaust thus imposed the vocation of writer upon Wiesel as it did upon other survivors living in France, such as Anna Langfus and Piotr Rawicz, who might never have written novels if it had not been for their concentration camp experience.[20]

Although Wiesel made a vow to keep silent for ten years after the war, during that time he read widely and thought constantly about the Holocaust in his travels around the world as a correspondent for Israeli and French newspapers. Conscious of the need to bear witness, he did not know how to approach a subject so overwhelming in its magnitude that words could only distort it. Nonetheless, the ten years of silent reflection prepared him for his meeting in 1954 with the French Catholic writer François Mauriac, who encouraged the young journalist to write about his journey into darkness. Mauriac became a kind of patron to him, a protector, a friend.

Two years after his interview with Mauriac (described in detail in *A Jew Today*), Wiesel published his first work, written in Yiddish, *Un di Velt hot Geshvign* (*And the World Remained Silent*), an eight-hundred-page [1956] *témoignage* of his life in the death camp universe. In 1958 he condensed it and translated it into French as *La Nuit*. Deeply moved by the book, Mauriac wrote the foreword. The text became a personal Bible for Wiesel, forming the nucleus of his subsequent volumes, the center around which all of his tales revolve. The publication also marked the beginning of his literary career and affirmed his task as *témoin:* never to forget the voices of those who perished in the Nazi concentration camps.

In effect, the desire to commemorate the dead and to give expression to their presence through his voice is one of the primary sources of Wiesel's will to bear witness. His words mourn and elegize his family, friends and the little *shtetl* of his youth peopled with rabbis, teachers, beggars, and madmen—figures who frequently reappear in his works. By building a monument to them in the form of tales and myths, he creates a memorial to a community deprived of its graves. The dead hover over him as he engraves his testimony onto the printed page: "When one writes, thinking of those invisible victims who should be his readers and are actually his writers (because he's writing their story), then one is very humble and very daring at the same time—in writing a sentence or when translating an image."[21] For Wiesel, the act of recording becomes analogous to inscriptions on a gravestone, a lasting message sculpted into the resistant matter: "For me writing is a *matzeva,* an invisible tombstone, erected to the memory of the dead unburied. Each word corresponds to a face, a prayer, the one needing the other so as not to sink into oblivion" (LT, 8).

The author's resolution to establish a permanent testament to those who have disappeared signifies a commitment to his faith. The Jews have been traditionally considered witnesses in the historical and religious sense,[22] upholding a legacy that commands them to record, transmit, and remember in order to assure the continuity of history. To be a Jew for Wiesel means to testify: "To bear witness to what is, and to what is no longer. . . . For the contemporary Jewish writer, there can be no theme more human, no project more universal" (OGA, 174). As a writer and a Jew (and Wiesel does not separate the two), he takes upon himself the entire destiny of his people from beginning to now and assumes the function of *le moi-somme,* or collective spokesman: "When I say 'I', I express a certain totality."[23] He believes that all events in Jewish history are linked: every Jew must see himself as having received the Torah at Sinai, having witnessed the destruction of the Temple, and having participated in the Holocaust. According to Wiesel, "Any Jew born before, during or after the Holocaust must enter it again in order to take it upon himself."[24] His strong sense of solidarity with his community has thus provided the framework for his position as a witness whose undying pledge is to work for the survival of his people.

The threat to the survival of the Jews is also a threat to mankind in general, and it is from his particular experience that Wiesel probes the more universal human condition, speaking out for nations oppressed and in danger of being destroyed: Cambodia, Biafra, Paraguay, and Bangladesh. "The Jewish and human conditions become one—a concentric circle, one within the other, not one against the other or one replacing the other," he declares.[25] The isolation, dehumanization, and devastation of one-third of the Jewish population during the Nazi regime reflect the violence and victimization of twentieth-century man *in extremis*. Wiesel continues to protest the injustice of a civilization that permitted the massacre of six million Jews and still tolerates torture and genocide. He believes that the task of the writer-as-witness is "not to appease or flatter, but to disturb, to warn, to question by questioning oneself" (JT, 108). His moral obligation is to awaken the conscience of an indifferent society.

Yet he has felt frustrated in his attempts to communicate and has gravitated toward silence as an alternative form of testimony. Throughout his texts there is an unresolved conflict between the urge to cry out and the need to remain silent, resulting in a complex thematic interplay. Silence is both destructive and beneficial: it is death, absence, betrayal, and exile, as well as purification and affirmation of being. Words, too, are double-edged: they can misrepresent what they aim to describe but have the power to create, reconstruct, and render immortal. The dialectic of silence and language—of transmitting silence through language—is at the core of the theme of the witness.

Wiesel finds himself in a paradoxical situation. He insists that it is impossible to write about the Holocaust, that Auschwitz negates the foundations of art, defies the imagination, and lies beyond the grasp of literature. He has sought to change his focus and widen his concentric circles by turning to historical and contemporary Jewish themes outside the realm of the Holocaust. Yet, he persists in remembering and in transmitting the legacy of Night through the enduring power of his words and silence.

"True despair," says Albert Camus, "is the agony of death, the grave or the abyss. If he speaks, if he reasons, above all if he writes, immediately the brother reaches out his hand, the tree is justified, love is born."[26] Elie Wiesel has chosen to reach out: he has given birth to a literary universe in which his protagonists testify for him. They tell his story, the story of how a young survivor, mute and passive, transforms himself into an articulate messenger. It is these characters—*the witnesses of the witness*—who provide insights for both the reader and the author. "Novelists ought not to speak," he observes. "Their mission consists in listening to other voices, including those of their own creations, of their own characters."[27] We, too, as readers, will listen to the voices from Elie Wiesel's inner landscape so that we may behold the other face of history and may preserve its memory: for to listen to a witness is to become one.

1

Witness of the Night

Dans la nuit, on trouve la mort, on atteint l'oubli. Mais cette autre nuit est la mort qu'on ne trouve pas, est l'oubli qui s'oublie, qui est au sein de l'oubli, le souvenir sans repos.
—Maurice Blanchot

Je fuis la nuit et je la porte sur mes épaules.
—Elie Wiesel

ELIE WIESEL's first book, *Night,* published originally in Yiddish in 1956, translated into French in 1958, and into English in 1960,[1] depicts the long journey into Holocaust darkness. The work defies all categories. It has been described as personal memoir, autobiographical narrative, fictionalized autobiography, nonfictional novel, and human document. Essentially, it is a *témoignage,* a first-hand account of the concentration camp experience, succinctly related by the fifteen-year-old narrator, Eliezer. With Kafka-like lucidity, the narrator initiates us, the readers, into the grotesque world of the Holocaust and compels us to observe the event taking place before our eyes. Before all else, Eliezer is a witness, who tells the tale in a direct and linear mode. He does not interpret or explain the facts but allows them to speak for themselves. The young boy lacks the self-consciousness of later Wieselean protagonists who are more aware of their mission to testify.

However, *Night* is more than a *témoignage,* and the narrator is more than a witness. While he effaces himself before the events, we also hear his own voice—a voice that recounts more than mere circumstances. "The child in *Night* is too old to write about children," Wiesel has remarked.[2] Indeed, the words of the author-narrator depict the metamorphosis of a child into an old man, his abrupt passage into the blackness and silence of nonbeing in one never-ending night. The voice of the child-witness reveals the effect of the landscape of violence upon the psyche of one individual. It communicates the vision of a nightmare: the voyage from a familiar to an unknown world, a son's perception of the slow death of his father and the spiritual death of himself. As François Mauriac, who wrote the foreword to *Night*, points out: "In truth, it is much less a deposition dealing with historical facts than the inner adventure of a soul who believed for a time that God, too, had been massacred—God, the eternally innocent."[3]

Ten years after the actual experience, Elie Wiesel brought forth this "inner" testimony and was thus able to reconstitute his fragmented memories in such a way as to form a structured and coherent narrative. The result is a text of literary quality, rich in themes that, lay the foundation for the author's subsequent works. A close examination of two of the book's principal motifs—*night* and *father-son*—help to shed light on the central theme of the witness, the generating principle of Wiesel's literary universe. For, to live through the forces of darkness and to care for another shows the persistence of self in a system principally designed to annihilate the self. To survive and to testify affirms the will to remain human in the aftermath of the inhuman. The event is unthinkable, the story impossible to transmit. Yet from another level of consciousness, the voice of the witness transcends *Night's* sovereignty and takes on a life of its own.

THE KINGDOM OF NIGHT

The theme of night pervades Elie Wiesel's memoir as suggested by the title itself, which encompasses the overall Holocaust landscape— *l'univers concentrationnaire*—a world synonymous with methodical brutality and radical evil. The dark country presented to us is self-contained and self-structured, governed by its own criminal gods who have created laws based upon a death-dominated ideology. Wiesel uses the word *Night* throughout his writing to denote this strange sphere, unreal and unimaginable in its otherworldliness.[4] He speaks of that "kingdom of the night where one breathed only hate, contempt and self-disgust" in "A Plea for the Dead" (LT, 191); and in one of his speeches, refers to "the dark kingdom which . . . represented the other side of Sinai, the dark face of Sinai." "We were the children of Night," he proclaims, "and we knew more about truth and the paths leading to it than the wisest philosophers on earth."[5]

Eliezer, the narrator of the book, is, in effect, a child of the Night, who relates the journey from the friendly Jewish community tucked away in the mountains of Transylvania to Auschwitz—the frightening and foreign capital of the kingdom of Night. During the course of the trip certain events take place which stand out in the narrator's memory and often occur during the nocturnal hours. The theme of night is linked to the passage of time in the account itself. Within the larger framework, more specific phases, characterized by the motifs of the *first* and *last* night, structure the descent into terror and madness, and point to the demarcations between the known and unknown.

Once Eliezer enters Auschwitz, he loses his sense of time and reality. Darkness envelops him and penetrates within: his spirit is shrouded, his God eclipsed, the blackness eternal. Pushed to his limits, the narrator experiences the *other* haunted and interminable night defined by Maurice Blanchot as "the death that one does not find"; "the borders of which must not be crossed."[6] The intermingling of particular nights with Night, the measuring of time alongside timelessness, corresponds to a style that interweaves a direct narration of events with subtle reflections upon the experience.

In 1941, when the narrative begins, Eliezer is a deeply Orthodox boy of twelve, living in the town of Sighet, situated on the Hungarian-Rumanian border. The word *night* is first mentioned with regard to his evening visits to the synagogue: "During the day I studied the Talmud, and at night I ran to the synagogue to weep over the destruction of the Temple" (N, 14). While this nocturnal lamentation is part of a religious tradition, its prominent position in the text can be interpreted as a prediction of the bleak shadow cast upon Jewish communities throughout twentieth-century Europe.

Eliezer spends many of his evenings in the semidarkness of the synagogue where half-burned candles flicker as he converses with Moché, his chosen master of the Kabbala; they exchange ideas about the nature of God, man, mysticism, and faith. Night, here, exudes a poetic and pious atmosphere as the time for prayer, interrogation and dialogue within the context of the secure and the traditional. Indeed, the narrator's experience of benevolent night begins to change with Moché's expulsion from Sighet. Deported because he is a foreign Jew, Moché is sent to Poland, driven to a forest along with hundreds of other Jews, and shot in front of freshly dug pits. Wounded in the leg only, he rises from the mass grave and miraculously makes his way back to Sighet to recount what he calls "the story of my own death." "Jews, listen to me," he cries out. "It's all I ask of you, I don't want money or pity. Only listen to me" (17). No one in the *shtetl*, including Eliezer, believes his tale, and Moché is forced into silence, Wiesel's first example of the unheeded witness whose futile warnings predict the fate of the entire Jewish community.[7] This occurs towards the end of 1942.

Without being explicit, Wiesel's narrative closely follows the historical events that led to the expulsion of the Hungarian Jews. The years 1942 and 1943 as rapidly described in the text were fairly normal for the Jews of Sighet. While anti-Jewish legislation was enacted and periods of calm alternated with those of turbulence, day still predominated over night. From 1938 to 1944, Hungarian prime ministers ranged from eager collaborators to those who collaborated reluctantly, resulting, in cycles of despair and hope for the Jews who were unable to assess their situation realistically.[8] In 1944 the Jewish community of Hungary was the only large group still intact. The circumstances changed drastically, however, in March, with the German takeover of the country and the installation of the pro-German Sztójay government. Adolph Eichmann, commander of the Special Action Unit (*Sondereinsatzkommando*), came to Hungary to personally carry out one of the most concentrated and systematic destruction operations in Europe. In the spring of 1944, with the end of the war in sight, the Nazis deported and eventually wiped out 450,000 Jews, 70 percent of the Jews of Greater Hungary. The Jews from the Carpathian region and Transylvania were among the first to be ghettoized and then rounded up. Of the fifteen thousand Jews in Sighet's community alone, about fifty families survived.

The Germans were notorious for their methods of deceiving their victims by dispelling notions of fear and creating the illusion of normality as they went about setting the machinery of extermination in motion. Eliezer speaks of life's returning to normal, even after the Nazis forced the Jews of Sighet into two ghettos fenced off from the rest of the population by barbed wire. At least, he remarks, Jews were living among their brothers and the atmosphere was somewhat peaceful. This deceptively secure setting was soon to be shattered.

"Night fell," says the narrator, describing an evening gathering of friends in the courtyard of his family's house in the large ghetto. A group of about twenty was listening attentively to tales told by his father, when suddenly a Jewish policeman entered and interrupted his father's story, summoning him to an emergency session of the Jewish council. "The good story he had been in the middle of telling us was to remain unfinished," Eliezer notes (22).

The theme of *the unfinished story* becomes a key to the entire text and to Wiesel's work in general, linking day and night, father and son, voice and silence. Suspended in the midst of its natural flow, the father's story is a metaphor for Jewish life and lives abruptly brought to a standstill in the middle of the *night*. When the father returns at midnight from the council meeting, he announces news of the deportation to be held the following day.

From this point on, time is defined by the first and last night. Eliezer refers to "our last night at home," spent in the large ghetto after watching the first transport of victims parade through the streets under the blazing sun, the infernal counterpart to Night. Then, there is the last evening in the small ghetto, where Eliezer, his parents, and three sisters observe the traditional Sabbath meal: "We were, we felt, gathered for the last time round the family table. I spent the night turning over thoughts and memories in my mind, unable to find sleep" (31).

Expelled from the small ghetto, Eliezer and his family, along with other members of the community, are thrown into cattle cars where they endure three long nights. Day is left far behind. The theme of night corresponds here to the reduction of space. Whereas the gentle gloom of the synagogue provided the framework for a boundless exploration of sacred doctrines, the ghetto period—in its progression from larger to smaller—serves as a transitional space, leading to the nailed-up doors of the cattle wagons, which plunge the prisoners into the confinement and extreme darkness of a night without limits.

The night of the cattle wagons is hallucinatory. Madame Schächter, a woman of fifty, who along with her ten-year-old son had been deported separately from her husband and two elder sons, starts to go mad. On the third and last night in the train, she screams out as if possessed by an evil spirit, conjuring up vivid images of fire and a furnace. Some of the men peer through the barred train window to see what Madame Schächter is pointing to, but all they can glimpse is blackness. Night is both within and without, surrounding the mad prophet who continuously cries out, as if to predict the end of the world, but who is forcefully silenced by those around her who do not want to believe in the foreboding signs. At the terminus, Birkenau–Auschwitz,[9] Madame Schächter gives one last howl: "Jews, look! Look through the window! Flames! Look!" (36). As the train stops, the victims, in disbelief, observe red flames gushing out of the chimney into the black sky.

The theme of fire is present, indeed, throughout the text, from the half-burned candles of the synagogue, where Eliezer and Moché attempt to illuminate the mysteries of the universe, to the relentless sun of the ghetto liquidation, culminating in the savage blaze of the death pits and crematoria. "Here the word 'furnace' was not a word empty of meaning," the narrator notes, "it floated on the air, mingling with the smoke. It was perhaps the only word which did have any real meaning here" (47). Fire is, indeed, an integral part of Night, as suggested by the term *Holocaust* itself, which signifies widespread destruction by fire or a sacrificial burnt offering.

When Eliezer sees the vivid flames leaping out of a ditch where little children are being burned alive, he pinches his face in order to know if he is awake or dreaming in this nightmarish atmosphere of "Hell *made immanent.*"[10] The young boy watches babies thrown into the smouldering pits and people all around murmuring *Kaddish* (the Jewish prayer for the dead) for themselves—the living dead—as they slowly move in a kind of *danse macabre.* They give the eerie impression that they are participating in their own funeral. For a moment, the narrator contemplates throwing himself on the barbed wire, but the instinct for survival prevails. As he enters the Holocaust kingdom on that first night he recites a ritualistic incantation, which marks his initiation into one long and never-ending night and commits him to remember it always:

> Never shall I forget that night, the first night in camp, which has turned my life into one long night, seven times cursed and seven times sealed. Never shall I forget that smoke. Never shall I forget the little faces of the children, whose bodies I saw turned into wreaths of smoke beneath a silent blue sky.
>
> Never shall I forget those flames which consumed my faith forever.
>
> Never shall I forget that nocturnal silence which deprived me, for all eternity, to the desire to live. Never shall I forget those moments which murdered my God and my soul and turned my dreams to dust. Never shall I forget these things, even if I am condemned to live as long as God Himself. Never. [43]

This invocation summarizes the principal themes of Wiesel's first book, joining the theme of night to those of fire, silence, and the death of children, of God, and of the self. The moment of arrival designates the end of the reality-oriented structure of "outer" night, and the shift to "inner" night, in which time is suspended. As dawn breaks Eliezer observes: "So much had happened within such a few hours that I had lost all sense of time. When had we left our houses? And the ghetto? And the train? Was it only a week? One night—*one single night?* . . . Surely it was a dream" (46).

Indeed, like a dream sequence, the events of the camp journey have been accelerated and condensed into a short interval. "One of the most astonishing things," says Wiesel, "was that we lost all sense not only of time in the French meaning of the word, of *durée*, but even in the concept of years. . . . The ten-year-old boy and the sixty-year-old man not only looked alike, felt alike and lived alike, but walked alike. There was a certain 'levelling.' "[11] This levelling process seems to occur in one night, a notion often repeated by the author:

> In a single night, a single hour, one acquires knowledge and grows up. The child finds himself an old man. From one day to the next, familiar structures and concepts vanish, only to reappear in different forms. One gets used to the new order in spite of everything. [*Entre Deux Soleils*, 71]

The concept of time that governs life in normal conditions thus changes radically in the concentrationary universe. But even more important than time is the highly organized and methodological procedure that deprives an individual of his humanness and transforms him into a thing while still alive.[12] The *défaite du moi*, the "dissolution of the self," is the worst kind of living death and is a recurring theme in Holocaust literature.[13]

After one single night in Auschwitz, Eliezer is turned into a subhuman, identified only by an anonymous number. Yesterday an active member of a community imbued with religious teachings and traditions, the boy is now bereft of all faith. A black flame, the demonic union of fire and night, has permeated his psyche. At the center of his soul lies a void:

> I too had become a completely different person. The student of the Talmud, the child that I was, had been consumed in the flames. There remained only a shape that looked like me. A dark flame had entered into my soul and devoured it. [46]

On the eve of Rosh Hashanah, the last night of the Jewish year, Eliezer experiences a deep sense of alienation as he stands among his praying and sobbing compatriots who are observing the holiday. The once fervent youth is now a spectator of himself, a stranger to his beliefs, and in revolt against an absent God who has betrayed his people by allowing them to be tortured, gassed, and burned. "I was the accuser, God the accused. My eyes were open and I was alone—terribly alone in a world without God and without man" (75). With blunted senses and branded flesh, the child turns away from his God and his heritage. His spirit is arrested in the confines of Night: the empire of darkness has taken possession of his inner being. For the boy of fifteen history has stopped.

Although time is essentially abolished in the kingdom of death, the narrator nevertheless continues to structure outer reality in the account itself by noting the nights that mark the principal stages of the trip. After three weeks in Auschwitz, he and his father are sent in a work transport to Buna, where they spend several weeks. The Germans finally evacuate the camp as Russian troops approach. Before the long cold voyage to Buchenwald, Eliezer meditates on the motif of *the last night*:

> The last night in Buna. Yet another last night. The last night at home, the last night in the ghetto, the last night in the train, and, now, the last night in Buna. How much longer were our lives to be dragged out from one 'last night' to another?[11] [89]

The march from Buna to Buchenwald takes place in blackness, amid glacial winds and falling snow. The boy realizes that the night he is leaving will be replaced by one even more unfathomable on the other side; the *invisible darkness* of the tomb. As the procession winds its way through the thick snow, numerous corpses are strewn upon its trail. After several days without food or water, the remaining prisoners are thrown into open cattle cars and transported to Buchenwald. For the starved skeletons who speed through the frozen landscape, "days were like nights and the nights left the dregs of their darkness in our souls" (105). Suddenly, on the last day of this seemingly endless journey, a fierce cry rises up from among the inert bodies of the entire convoy—a collective death rattle that seems to emanate from beyond the grave. This shared song of death when no hope is left is a protest to the world which has abandoned them. A brutal expression of the agony of those who have reached their limits, this massive convulsion *is* the primeval language of Night. Finally, late in the evening, twelve survivors out of the hundred who started out reach Buchenwald.

The last night—and the most significant—is January 28, 1945. Eliezer's father, sick with dysentery, his head bloody from the blows of an SS guard, lies curled up miserably on his bunk bed. When his son awakens the next day, he realizes that his father has been carted away before dawn—perhaps still alive. It is the finality of this moment that virtually ends the narrative, plunging Eliezer into a realm where no light penetrates and where, on some level, the *child of Night* remains for the rest of his life.

FATHER AND SON: A RESIDUE OF HUMANISM

If the nocturnal forces of death envelop and endure, miraculously, from within the depths of the Holocaust universe surges the will to survive. Father and son struggle to remain human, acting as lifelines for each other.[14] They fight to keep alive by mutual care and manage to create a strong bond between them in the most extreme of circumstances. Yet competition for survival causes a conflict between self-interest and concern for the other. Close ties break down in the kingdom of Night and even the solidarity built up between Eliezer and his father is undermined by feelings of anger and ambivalence brought about by Nazi techniques specifically designed to destroy human relationships.

"A residue of humanism persists illogically enough in our world, where there is a 'void' at the center of things," Wylie Sypher observes, in *Loss of the Self in Modern Literature and Art.*[15] For a child of fifteen entering the perverse world of the concentration camp, the "residue of humanism" is the presence of his father. Separated from his mother and three sisters upon their arrival at Birkenau, Eliezer becomes obsessed with the need to hold on tightly to his father's hand, the only object of life in a universe where every moment holds the possibility of death. "My hand shifted on my father's arm. I had one thought—not to lose him. Not to be left alone" (39). Warned by an anonymous prisoner to lie about their ages, the fifteen-year-old boy and the fifty-year-old man instantly become eighteen and forty, and are thus able to follow Dr. Mengele's wand to the left-hand column (life) instead of the right-hand one (crematoria).

The fear of being torn apart from his last family link haunts the narrator throughout the book. During the "levelling" process, as he is being stripped bare of all possessions, he is fixated on one thought—to be with his father. Later, when the boy is recovering from a foot operation in the Buna hospital and finds out that the camp is about to be evacuated, he runs outside into the deep snow, a shoe in his hand because his foot is still swollen, and frantically searches for his father: "As for me, I was not thinking about death, but I did not want to be separated from my father. We had already suffered so much together; this was not the time to be separated" (88). Upon arrival in Buchenwald after the long torturous convoy in the open wagons, Eliezer is again haunted by the familiar fear and fiercely clutches his father's hand.

This obsession to hold on to the father has been interpreted by the French scholar André Neher as juvenile. He feels that "Elie remains a small, dependent child in spite of the overabundant maturity resulting from his experience."[16] However, if the gesture of grasping the hand is somewhat childlike, and the son's vow never to be severed from his father has a desperate tone, the primary relationship between father and son appears to be more an interdependency based upon mutual support in the midst of surrounding evil. Father and son, joined together in front of the sacrificial altar, recall the Biblical story of Abraham and Isaac (the *Akeda*), described by Wiesel in *Messengers of God* with the emphasis on commitment in a world threatened by destruction: "And the father and son remained united. Together they reached the top of the mountain; together they erected the altar; together they prepared the wood and the fire" (82). Wiesel cites a text from the Midrash in which the Biblical pair are envisaged as "victims together," bound by their communal offering.

Until the last pages of *Night,* reciprocal devotion sustains both Eliezer and his father and is linked to the recurring Wieselean theme of rescue—saving the life of another human being and thereby saving one's own. The narrator reports several instances during which his father's presence stops him from dying. When Eliezer files past the fiery pits on the first hallucinatory night in Auschwitz, he has thoughts of suicide. He is deterred from killing himself by the voice of his father who tells him that humanity no longer cares about their fate, and that at this time in history everything is permitted. The father's voice, though sad and choked, represents a life force, which combats the all-encompassing blackness.

During the long march from Buna to Gleiwitz, the prisoners are forced to gallop through the snow, and Eliezer, pained by his throbbing foot, is again drawn to death as an escape from suffering. Once more the paternal presence helps him to resist the appeal of death. Because he feels that his father needs him, the son does not have the right to succumb. His will to survive is ultimately linked to the existence of his father:

> Death wrapped itself around me till I was stifled. It stuck to me. I felt that I could touch it. The idea of dying, of no longer being, began to fascinate me. Not to exist any longer. Not to feel the horrible pains in my foot. . . . My father's presence was the only thing that stopped me . . . I had no right to let myself die. What would he do without me? I was his only support. [92–93]

After seventy kilometers of running, as morning approaches, the survivors are allowed to rest. The narrator sinks into the soft snow, but his father persuades him to go into the ruins of a nearby brick factory, since to sleep in the snow means to freeze to death. The open shed, too, is crusted with a thick cold carpet enticing its weary victims, and Eliezer awakes to the frozen hand of his father patting his cheeks. A voice "damp with tears and snow" advises the boy not to be overcome by sleep. Eliezer and his father decide to watch over each other: they exchange vows of protection, which bind them together in revolt against the death that is silently transforming their sleeping comrades into stiffened corpses.

Later on, when the men pile on top of each other in the barracks of Gleiwitz, Eliezer struggles to rid himself of an unknown assassin slowly suffocating him with the massiveness of his weight. When he finally liberates himself and swallows a mouthful of air, the boy's first words are to his father whose presence is acknowledged by the sound of his voice, "a distant voice, which seemed to come from another world" (100). The voice once again is a lifeline, a reassurance against death. Yet the otherworldliness of the father's speech suggests that he is beginning to lose hold of his vital forces; eternal night beckons to him.

The last time the father rescues the son is in the open cattle car shuttling the victims from Gleiwitz to Buchenwald. On the third night of the trip, the narrator suddenly wakes up: somebody is trying to strangle him. He musters enough strength to cry out the one word synonymous with survival—"Father!" Too weak to throw off the attacker, his father calls upon Meir Katz, an old friend from his home town, who frees Eliezer. The father thus saves his son's life through a surrogate, one of the most robust in the group, but one who dies before the men reach Buchenwald and whose abandoned corpse is left on the train.

During the various phases of the nocturnal journey the other side of the rescue motif is also apparent: the son carefully watches over his father and at times delivers the latter from death. These brief moments of solidarity disrupt the machinery of destruction and prove to be examples of human resistance in the face of the inhuman. When Eliezer's father is selected for the gas chamber in Gleiwitz, the youth runs after him, creating enough confusion to finally reunite father and son in the right-hand column, this time the column of life. Shortly after this episode, Eliezer saves his father's life in the convoy to Buchenwald. Lying inert in the train, his father is taken for dead by the men who are throwing out the corpses. Eliezer desperately slaps his father's nearly lifeless face in an attempt to revive him and succeeds in making him move his eyelids slightly, a vital sign that he is still alive. The men leave him alone.

Upon arrival at the camp, the father reaches the breaking point. He sinks to the ground, resigned to dying. Eliezer is filled with rage at his father's passivity, and realizes he must now take charge. "I found my father weeping like a child," he says when later he finds him stretched across his bunk, crying bitterly after being beaten by the other inmates for not properly taking care of his bodily needs (114). The boy feeds his helpless father and brings him water. We see here the reversal of roles: the transformation of the once-powerful paternal authority into a weak, fearful child and that of the dependent child into an adult.[17] By assuming responsibility for the sick old man, the son becomes a kind of father figure, illustrating Wiesel's contention that in the inverted world of the concentration camp, old men metamorphosed into children and children into old men in one never-ending night.

The reversal of roles in *Night* has been viewed by André Neher as "an anti-*Akeda:* not a father leading his son to be sacrificed, but a son guiding, dragging, carrying to the altar an old man who no longer has the strength to continue." Wiesel's text, he observes, is "a re-writing of the *Akeda* under the opaque light of Auschwitz. It is no longer a narrative invented by the imagination of a poet or philosopher. It is the reality of Auschwitz."[18] This reality offers a sharp contrast to the Biblical event. Whereas in the Bible God saves Isaac from being sacrificed by sending a ram to replace him, He does not intervene to save the father at the altar of Auschwitz. God allows the father to be consumed by Holocaust flames and the son is forced to recognize the inevitable—that he is impotent in the face of death's conquest and God's injustice. He must slowly watch his father acquiesce to death. Symbol of reason, strength, and humanity, the father finally collapses under the barbaric tactics of the Nazi oppressor to which Eliezer is a silent witness.[19]

If the theme of father-son is characterized, in general, by the reciprocal support necessary for survival in extremity, the sanctity of the relationship is nevertheless violated by the camp conditions. In contrast to the son's need to protect and be protected by his father, there appears the opposing motif: the abandonment of the father. The Nazi technique of attempting to eradicate all family ties and creating a state of mind in which men view each other as enemies or strangers—what can be called the *concentration camp philosophy*—is demonstrated in *Night* through a series of incidents showing the competition for survival between fathers and sons.

Bela Katz, the son of a merchant from Eliezer's hometown and a member of the *Sonderkommando* in Birkenau, is forced to shove the body of his own father into the crematory oven. A *pipel* in Buna beats his father because his father does not make his bed properly.[20] A third instance, and the one the narrator constantly uses as a measure of his own behavior, is the deterioration of relations between Rabbi Eliahou and his son. Shunted from camp to camp for three years, the boy and his father have always managed to stay together. But after the seventy-kilometer march from Buna to Gleiwitz they are separated. The Rabbi reaches the shed and looks for his son. He tells Eliezer that in the obscurity of the night his son did not notice him fall to the rear of the column. However, Eliezer remembers seeing the youth run past the staggering old man and is horrified by this clear example of abandonment:

> A terrible thought loomed up in my mind: he had wanted to get rid of his father! He had felt that his father was growing weak, he had believed that the end was near and had sought this separation in order to get rid of the burden, to free himself from an encumbrance which could lessen his own chances of survival. [97]

Eliezer prays to God to give him the strength never to do what Rabbi Eliahou's son has done.

Perhaps the most devastating example of the breakdown of human bonds occurs in the cattle cars going to Buchenwald during the final phase of the journey. Some workers amuse themselves by throwing pieces of bread into the open wagons and watching the starved men kill each other for a crumb. Eliezer sees an old man about to eat a bit of bread he was lucky enough to snatch from the crowd. Just as he brings the bread to his mouth, someone throws himself on top of him and beats him up. The old man cries out: "Meir, Meir, my boy! Don't you recognize me? I'm your father . . . you're hurting me . . . you're killing your father! I've got some bread . . . for you too . . . for you too . . ." The son grabs the bread from his father's fist; the father collapses, murmures something and then dies. As the son begins to devour the bread two men hurl themselves upon him and others join them. The young narrator is witness to the entire event: "When they withdrew, next to me were two corpses, side by side, the father and the son. I was fifteen years old" (106).

Having witnessed fathers beaten, abandoned, and killed, the author, through his narrator, has chosen to represent the *son's betrayal of the father* and has omitted situations in which the father mistreats the son. As Terrence Des Pres has pointed out in *The Survivor*, the principle of jungle rule in the camps is frequently belied by examples of human solidarity.[21] Wiesel elects to record the acts of care and decency performed by his father. By not being critical of the paternal figure in a world too often governed by viciousness, the author protects his father's image and honors his memory. This unconscious process of selection reveals the subjective aspect of the eyewitness account and of the survivor's perceptions. The focus upon the abuses of the sons is perhaps a projection of the author-narrator's own feeling of guilt; he identifies with them at the same time that he condemns them for having let their fathers perish. Despite Eliezer's efforts to save his father's life throughout the camp experience, the boy is critical of his own reprehensible behavior, and ultimately takes the blame for his father's death upon himself.

From the first day, the son helplessly witnesses the debasement of his father. When Eliezer's father is seized with colic and politely asks the *Kapo* where the lavatories are, he is dealt such a heavy blow that he crawls back to his place on all fours like an animal.[22] Instead of defending his father's honor by striking the *Kapo*, Eliezer remains paralyzed, afraid to speak out. This fear makes him aware that his values are changing:

> I did not move. What had happened to me? My father had just been struck, before my very eyes, and I had not flickered an eyelid. I had looked on and said nothing. Yesterday, I should have sunk my nails into the criminal's flesh. Had I changed so much, then? So quickly? Now remorse began to gnaw at me. I thought only: I shall never forgive them for that. [48]

This feeling of impotence is repeated in Buna when Idek, the *Kapo*, in a fit of madness beats Eliezer's father with an iron bar. The son's reaction is not simply that of a passive onlooker; he is furious at his father:

> I had watched the whole scene without moving. I kept quiet. In fact I was thinking of how to get farther away so that I would not be hit myself. What is more, any anger I felt at that moment was directed not against the *Kapo*, but against my father. I was angry with him, for not knowing how to avoid Idek's outbreak. That is what concentration camp life had made of me. [62]

At the end of the narrative, when an SS guard strikes the sick father on the head with his bludgeon, Eliezer again looks on without moving, terrified of being beaten himself.

We see here the brutal effect of concentration camp life upon an individual psyche. Rage against the aggressor has been displaced onto the victim, and concern for the other has regressed into a preoccupation with self-survival, reduced to primitive and instinctual bodily needs. Eliezer is condemned to the role of the impotent witness, incapable of crying out, of seeking revenge, or, finally, of saving his father's life. Although he has fantasies of destroying his father's assassins, he can only behold his bloody face in despair. He is unable to respond to his father's last summons for help—an utterance of his name, "Eliezer."

Yet more than the sense of complicity, after the father dies the son feels ambivalent and even somewhat liberated. Earlier in the text, his mixed emotions surface during an alert in Buchenwald, when Eliezer, separated from his father, does not bother to look for him. The next day he sets out but with highly conflicting feelings:

> Don't let me find him! If only I could get rid of this dead weight, so that I could use all my strength to struggle for my own survival, and only worry about myself. Immediately I felt ashamed of myself, ashamed forever. [111]

Eliezer's desire to rid himself of his oppressive burden, to lose his dependent father in the crowd, makes him recall with horror Rabbi Eliahou's son during the evacuation from Buna. When the narrator finally locates the feverish and trembling old man lying on a plank outside, he frantically claws his way through the crowd to get him some coffee. Later, he halfheartedly offers his dying father what is left of his own soup. While his deeds demonstrate care and devotion, his thoughts are of withdrawal and abandonment. Actions and intentionality, behavior and fantasies, do not correspond. The fifteen-year-old judges himself guilty: "No better than Rabbi Eliahou's son had I withstood the test" (112).

The head of the block tells Eliezer that it is too late to save his old father and that instead he should be eating his father's ration. In his innermost recesses, Eliezer believes that the *Kapo* is right, but is torn by shame and runs to find more soup for his father. We see here the clashing principles for survival that dominated the death camp universe. On one hand, the rule of eat or be eaten, devour or be devoured prevailed. In the struggle of all against all, the *Kapo* teaches Eliezer, "every man has to fight for himself and not think of anyone else. Even of his father. Here, there are no fathers, no brothers, no friends. Everyone lives and dies for himself alone" (115). And yet on the other hand, a *Kapo* tells the prisoners: "We are all brothers, and we are all suffering the same fate. The same smoke floats above all our heads. Help one another. It is the only way to survive" (50).

In Wiesel's tale "An Old Acquaintance," a similar situation reveals human beings at odds with themselves. In this instance the father offers his half-full bowl of soup to the son, who refuses it. Seeing this occur several times, the *Kapo* finally orders the son to eat his father's soup. As the son gulps it down, he has contradictory feelings: "At first I wanted to vomit but soon I felt an immense well-being spread through my limbs. I ate slowly to make this pleasure, stronger than my shame, last longer" (LT, 48). He hates the *Kapo* but is grateful for his intervention. These mixed sensations of nourishment and regurgitation, well-being and disgust, are indicative of the opposing emotions constantly created in the camp inmates as their dignity, loyalty, and honor are assaulted by the barbaric choices they are forced to make.

The ambivalent feelings of the fifteen-year-old with regard to his father and food are intensified after his father dies:

> I did not weep, and it pained me that I could not weep. But I had no more tears. And in the depths of my being, in the recesses of my weakened conscience, could I have searched it, I might perhaps have found something like—free at last. [116]

The relief soon turns into a deep sense of guilt, for having failed to save his father, for having survived in his place, and for having thoughts of being liberated by his death. The protector has been transformed into a betrayer. Unconsciously, the youth may even feel that he has acted out a son's worst Oedipal fear: he has psychically become "his father's murderer."[23]

The survival guilt that Eliezer painfully endures culminates with the face in the mirror at the end of the narrative. Several days after the liberation of Buchenwald by American soldiers, and after a severe bout of food poisoning during which the boy almost dies, he looks at himself in the mirror for the first time since the ghetto. A stranger—a child of Night—peers at him, and the text concludes with the dark image of death itself: "From the depths of the mirror, a corpse gazed back at me. The look in his eyes, as they stared into mine, has never left me" (119). The distinction made between *his* eyes and *mine*, conveying the notion of the fragmented self, is stressed in the original French: "Son regard dans mes yeux ne me quitte plus" ("His look in my eyes no longer leaves me") (*La Nuit*, 178). The staring corpse is a permanent reminder of the "dead" self, that part of the narrator which was engulfed by the black smoke of Auschwitz and which will plague him for the rest of his life.

The cadaverous reflection in the mirror also suggests the son's identification with his dead father, to whom he remains attached. According to Robert Jay Lifton, survival guilt is related to "the process of identification—the survivor's tendency to incorporate within himself an image of the dead, and then to think, feel and act as he imagines they would."[24] At the end of the night, Eliezer incorporates his father into his own psyche and projects this image onto the mirror as his double. The haunting specter with its penetrating glance serves to keep the paternal presence alive and is the son's means of defending himself against his loss. The mirror image epitomizes Eliezer's state of mourning and his desire to join his father, whose death is experienced as a death of the self. "When my father died, I died," Wiesel reveals. "That means that one 'I' in me died. . . . At least, something in me died."[25]

THE UNFINISHED STORY

If Eliezer is spiritually reunited with his father in the ghostly visage of the glass tomb, the guilt-ridden, numbed, and nearly lifeless son is nevertheless condemned to survive. The "surviving" self emerges as witness and counteracts the "dead" self, an important theme in Wiesel's works, linked to the theme of father-son. In order to continue the succession, the son must take his father's place. An imperative reaching far beyond himself compels him to complete the story his father was in the midst of telling the night in the ghetto before news of the deportation interrupted his words; The son himself must become a storyteller, for the story is a mode of transcendence, and the power of the word a protest against the nihilism of the Holocaust. As heir to the aborted tale, the son's task is to bring the destroyed Jewish communities and their inhabitants back to life. The need to remember transcends the particular to include an entire tradition that has vanished in the night. Before all else, the author-narrator seeks to resurrect his father and to prolong his voice: *the father's unfinished story becomes the story of the father.*

The struggle to recover one's words in a dissolving world, to fight against silent suffocation in a universe where daily events all but fatally constrict one's breath, is dramatized through the theme of the voice—a counterforce to Night. With the progressive decay of the body, the human voice alone remains a sign of life. The Hungarian Jew dying next to Eliezer in the hospital room is a faceless mass of skin and bones, and yet is able to speak out and warn the boy to leave the hospital before the next selection. The man's ability to articulate is synonymous with survival. "I could only hear his voice," the narrator says; "it was the sole indication that he was alive. Where did he get the strength to talk?" (84).

In the dark shed of Gleiwitz where exhausted men pile on top of each other, Eliezer wrestles against death. As he gasps for air under the heap of dying bodies, a weak but familiar voice cries out for help beneath him. He realizes that it is Juliek, the boy from Warsaw who played the violin in Buna. The narrator struggles to move away from his friend—to breathe and to let him breathe. He calls out to the young musician: " 'How do you feel, Juliek?' I asked, less to know the answer than to hear that he could speak, that he was alive" (99). The act of speaking becomes an act of resistance, the disembodied voice a vestige of humanity in a thoroughly dehumanized universe. After a long while, the hallucinatory notes of Juliek's violin miraculously punctuate the oppressive silence of the pitch-black living tomb and, for a brief moment, evil is eclipsed by tones of purity and innocence. "I shall never forget Juliek," Eliezer says. "How could I forget that concert, given to an audience of dying and dead men!" (101). In the morning, the corpse of Juliek lies next to his shattered instrument.

Whereas the utterance of sounds signifies life, death is the collapse into silence. At the end of the text, when Eliezer's father lies across his bunk bed, aware that his life is drawing to a close, he puts his parched lips to his son's ear and feverishly races against the end. Fearful that he will not have time to tell him everything, he verbally passes on his meager heritage to his successor. Eliezer listens carefully to his father, who can barely pronounce his final words. When the doctor comes and does nothing as the old man slowly dies, Eliezer is furious: "I felt like leaping at his throat, strangling him. . . . Oh, to strangle the doctor and the others! To burn the whole word! My father's murderers! But the cry stayed in my throat" (113–14). The soundless scream is a form of death-in-life. This inability to protest further alienates Eliezer and severs him from his last living tie to the past. Unable to avenge his father's death by choking the enemy, it is inevitably the son who is stifled by impotent rage.

The theme of the stifled voice permeates the fiery landscape of *Night*, where the inmates can barely whisper because of "the thick smoke which poisoned the air and took one by the throat" (46). In this polluted atmosphere, the cutting off of breath is most tragically exposed in the scene describing the hanging of the young boy with the face of a sad angel. The youth, who took part in an attempt to blow up the electric power station at Buna, is discovered and tortured for several days. He refuses to give the names of his accomplices and is condemned to be hanged along with two other men. The entire camp is summoned to witness the execution. The two adults die quickly, but the child, because his body is so light, suffers a delayed agonizing death. As the camp prisoners march past the gallows in total silence and look the child in the face, Eliezer hears a man behind him ask: " 'Where is God now?' And I heard a voice within me answer him: 'Where is He? Here He is—He is hanging here on this gallows . . .' " (72).

The death of an innocent child calls to mind religious sacrifices of other sons—Isaac bound to the altar, and the crucifixion of Jesus. However, in Buna, God does not intervene to substitute a ram, nor does he resuscitate the young boy slowly dying on what Lawrence Langer calls a "gallows-crucifix." The camp ceremony is, as Langer observes, "the ritual of death ungraced by the possibility of resurrection."[26] God Himself died on the gallows of Auschwitz, Wiesel has declared:

> I had the impression in Buchenwald of being present at the death of God. I have remained haunted by it. God died in each one of these deported children. I survived, but not completely. My heroes seek a supplementary death.[27]

Friedrich Nietzsche's prophecy of the "death of God" is literally enacted here upon the death camp altar. However, Nietzsche points to man's abdication of religious values while advocating the establishment of a human deity to replace the state of godlessness. Wiesel's statement is more than an accusation against the God who has betrayed his people, "the God who kills, and therefore can kill himself."[28] For Wiesel, no new order of human divinity can replace God; the loss of faith extends to all of mankind: "At Auschwitz, not only man died but also the idea of man. . . . It was its own heart the world incinerated at Auschwitz" (LT, 190).

The scene of the hanging child has been viewed by many as the central event in *Night* because the death of God as experienced by a fifteen-year-old is inscribed into the concentrationary landscape. In his foreword to the book, François Mauriac speaks of the horror produced by the "death of God in the soul of a child who suddenly discovers absolute evil" (9). This French writer sees in the dark, penetrating eyes of Wiesel "the reflection of that angelic sadness which had appeared one day upon the face of the hanged child" (11). Alfred Kazin describes the hanging as

> the one particular scene that has already made this book famous in Europe. . . . It is the literal death of God and absolute emptiness in the soul, the blackness that in his mind means that there is no longer any light from a divine source, that Wiesel experienced most in the endless night of Auschwitz.[29]

The figure of the innocent, saintly boy whose breath is cut off and whose young voice is permanently stilled on the camp gallows mirrors for Eliezer the annihilation of his own self—the self that once believed in God and humanity. But at the same time that he identifies with the strangled child, he is destined to survive as his witness. For the rest of his life, the author-narrator is torn by these conflicting selves: the self that has died, choked into stillness by the thick fumes of the death camps, and the one fighting to preserve itself in a post-Holocaust era.

Ultimately, the voice of the witness fills Night's void. The deaths of the child, the father, and God compel Eliezer to search for something to believe in.[30] This "something" is his own ability to answer the disembodied voice from behind asking where God is as the youth swings from the gallows: "*And I heard a voice within me*" (my emphasis). What the narrator beholds lies infinitely beyond speech and can only be acknowledged in awesome silence. Yet the very existence of an inner voice is a sign of life—a trace of human identity in the universe of darkness.

This *voice from within* is the generative principle of the will to bear witness, source of survival, and residue of life in the kingdom of death. The narrator of *Night* has been reduced to a disembodied voice: the narrator *is* his voice. Yet this struggle against suffocation is what transforms the passive spectator into the active witness who must tell future generations what he has seen and lived through in order to warn them that fathers and sons have been murdered, that God is dead. The power to articulate emanates from a deeper level of the self and reaches far beyond words. What the narrator ultimately recounts is not only the outer reality but also the inner reality of the experience, thereby creating a new reality that combats "the finality of the event," as Wiesel points out:

> In *Night* I wanted to show the end, the finality of the event. Everything came to an end—man, history, literature, religion, God. There was nothing left. And yet we begin again with Night.[31]

The author reveals here a basic contradiction—that of Night as the end and the beginning. This apparent opposition can be interpreted in light of the writing process. The world of death and degradation gives birth to the narrative. Ten years have distanced the survivor from the pain of the immediate but have given him the perspective and the courage, on the one hand, to detach himself from the experience and, on the other, to reenter it through the eyes of a fifteen-year-old. He has been able to relate and to order the events so as to transmit a coherent literary work. Language and memory are mobilized as instruments of healing, and telling the story becomes an act of restitution, as well as a protest against forgetfulness. By bearing witness the author transforms his voice into a life-giving force, so that he may infuse his dead father, the hanging child, and other victims of the Holocaust with breath.

Night terminates in silent darkness. The tomblike glass image looms before Eliezer, a terrifying conclusion to the child's unfathomable journey into the realm of the dead. Nonetheless, it is this unrecognizable reflection of himself that inspires Elie Wiesel to become a writer:

> One day as I was looking in a mirror, I didn't recognize myself . . . I then decided that since everything changes—even the face in the mirror changes—someone must speak about that change. Someone must speak about the former and that someone is I. I shall not speak about all the other things but I should speak, at least, about *that* face and *that* mirror and *that* change. That's when I knew I was going to write.[32]

The author rises from the grave to tell the tale, a tale which depicts the zero point of existence, but which is also the point of departure for his future works:

> *Night*, my first book, became the basis of my entire edifice. Afterwards, I tried to construct concentric circles around this testimony. For me, the war represents the year zero and Auschwitz is as important as Sinai.[33]

Night testifies to the destruction of man. At the same time, this work provides the foundation upon which Elie Wiesel rebuilds a structure for his life, and sets forth his legacy as witness to the Holocaust.

2

The Return of Lazarus:
Messengers from the Grave

If a man die, may he live again?
—Job 14:14

I am Lazarus, come from the dead,
Come back to tell you all, I shall tell you all.
—T. S. Eliot

THE corpselike image that Eliezer sees in the mirror at the end of *Night* is a relentless reminder of his "dead" self. This sinister reflection is passed on to his successors in *Dawn* and *The Accident*, the latter of which in French is entitled *Le Jour* (*"Day"*). Along with *Night* the two novels form a trilogy: Elisha in *Dawn* and the nameless narrator of *The Accident* are heirs to Eliezer's somber legacy.[1] They, too, are concentration camp survivors whose encounter with death has left them psychically numbed, spiritually isolated, and emotionally paralyzed. Like the Biblical Lazarus, they have crossed over the border and returned from the other side. But a great abyss sets them apart from the world of the living and they hover precariously on its edge. That part of themselves which has died along with the victims resists the part attempting to emerge from the tomb. The protagonists of Wiesel's early novels are Lazarene witnesses who have come back from the dead but are not yet resurrected.

The theme of Lazarus pervades *Dawn* and *The Accident*, as it does the condition of the survivor in general. Those who survived the Nazi assault upon the human species are described by Hannah Arendt in *The Origins of Totalitarianism* as "inanimate men, i.e., men who can no longer be psychologically understood, whose return to the psychologically or otherwise intelligibly human world closely resembles the resurrection of Lazarus."[2] Yet unlike the Biblical figure whose resurrection promises hope and redemption, the post-Auschwitz Lazarus lingers on the threshold of the grave. His very ghostlike appearance conveys his inability to return to the life he left behind. Upon meeting Elie Wiesel for the first time, François Mauriac was struck by "that look of a Lazarus risen from the dead, yet still a prisoner within the grim confines where he had strayed, stumbling among the shameful corpses" (N, 10).

Jean Cayrol, survivor, author of several novels, and screenwriter of Alain Resnais's film *Nuit et Brouillard (Night and Fog)*, wrote two essays in 1950 in which he attempted to formulate the aesthetics of an art born of the death camps, and to define the Lazarus-like character—"*le personnage lazaréen*"—whom he envisages as a likely character in fiction.[3] Called by Roland Barthes "the first junction of the camp experience and literary thought,"[4] Cayrol's "Lazare parmi nous" and "Pour un romanesque lazaréen" offer general observations on the concentration camp experience and how it has seeped into postwar literature, psychology, sociology, and art. The author believes that the event is inseparable from the uncertain condition of modern man and cannot be seen as a myth but rather as a reality of everyday life. He calls for writers who are not afraid of exposing the myth and granting readers access to the "*réalisme concentrationnaire*," which has "shaken the very foundations of our conscience" (RL, 202–3).

Although Cayrol feels that every survivor has been affected by "*cet Insaisissable Camp*" ("this Ungraspable Camp") in a different way, he notes certain characteristics which distinguish *le personnage lazaréen*. Solitude is one of the primary aspects of the Lazarene existence: the character dwells in an enclosed space, a tomblike prison. But the prison is also a kingdom, for solitude like a minotaur both devours and nourishes the protagonist cloistered in his special universe. Cayrol points to an active solitude which serves as a private refuge for the survivor's memories and obsessions, a means of preserving the secret of his inner "camp," and an impenetrable weapon used to protect his vulnerability. At the same time, this isolation cuts the protagonist off from physical and emotional contact with other human beings. Suspicious and fearful of contaminating others, he abstains from any display

of tenderness or affection. If ties are established with another individual, the victim-executioner relationship of the camp is often reenacted,
with the Lazarene character alternating between the roles of the
oppressed and the oppressor.

According to Cayrol *le personnage lazaréen* lives in a state of
anonymity and has lost the desire to repossess the identity taken from
him in the camp through the methodical Nazi processes of dehumanization. His universe excludes all notion of the human, since for him
"the world no longer has a human face" (RL, 221). Impassive,
somnolent, he often appears paralyzed by an overall feeling of
heaviness and an inability to act.

The notion of time has taken on a particular dimension for the
Lazarene character; suspended somewhere between his inner landscape of fragmented memories and the alien world he has reentered,
he possesses what Cayrol calls "*le pouvoir de dedoublement*" ("the ability to
live on two levels at the same time"). In the camps, prisoners developed
this mechanism to detach themselves from the pain of the situation,
and Cayrol analyzes the "*rêves cellulaires*" ("prison dreams"), which
enabled the inmates to mentally escape their suffering. However, the
fluctuation between two levels of reality has the reverse effect on the
survivor, who drifts in and out of his nightmares, continuing to relive
the terror of the camps in his dreams as well as during his waking
hours. The slightest associations trigger images that open up tender
scars. This perpetual state of mental vagabondage divides the survivor
within himself. He comes to doubt the credibility of his own recollections, and wonders if he has imagined the whole experience. His past
seems as uncertain as his present.[5]

Because *le personnage lazaréen* has been on one level permanently
"deported," his life in the aftermath can never be the same. He
constantly vacillates between staying in the tomb and abandoning it.
Uprooted, cast out, exiled in the loneliness of his internal prison camp,
he is the paradigm of twentieth-century disinherited man, forced to
bear the stigmata of inhumanity and injustice. As René Prédal declares
in his book on Alain Resnais: "The Lazarene hero is thus the representative hero of our era: solitary, anonymous, set *[figé]* in an unstable
equilibrium, traumatized and abused by all the misery of the world."[6]

The protagonists of *Dawn* and *The Accident* are Lazarene witnesses
who have endured atrocities of every kind and who now live at life's
edge, angry and guilty for having survived. Death's presence lies at the
core of both novels. The lifeless self of the protagonist, or what
Maurice Blanchot in *La Part du feu* calls "le Lazare du tombeau . . . le

Lazare perdu" ("Lazarus of the tomb, the lost Lazarus") predominates over the self attempting to emerge from the grave—"le Lazare sauvé et ressuscité" ("Lazarus saved and resurrected").[7] Elisha in *Dawn* and the narrator of *The Accident* are haunted by the dead with whom they identify. They dwell in a state of solitude and anguish, perceiving themselves more dead than alive. "I had died and come back to earth, dead," Elisha silently tells Catherine, the young woman who wants to make love with him in the Normandy youth camp where a rescue committee has sent him after the war (D, 165). And, as he lies paralyzed on a hospital bed, the narrator of *The Accident* thinks back to how he felt when he left the camps:

> I thought of myself as dead. I couldn't eat, read, cry: I thought I was dead and that in a dream I imagined myself alive. I knew I no longer existed, that my real self had stayed *there*, that my present self had nothing in common with the other, the real one. I was like the skin shed by a snake. [A, 246]

The wide gap between the "dead" self and the "surviving" self causes these protagonists to lose their sense of boundaries: they can no longer distinguish between memory and reality. Their lives take on the unreal aspect of a dream or rather a nightmare in which they are relentlessly assailed by past traumas. Unable to relate to the world around them, strangers to themselves and to others, they often prolong their camp experience by playing the familiar parts of executioner and victim.

The tainted figures of Wiesel's early novels seem to perform what Robert Jay Lifton calls a "psychic *danse macabre*" around the dead, whom they keep alive within themselves and whose presence governs their existence.[8] Through the silence of their despair, they dialogue with those who have perished. Nevertheless, there are signs that point to the resurgence of a life force. Despite an obsessive yearning to join the victims, the will to survive and to speak out asserts itself, albeit in a limited way. In both *Dawn* and *The Accident* the theme of the witness is suggested by the Lazarene character's tortured efforts to crawl out of the grave and return to life—as a messenger from the dead.

THE SURVIVOR AS EXECUTIONER: *DAWN*

The black night of *l'univers concentrationnaire* gives way to the bleak dawn of post-Holocaust survival which, instead of announcing daylight, perpetuates the state of darkness. The same dawn that brings death to the father in *Night* inflicts a living death upon the young protagonist of *Dawn*. Elisha, an eighteen-year-old survivor who lives in Paris after his liberation from Buchenwald, is a Lazarus-like figure from another kingdom, situated halfway between the land of the living and that of the dead. He spends most of his time alone in his room, reading books and ruminating about the events that deprived him of his family, his friends, and his God. Desperately, he tries to understand the meaning of history, knowing all the while that it is impossible.

One night, a mysterious young visitor named Gad knocks on his door and invites him to join the Jewish resistance movement in Palestine. Elisha accepts because he has nothing and no one to lose. By departing from the oppressive space of his solitary quarters, Elisha seeks to break out of his tomb, to step across the threshold separating the "dead" self from the one struggling to survive. But the confinement of the lonely room is merely replaced by the stifling chamber in Palestine where the protagonist spends a long hot night preparing to become an executioner. If Gad promises Elisha a fiery Middle-Eastern dawn—sign of revolution, blood, anger, and perhaps hope—the dawn that Elisha eventually perceives in Palestine is enveloped by "a grayish light, the color of stagnant water" (D, 204), identical to the one he has abandoned in Paris: "a pale, prematurely weary light, the color of stagnant water" (137). For Elisha, the outer and inner landscapes are indistinguishable: the torpid atmosphere beyond the window of the room reflects his innermost self, which the Holocaust has left behind as a polluted lifeless being, bereft of feeling, and dwelling in the silent gray zone of dawn. And as Jean Cayrol observes: "*Le personnage lazaréen* is neither the man of day nor of night, but of dawn, the light of Purgatory" (RL, 228).

The novel focuses on the metamorphosis of the victim into victimizer and his inability to see himself in this new role. The confused self-identity of the main character is revealed principally through the motif of the mirror, manifested by the recurring window image. The book commences and terminates with Elisha in front of a window. In the beginning, before the act of execution, the young survivor looks through a window in Jerusalem to see twilight fall just before night approaches; at the conclusion of the narrative, after he has killed a man, he gazes through the same window to see dawn rising over the sleeping city. The city appears unreal and far away under the somber light. Only the piercing cry of a child lends some reality to the muted landscape.

Elisha stands near a window every evening at dusk looking for a face on the other side. As a child he was taught by a beggar the art of separating day from night. He was told that in order to know night had come he had to look for a face in a window, and if that were not possible, to look into the eyes of another human being. "For, believe me," the beggar had declared, "night has a face" (D, 126). Every evening since, Elisha approaches a window as darkness descends.

The reflection changes according to the night. At first, he sees the face of the beggar; after his father dies, the paternal image looms at the window's edge. Then, the multitude of sad and smiling faces of the unknown dead mutely stare at him from behind the transparent glass. On the night before he is to kill John Dawson—a British army officer held hostage by the Jewish resistance fighters in retaliation for David ben Moshe, one of their members captured by the British and threatened with execution—Elisha is shocked when he perceives the features emerging from the blackness: "I looked out the window, where a shadowy face was taking shape out of the deep of the night. A sharp pain caught my throat. I could not take my eyes off the face. It was my own" (D, 126). The vision mirrored in the window comes from the nocturnal depths and is composed of its tenebrous fragments. The theme of the mirror, then, is closely allied to that of night, for night defines the self: there is no distinction between the countenance of night and the face of Elisha.

Night has both positive and negative qualities in the novel. Source of beauty and serenity, it is the time when one gravitates into the labyrinths of the unconscious. The gentle gloom lends itself to the probing of mystical truths. In *Night*, Eliezer and Moché, the beadle, sit for hours in the dimly lit synagogue of Sighet, meditating about God, the universe, and eternity. Like Moché, the beggar in *Dawn* comes to the synagogue in the evening to pray, and there meets the child Elisha. He tells him not to be afraid of the dark: "Night is purer than day; it is better for thinking and loving and dreaming. At night everything is more intense, more true" (D, 125).

If in *Dawn* night is a fitting landscape for the Jewish terrorists' fierce fight to gain independence, the darkness is also the time of destruction and despair—the ally of the assailant. The novel ends with the image of night as death. After Elisha has executed the British hostage, he again recognizes in horror his own face suspended in midair on the other side of the window: "Fear caught my throat. The tattered fragment of darkness had a face. Looking at it, I understood the reason for my fear. The face was my own" (204).

Just as Eliezer in *Night* looked into a mirror and saw a corpse, Elisha's image, stained with darkness, is the reflection of that part of himself which has been spiritually destroyed. The mirror-window is like a glass tomb through which the "surviving" self glimpses the shadow of the "dead" self. Elisha the survivor is the inheritor of Eliezer's cadaverous profile and is thus incapable of separating day from night, life from death. He exists in a state of *dédoublement*, dwelling on both sides of the mirror at the same time.

Linked to the motif of the mirror is that of the gaze, depicted in the text by an abundant use of eye imagery. As Elisha faces the task of executioner, he begins to see himself as all eyes. The underlying connection between death and eyes is found in the Kabbalistic notion taught to the young Elisha by his old master Kalman: "Death is a being without arms or legs or mouth or head; it is all eyes. If you ever meet a creature with eyes everywhere, you can be sure that it is death" (140). The "evil eye" cannot be warded off by the strength of the loving eye since God "has no eyes at all" (57). Indeed, God's absence is marked by his lack of eyes.

By allying himself with the death-dealing force, Elisha, too, becomes all eyes: he is the spectator or *eye*witness of himself: This is demonstrated by the recurring motif of the "gaze gazing at itself." A self of eyes stares back at the protagonist from the mirror when he realizes he has to kill another human being. He almost cries out in horror at the sight of his own eyes everywhere. As he thinks of the hostage's mother in the London suburbs, he imagines her looking into the lonely night from the window of her flat, silently awaiting dawn. Before her looms the face of her son's executioner—a face composed of eyes. When Elisha enters John Dawson's narrow white cell an hour before sunrise, he knows that the victim suddenly perceives that "I had neither arms nor legs nor shoulders, that I was all eyes" (191). The sight and smell of death that the protagonist brings with him seals off all exits. One of the most terrifying aspects of Elisha's ordeal, then, is his insight: the act of seeing himself and being seen as the aggressor. In dread of his image, he fears it comes close to the new SS. And as Jean Cayrol has warned at the conclusion of *Nuit et Brouillard:* "Who among us looks out from this strange watchtower to guard us against the new oppressors? Do they really have a face other than our own?"[9]

The protagonist spends a long agonizing night questioning his ability to adopt the role of the executioner, which for him is the incarnation of pure cruelty and radical evil. The word itself fills him with disgust and burns his mouth even as he pronounces it. Elisha considers putting a mask on Dawson or wearing one himself in order to depersonalize the act of killing. But he knows that an executioner's mask will not hide his eyes and, therefore, cannot offer any form of disguise. On the contrary, once donned, the mask will be glued to his skin forever. Never will he be able to rid himself of the oppressor's identity:

> There are not a thousand ways of being a killer; either a man is one or he isn't. . . . He who has killed one man alone is a killer for life. He may choose another occupation, hide himself under another identity, but the executioner or at least the executioner's mask will be always with him. There lies the problem: in the influence of the backdrop of the play upon the actor. War had made me an executioner, and an executioner I would remain even after the backdrop had changed, when I was acting in another play upon a different stage. [177–78]

The notion of role playing and the use of theatrical allusions to depict victimizer and victim recur throughout Wiesel's texts. In the essay "A Plea for the Dead," he observes: "executioners are usually romantic types who like perfect productions: they find in darkness a stage setting and in night an ally" (LT, 175). He speaks of "the cold cruelty of the executioner and the cry which strangled the victim, and even the fate that united them to play on the same stage, in the same cemetery" (LT, 178). The killing of Jews in front of open pits in the forest is described in *A Beggar in Jerusalem* as a well-rehearsed theatrical production in which the stage is carefully set. Dramatically, ceremoniously, the aides transmit the lieutenant's orders to kill, and the troops methodically adjust their machine guns as they prepare to destroy an entire community. "The executioners have known their roles for a long time, forever," Wiesel tells us (BJ, 76).

The parts thrust upon the oppressor and the oppressed, perversely uniting them upon the same stage, embody the tragedy of the human condition in which men at both extremes act out the destinies imposed upon them. In *Dawn*, Elisha and John Dawson assume the archetypal roles of executioner and victim forced by circumstances far beyond their control to participate in a macabre cosmic play, where God perhaps makes his presence felt through the absence of hatred and the feeling of pity. In effect, the classical structure of the novel lends itself to theatrical interpretation and has even been outlined as a play by a French critic, Luc Estang, who envisages the possibility of staging the piece in the form of a trial that would take place in the course of one long night.[10] In the first act, Elisha would set himself up as his own witness and judge, subjected to the torments of a private tribunal. In the second act, he would defend his position in front of the dead, called upon to be his witnesses and judges. The third act brings the play to a tragic conclusion through a confrontation of the executioner and his victim, the British hostage.

A trial does, indeed, seem to be occurring during Elisha's anguished night in the bleak antechamber, a trial commanded by the presence of the dead. According to Jewish tradition, the dead rise from their tombs at midnight to pray in the synagogue.[11] From midnight on, the numberless friends and family of the protagonist, as well as strangers, parade into the room of the resistance fighters. A multitude of faces without names and names without faces, they are invisible to all but Elisha. They appear as "sad, funereal, hostile" shadows at one with the darkness. They stay with Elisha through the night, even accompanying him into Dawson's cell. At daybreak, they vanish.

The phantoms communicate chiefly through their eyes. The young boy representing Elisha's child self silently speaks to the adult Elisha with a penetrating gaze that has a voice of its own. The ghost of Elisha's father stares at him with "his large eyes in which I had so often seen the sky open up" (167). The eyes of Kalman, his former master, are "two globes of fire, two suns that burned my face" (167–68) and the most powerful look of all, the mystical, loving and otherworldly gaze of the beggar, makes Elisha doubt for a moment, and then acknowledge, his own existence. The beggar takes Elisha's head in his hands, looks him in the eyes, and tells him that he may not execute John Dawson without involving all present in the room.

The congregation of the dead crowded into the small chamber, too hot and too narrow to hold so many visitors, is an integral part of Elisha's past and present. The ghosts perform a hallucinatory dance around the protagonist, stepping lightly to their own rhythm without touching the ground. Elisha feels like an orchestra leader, directing their movements with his words, which serve as a baton. He is their collective representative, the sum total of what they had been and would have become had they lived: "We're present wherever you go; we are what you do," the young Elisha tells his older self (182). While the protagonist remains on the circumference of the circle of the living, he finds himself at the fixed center of this eerie kingdom inhabited by ghosts, the meeting ground of two worlds. All that he does involves those who have contributed to his personal history: "An act so absolute as that of killing involves not only the killer but as well, those who have formed him. In murdering a man I was making them murderers" (169).

Implicating the dead in his act reinforces Elisha's sense of guilt. Their suffocating silence and mute stares fiercely accuse the would-be resistance fighter, who is uncomfortably conscious of the soundless tribunal behind his back. Wherever he goes in the room, he feels they are watching him. He thinks that he has doubly betrayed these people from his former life, first, by staying alive when they died, and then, by assuming the role of the executioner. He struggles to vindicate himself in their reproachful eyes and implores them not to judge him but to judge God. However, the dead make it clear that they have come not to be judges but rather witnesses at the execution. They are present simply because he is, and must accompany him to the end. "We *are* silence. And your silence is us. You carry us with you. . . . Your silence is your judge," says the boy (183).

Yet if the dead do not condemn Elisha, throughout the night he wrestles with his predicament: the fact of killing strongly contradicts the precepts of Judaism, but there is a higher cause at stake, the establishment of a Jewish state. In *Dawn*, as Lothar Kahn puts it, "traditional Judaism debates with modern national Judaism."[12] Elisha wants to believe that he is not an assassin but a fighter for freedom, an idealist who has chosen life over death. He tries to reject the conventional role of the passive Jew, the persecuted, neurotic, spineless victim—"the trembling of history"—in favor of the new aggressive Jewish man of action, "the wind which made it tremble" (135). But unlike Gad and the other members of the Resistance movement in Palestine—Jacob, Gideon, Ilana—the protagonist cannot evoke the rule of "an eye for an eye, a tooth for a tooth." Torn by ambivalence, filled with fear and disgust, he is unable to break with his past. Precisely because he has entered the realm of death and has survived, his inner struggle grows all the more intense.

In the course of the painful debate occurring within his conscience, the protagonist recalls Kalman's words: "Why has a man no right to commit murder? Because in so doing he takes upon himself the function of God" (144). Elisha pictures both himself and an anthropomorphic God, in a dark gray SS uniform. But this is too disturbing to him and God the executioner becomes God the terrorist. The God who died on the gallows of Auschwitz in *Night* is reborn in *Dawn* as a resistance fighter striving to create a country for the homeless Jews.

Despite a desperate attempt to overcome his doubts, Elisha is never able to accept the role of the aggressor. At the end of the novel, surprisingly enough, he finally pulls the trigger, but unwillingly, as if directed by a force higher than himself. Because the protagonist seems to be controlled by the circumstances in which he finds himself, and because his act seems to be his and not his at the same time, he has been compared to other existential characters. Irving Feldman states:

> The character does not act into his acts—he awakes to them as to *faits accomplis*—but only into the situation they have provoked. . . . So here in *Dawn*, Elisha's voice is detonalized by his Stranger-like 'for some reasons' and like other existentialist murderers, he pulls the trigger only because the gun is in his hand.[13]

Elisha's passivity is not unlike Meursault's remoteness in Albert Camus's *The Stranger*, to which Feldman is clearly alluding. However, the Wieselean protagonist's night of probing and uncertainty prior to the hostage's execution hardly resembles Meursault's motiveless shooting of the Arab on the Algerian beach. Meursault is morally indifferent; Elisha battles with the conflicting alternatives of his dilemma, well aware of their moral implications. While Meursault's act awakens his consciousness, Elisha's plunges him into a void provoked by the idea itself of killing: "The earth yawned beneath my feet and I seemed to be falling into a bottomless pit, where existence was a nightmare" (130). For a brief moment as he holds the revolver, he feels especially lucid and sure of himself. But the bullet shot through John Dawson's heart returns Elisha to a deathlike stance:

> There was a pain in my head and my body was growing heavy. The shot had left me deaf and dumb. That's it, I said to myself. It's done. I've killed. I've killed Elisha. [203]

This sense of physical heaviness, also experienced when Elisha first encountered Dawson ("I felt my body grow heavy" [191]), is a bodily expression of the psychic numbness particularly Lazarene in nature. The protagonist is weighed down by the awesome burden he has assumed—the authority of dealing death. He has violated one of the major commandments of Judaism: "Thou shalt not kill." No death can be justified, even if for a higher cause. The finality of the pulled trigger dehumanizes Elisha and prolongs his state of mourning. For he mourns not only the murdered hostage, with whom he identifies, but that part of himself which he has assassinated. All murder is suicide and every suicide a murder, Wiesel observes throughout his writing: "Whoever kills, kills his brother, and when one has killed, one no longer is anyone's brother. One is the enemy" (MG, 59).[14] The corpselike assailant ends up seeing himself as the "Lazarus of the tomb," once again the victim—and enemy of himself.

Elisha's strong identification with Dawson both before and after his death reflects a tragically human dimension in the victim-executioner relationship. In contrast to the detached and merciless treatment of their victims by the Nazis, Wiesel's portrayal is intimate both physically and emotionally. The act of execution itself is personalized:[15] Elisha kills his hostage at close range, looks him in the eyes (Dawson rejects the blindfold offered to him) and shoots him not in the neck as is customary but through the heart. The protagonist tries to depersonalize Dawson by making him into the archetype of the hated enemy—the incarnation of evil, the SS, assassin of his own parents, "the man who had come between me and the man I had wanted to become, and who was now ready to kill the man in me" (198). He focuses on his compatriot David ben Moshe, about to be killed by the British, but despite his concentrated efforts is unable to muster enough hatred to give meaning to his act.[16] The alliance between Elisha and Dawson appears more like a friendship than a clash between antagonists, a notion developed in the novel through the themes of identification and substitution.

Clearly identifying with Dawson and linking their destinies, Elisha is aware of the eternal bond between the oppressor and the oppressed. At the moment of confrontation between these so-called enemies, they seem to comprehend each other in a particular manner:

> The seated victim, the standing executioner[17]—smiling and understanding each other better than if they were childhood friends. . . . There was harmony between us; my smile answered his; his pity was mine. No human being would ever understand me as he understood me at this hour. [192]

The affinity between these two men suggests an unmistakable tie that transcends the immediate situation, a kinship even closer than that of childhood friends.

The rapport between Dawson and Elisha resembles, in effect, that of a father and his son. Towards the end of the novel, the British officer makes a comparison between Elisha and his own son, who are the same age. His son is studying at Cambridge and is not at all like Elisha: he is blond, strong, healthy, likes to eat, drink, go to the movies, and go out with girls. "He has none of your anxiety, your unhappiness," the British officer tells his assailant (192). This conscious effort to distinguish the young executioner from his own son leads us to believe that the two boys are surely inseparable in Dawson's mind.

The father-son relationship also manifests itself through the theme of the name. One of the first questions Dawson asks Elisha is "What is your name?" Troubled by the question, the youth explains that he was named after a prophet traditionally said to represent a life-giving force. Elisha, the disciple and successor of Elijah, is the prophet of resurrection.[18] "He restored life to a little boy by lying upon him and breathing into his mouth." the protagonist says (191), and the hostage ironically acknowledges that his would-be executioner is acting contrary to tradition. But when the bullet finally pierces Dawson's heart, his last word is "Elisha," which he repeats twice: "A dead man, whose lips were still warm, had pronounced my name: Elisha" (203).

There is a parallel treatment of the theme of the name in *Night*, when the narrator's dying father calls out "Eliezer" twice before he is silenced by the club of an SS guard. His son hears his last appeal and does not move. Although in *Night* the father is still alive while calling out the name and in *Dawn*, the father figure dies at the moment of speaking, in both books the name can be seen as a summons for help as well as a condemnation of betrayal. The dying victim utters the name twice, almost in incantation, while the survivor remains mute. The invocation of the name is a means of passing on the heritage, race, and identity from the father to his successor, who unwillingly emerges from the Night to be the "son of Dawn" (Dawson)—the dusty gray dawn of death-in-life.

Wiesel has transposed his autobiographical account of *Night* onto the fictional narrative *Dawn*, creating characters who live out the ambiguities of the father-son relationship. If Eliezer feels responsible, first for having let his father die and then for having "stolen life" from him by surviving in his place, the fictional character of Elisha actually does become the murderer of a father figure, thus carrying the son's unconscious death wishes and guilt feeling to the extreme. As Robert Jay Lifton points out in *Death in Life* with regard to the survivor: "The unconscious self-accusation 'I am responsible for his death' can easily become 'I killed him.' "[19] Elisha, heir to Eliezer's guilt and hence to his sense of betrayal, violently relives the most horrifying and hostile impulses incurred by the death camp experience.

Nevertheless, Elisha does not accept the role of assassin without a struggle. He desperately hopes to change the course of events by substituting himself for the victim in an attempt to save the man's life, a theme that prevails throughout Wiesel's works:

> I felt powerless to change anything, least of all myself, in spite of the fact that I wanted to introduce a transformation into the room, to reorder the whole of creation. . . . To have such power I should have had to take the place of death, not just of the individual death of John Dawson. [158]

So intense is Elisha's will to die in the place of Dawson that when he enters his hostage's cell, he has the impression that he is going to his own execution. Yet, in spite of his overwhelming desire to change places with the victim, it is ultimately impossible to "reorder" creation, and the figure of the son both in *Night* and *Dawn* is condemned to survive while the father dies. The son is forced, in a sense, to replace his father, to "become" him. As the "surviving" self, he inherits the task of carrying on the tradition and continuing the succession. At the same time, he feels guilty about taking his father's place: the "dead" self holds on to the image of the father and identifies with him. This state of ambivalence defines the Lazarene character who exists halfway between the world of the living and the world of the dead.

The theme of substitution, as evidenced by the protagonist's obsession to change places with the father surrogate in *Dawn*, is extended to the ghost of Elisha's real father, who appears in the waiting room along with the other dead members of his family. Elisha's deepest wish is to transfuse the life and blood of his own body into his father. Like the prophet of resurrection for whom he is named, Elisha wants to bring his father back to life. The act of transfusion is the ultimate form of substitution:

> I stood in front of him, not knowing what to do with my head, my eyes, my hands. I wanted to transfer the lifeblood of my body into *my voice*. At moments I fancied I had done so (180; my emphasis).

The theme of substitution is related here to that of the voice. Despite Elisha's inability to resuscitate his deceased father, his belief that he has partially succeeded in transmitting life through his voice is a positive sign. The transfusion of life by means of the voice becomes a metaphor for the creative act capable of transcending death by breathing life into a dead object. The voice may be fragile, as Roland Barthes points out in his essay on Jean Cayrol, but it has a permanent quality that surpasses the material world:

> It [the voice] is thus the sign of the unnamable, what is born or remains of man if one takes from him the materiality of his body, the identity of his face or the humanity of his gaze; it is both the most human and most inhuman of substances.[20]

The body decays but the voice is ever-present. By writing about his father, Wiesel has given him back his *voice*.

If the voice is a life-giving force, it can also be a powerful weapon. Ilana, a member of the resistance movement, whose legendary, warm, and resonant "Voice of Freedom" is heard every night on the radio by all of Palestine, knows that her dangerous words provoke the British. Each person kills in his or her manner, she informs Elisha. "There are those, like you, who kill with their hands and others—like me—who kill with their voices" (177). For the entire world, with the exception of five people in the terrorist movement, Ilana lacks "the identity of a face" and "the humanity of a gaze." Her spoken language *is* her identity and her form of combat. The voice, therefore, can restore life and hope but can be the source of death as well. Pushed to both of these extremes, the voice is more potent than fragile.

The voice in *Dawn* falls into a third category: a symbol of purity and tranquility. Ilana's speech is described as golden, clear, deeply moving, "as pure as truth, as sad as purity" (175). Her sensitive, gentle tone and choice of vocabulary remind Elisha of his mother, whose bedtime stories created peace and harmony for him every night until he was about nine or ten: "Like the voice of God it had the power to dispel chaos and to impart a vision of the future which might have been mine" (176). Both Ilana and Elisha's mother speak forth in a way that soothes and caresses. No longer a weapon or an instrument of restitution, the voice here is an expression of human tenderness.

The last category of voice portrayed in the novel—and perhaps the most awesome—is that of the messenger. Gad, the mysterious *Meshulah* of Hasidic legends, charged with transforming Elisha's destiny, is distinguished by his voice, which frightens and attracts the youth by its intense and unconditional quality:

> His voice is such as to make a man tremble, for the message it brings is more powerful than either the bearer or the recipient. His every word seems to come from the absolute, the infinite and its significance is at the same time fearful and fascinating. [134]

Gad, whose name means *good fortune*, appears as a modern-day prophet, a kind of Messianic figure. He is the master who transmits the word; his voice transcends his being. When he gravely announces "I am Gad," he sounds "as if he were uttering some kabbalistic sentence which contained an answer to every question" (133). But Gad's teachings do not come from the mystical doctrine of the Kabbala. He tells tales of Palestine and of the struggle for the future Jewish state. Sent to deliver messages of hope and redemption, his mission is to bring Elisha to the Promised Land.

Gad's words encourage the young protagonist to join the Palestinian resistance movement, where he becomes a messenger in his own right, but of a different sort. Shortly before John Dawson's execution, the British officer asks Elisha for some paper and pencil in order to write a note to his son. At first Elisha tears out some pages from his notebook and hands him his own pencil, then gives him the entire notebook. Silence dominates the room, broken only by the sound of the pencil etching out a meager legacy. Elisha's gesture is charged with significance for he furnishes the material for the message, providing the instrument by which the hostage can bear witness.

The victim is obsessed with the idea that his testament be transmitted to his heir. Twice he asks Elisha to send the note to his son: the first time about forty minutes before the execution, and again, five minutes before his death, he repeats insistently: "The note. You won't forget, will you?" (202). Elisha promises to mail it that very day. The father here is the chronicler and the son inherits the chronicle. Elisha's position is that of the courier, news bearer, and letter carrier, who receives the father's message and passes it on to the son, thus insuring the continuity of generations. The figure of the letter carrier can be extended to that of the writer bearing words endowed with creative and sacred powers, which is to say, bearing witness.[21]

If *Dawn* ends in a state of self-laceration and fear, reflected by the protagonist's death mask suspended on the other side of the window, the role of the messenger nonetheless points to a more positive side of the theme of the witness. Elisha as the Lazarene witness is a messenger of the dead, but by serving as intermediary between father and son he assumes an important function: the link between past and present. The act of transmission itself becomes the primary mode of survival and, in its own way, restores a sense of connection to life.

THE VICTIM'S SECOND DEATH: *THE ACCIDENT*

The stagnant dawn breaks through to the sterile light of day in *Le Jour* (or *The Accident*, as Wiesel's second novel is entitled in English). Elisha, whose name was repeated by the victim at the moment of execution, is replaced by the narrator of *The Accident*, who has lost his name. Elisha looks for a face in the window and fearfully sees his own death image; the "I" of *The Accident* categorically refuses to look at himself in a mirror. If by executing another, Elisha spiritually annihilates a part of himself, the narrator-protagonist of the book that follows actually does attempt to commit suicide. Elisha is kept alive by the dead preserved inside of him, but his successor can no longer cope with the anguish of his memories. The only way he can turn his back on the past is to destroy himself.[22]

One hot summer evening in Times Square, the narrator is hit by a taxi. To his dismay he is brought back to life by his doctor, Paul Russel, his girlfriend, Kathleen, and his artist friend, Gyula. At the time of the accident, the narrator is a correspondent for an Israeli newspaper in New York; he is also a concentration camp survivor. Because he has been severely injured, he is forced to remain in traction, totally immobilized for weeks in a plaster cast, as he hovers between life and death. The oppressive setting of the hospital room is similar to the circumscribed space of Elisha's room in Paris, the antechamber of the terrorists, and the basement cell in Palestine. In *The Accident*, the cast further circumscribes the space of the main character by enclosing him in a private impenetrable world, cut off from others. The bandage serves as a shell that paralyzes and imprisons him, but also protects him.

The swaddled figure of the protagonist in his mummified bandaged state resembles, in effect, the dead Lazarus of the Bible, "his hands and feet bound with bandages and his face wrapped with a cloth" (John 11:44). Both the Biblical and fictional characters are bound and constricted and dwell in the kingdom of the dead. Lazarus was in the tomb for four days before Jesus brought him forth. Likewise, Wiesel's narrator regains consciousness on the fifth day after the accident. Lazarus is resurrected as a miraculous sign of victory over death, just as Dr. Russel brings his patient back to life from the edge of the grave.

Yet, unlike the Biblical Lazarus, the Lazarene character in the novel resents the light of day. He prefers the darkness of the tomb and the familiar faces of the dead to the foreign ones of the living. The survivor mending on his hospital bed is angry at medicine's apparent triumph and feels cheated by having failed a second time to join his loved ones. His sterile reentry into life reinforces his sense of isolation and he considers himself half-dead, a monster, an outcast, and most of all a stranger to himself and to others, an image revealed mainly through the motif of the mirror.

As in *Dawn*, the theme of the mirror is represented by the image of the window, but instead of reflecting the protagonist's fragmented face, in *The Accident* the glass becomes his eye or opening to the outside world. The window overlooking the East River is his only access to the landscape beyond the confinement of the hospital room. However, like Elisha, the narrator does not distinguish between inner and outer space: what the eye or "I" sees beyond the room reproduces its own sense of self. When Dr. Russel goes to the window and comments about the beautiful view of the East River, his patient replies cynically that it is just like himself, "it hardly moves." "Sheer illusion!" the doctor retorts. "It is calm only on the surface. Go beneath the surface, you'll see how restless it is" (A, 254). The window serves here as a passageway to a body of water that takes on the function of a mirror, revealing the protagonist's state of mind and body. The illusory immobility of the river, like the frozen self, masks the fierce tension and agitation within.

The image of stilled water is mentioned earlier in the novel during one of the protagonist's many flashbacks. Recalling his first night with Kathleen in Paris and their silent walk along the Seine, he muses: "The Seine, reflecting the sky and the lampposts, now showed us its mysterious winter face, its quiet cloudiness where any life is extinguished, where any light dies. I looked down and thought that someday I too would die" (229). The unmoving water, mirror of the cosmos at a standstill and of the soul fixed unto itself, is an icy embodiment of silence and death. The protagonist suddenly recalls how on a boat trip to South America he understood Narcissus' desire to jump into the water. He, too, yearns to be one with the sea, but not because he is in love with his own image: the sea attracts him by its promise of eternal peace, and end to suffering.

The "I" of the novel is, indeed, the opposite of Narcissus; he hates his own visage and refuses to look in the mirror about to be handed to him by the nurse who has shaved his face. When he threatens to break the mirror if she gives it to him, the nurse is manifestly disturbed; she cannot comprehend why the patient is repelled by his self-image. Disgusted and guilt-ridden at being reminded that he is still alive, he prefers to remain anonymous and invisible, prolonging the depersonalization of the camps where he was considered a number, an object, a subhuman without an identity. He rejects the meeting with the stranger in the mirror and fears the creation of a new form out of the formlessness that envelops and protects him. He refuses the long painful process involved in developing a new sense of self.

Faceless and nameless, the narrator of *The Accident* echoes Elisha's feelings of isolation, but in a more bitter and melancholic mode: "I had nothing to lose, nothing to regret. I wasn't bound to the world of men. All I cared for had been dispersed by smoke" (241). The world for him is now desolate as an arid desert. True life lies far beyond in that other universe he has never left. One can note resonances of the nineteenth-century solitary hero who felt alienated in the society of his times, but the underlying despair comes closer to existential solitude. The word *alone*, for example, appears throughout the text: "I felt alone, abandoned" (218); "Now I was alone. Alone as only a paralyzed and suffering man can be" (222); "I'm not afraid of being alone, of walking the distance between life and death" (221); "A man who has suffered more than others and differently, should live apart. Alone" (304).

Yet, no analogies can convey the solitude of the survivor, for it transcends all other kinds. Wiesel's narrator feels cut off from others around him who are capable of laughing, loving, praying, suffering, and leading normal lives; he sees himself as "a grave for the unburied dead" (247). His will to live has been "amputated" and he no longer knows if he is dead or alive. He is a twentieth-century Hamlet issued from the death camps.

> The problem is not: to be or not to be. But rather: to be and not to be. What it comes down to is that man lives while dying, that he represents death to the living, and that's where tragedy begins. [275]

The extreme alienation experienced by the main character in *The Accident* is translated textually through the theme of paralysis. Bodily paralysis reflects the death-in-life condition of the Lazarene protagonist, and is one of the dominant motifs of the novel. As the narrator walks around Times Square on a hot July evening before the accident occurs, he feels tired, oppressed, sluggish. One has the impression that he is a walking corpse, an automaton propelled into "the human whirlwind" of the carnivallike urban crowds: "I felt stunned, heavy, a thick fog in my head. The slightest gesture was like trying to lift a planet. There was lead in my arms, in my legs" (208). The sensation of heaviness evoked by the leaden parts of the body recalls Elisha's intense feeling of being weighed down before and after he has killed John Dawson. ("I felt my body grow heavy. The next day it would be heavier still. . . . it would be weighted down by my life and his death" [D, 191–192]). In both novels, the psychic numbness of the characters is manifested through body language.

With the advent of the accident, the theme of paralysis is carried to its extreme. The protagonist's near death is depicted by his physical immobility and loss of sensation. Like the face, the inert arms and legs have become detached from their owner, who has lost control of them. A foreign object, his body no longer belongs to him, a motif prevalent in Holocaust literature.

"My body escapes me," says Robert Antelme in *L'Espèce humaine*,[23] and Primo Levi in *Survival in Auschwitz* states: "I turn rotten in the rain, I shiver in the wind; already my own body is no longer mine."[24] "Our bodies moved apart from us. Possessed, dispossessed. Abstract. We were unfeeling. . . . We marched. Automatons marched. Statues of frost marched," Charlotte Delbo recollects in *None of Us Will Return*. She is obsessed with the theme of immobility represented by the numbed body. The camp prisoners, glacial figures, have become a part of the paralyzed landscape of Auschwitz: "And us, we were immured in ice, in light, in silence."[25] Gestures and words are abolished in this soundless, timeless, frozen present.

The theme of paralysis is linked to the frozen body in *The Accident* as well. Just before losing consciousness during his accident, the protagonist dreams of "a summer night when my body was frozen" (215). Rushed to the hospital his mouth full of blood, deaf and mute, he is unable to move. He lies on the hospital bed, as stiff as a statue: "The muscles in my face were motionless, frozen. . . . the muscles in my face didn't obey me. I was too cold" (223). The image of the desensitized self is associated then with the theme of cold, which also serves as a transition from the present to the past.

Dying of cold on his hospital bed, the protagonist flashes back to the chilly winter evening in Paris when he first met Kathleen. He remembers the icy wind whipping his face as he and Kathleen walked along the frigid Seine. The cold seemed to punish him and prevent him from forgetting the haunting black and white figure of his grandmother, who like some shadowy figure of Chagall hovered over him about to drop out of the sky. "No! I haven't forgotten. Every time I'm cold, I think of you, I think only of you," he cries out to his dead grandmother as he jumps away from Kathleen, who reaches over to touch his arm. The piercing cold is a contact with death, "the cold of a grave," beckoning to the survivor, who yearns to join his old grandmother adrift in the freezing wind.

At the same time that the body is numbed by cold, it is also the source of intense heat, burning with fever and transformed into a furnace. The themes of cold and heat are juxtaposed. The fever flings the narrator from one extreme to another, "throwing me from one world into another, up and down, very high up and very far down, as if it meant to teach me the cold of high places and the heat of abysses" (221). His hell is the fire that burns from within and freezes at the same time. "Hell isn't others. It's ourselves. Hell is the burning fever that makes you feel cold" (220), says the narrator.

The theme of heat also ties the past to the present. As the narrator suffers from the sensation of burning and unquenched thirst, he identifies with his grandmother dying of thirst, crushed by bodies, and suffocating from the heat of the gas chambers: "Grandmother would have understood. It was hot in the airless, waterless chambers. It was hot in the room where her livid body was crushed by other livid bodies. Like me, she must have opened her mouth to drink air, to drink water. But there was no water where she was, there was no air" (223).

The fiery heat of the crematorium that killed his grandmother is transformed into the tragic symbol of the black sun. The narrator envisages his grandmother as a flame that has chased and replaced the sun, blinding and darkening the vision of future generations. This new sun casts a long shadow on the post-Auschwitz epoch. The black sun is also linked thematically to the black shawl worn by the grandmother, representing a kind of shroud that frightens her grandson but offers him refuge and union in death. Moreover, the dark sun is associated with the black clouds of smoke hanging over the death camps—the only monument to the homeless dead.

The theme of death through heat and fire is brought to its conclusion at the end of the text with the burning of the portrait. Gyula, a painter of Hungarian origin and a good friend of the narrator, comes to the hospital room every day to work on a portrait of his paralyzed comrade. The day before the protagonist is to leave the hospital, Gyula presents him with the sinister portrait. The "I" of the novel is portrayed as death, his eyes a throbbing red in the manner of the artist, Soutine. The sky is painted in thick blacks and the sun is dark gray, repeating the motif of an eclipsed civilization. The eyes in the portrait reflect the presence of the narrator's dead family and especially his grandmother with her dark shroud that promises to envelop him securely in a long-sought tomb and remove him from his exile on earth. From the depths of the portrait, she speaks to him: "I'll take you with me. In the train that goes to heaven. And you won't see the earth any more. I'll hide it from you. With my black shawl" (317).

Gyula, who represents a life-force and movement pitted against death and paralysis, has tried to objectify the dead self of his friend in this portrait. The artist dramatically takes a match, and defiantly sets fire to his creation in order to exorcise the past. Heat or fire is utilized here for purification or purging, but the narrator clearly remains a Lazarene character, left with the ashes of his own image—grotesque remnants of his deathlike state. The burned portrait serves as a mirror of the "I" 's self-immolation through attempted suicide, a frightening expression of his seared psyche and scarred soul.

The burning of the portrait is for the narrator the "second burning" of his grandmother, and makes him more than ever aware of his second failure to join her. Too weak to stop Gyula's action, he can only protest impotently through tears. However, the theme of tears, which concludes the novel, is important, for it is linked to that of fire. The narrator says that his grandmother's tears are "so hot that they burn everything in their path" (234). These burning tears leave scars. In effect, the survivor's tears recall the wounds and stigmata of the deep burns of the past—embers of the devouring fire.

Yet if tears, like memory, reactivate the wounds, they also wash away the lingering pain. The narrator notes that he has inherited his grandmother's tears, "which as it is written, open all doors" (235). In contrast to the "scar-tears," these tears of deliverance help to release suffering and to thaw the frozen water. Crying, then, is part of the renewal process, of moving away from death and learning to feel again.[26] It is a means of extinguishing the fire of the Holocaust.

If there is an affirmative element in *The Accident*, it is not conveyed through the ambivalence of the final tears, which both burn and cleanse. Rather, it is the voice that offers a possibility of piercing the thick cast of plaster imprisoning the survivor-protagonist. Images from the past, triggered off by the slightest provocation, turn into the mental dictators of the present. Deeply embedded within, like time bombs they explode, bringing the shame, guilt, and madness of humanity to the surface. "What you lived remains planted in you like a jagged crystal that starts growing slowly, slowly, until there is no room for anything else and you become one searing pain, bursting its shell."[27] The protagonist of *The Accident* is obsessed with these erupting time bombs. His memories set him apart from those around him, and he remains alienated from other human beings, afraid of loving or accepting love. The fragmented mosaics of his vanished life are his burden and his nourishment. Yet, in spite of his self-imposed isolation, the need to speak out and be heard begins to bring this Lazarus-like figure back to life.

Loss of voice in the Wieselean thematic network implies loss of self, the condemnation to a silent death. Fear of not being able to hear his own voice haunts the narrator-protagonist, whose parched throat burns feverishly with thirst as he lies on his hospital bed. He tries to shout but the inarticulated noises stick in his throat. When finally he realizes that the power of speech still belongs to him, though his utterances are barely a whisper, he is overwhelmed by a strong feeling that breaks through his numbness: "That I was still alive had left me indifferent or nearly so. But the knowledge that I could still speak filled me with an emotion that I couldn't hide" (218). The sound of the disembodied voice is a means of escape from the prison of plaster; it is the first step towards resuscitating the dead self. "Suddenly I felt a strange need to speak out loud," the narrator proclaims. "To tell the story of Grandmother's life and death" (233).

The desire to speak out suggests a shift from inner to outer, from absence to presence, from death to life. In order to feel that one is alive, it becomes necessary to express oneself aloud. The narrator of *The Accident* finds it difficult to reenact the past in the solitude of his memory; an inner monologue is not sufficient to sustain his existence. The subject needs an object to whom he can tell his story, the speaker needs a listener. The verbalization of thoughts and the externalization of events in the presence of another create a reality of their own that helps to alleviate the isolation of the survivor. Speaking becomes a mode of survival.

But if using one's voice to bear witness is the beginning of the healing process, the voice in this novel is tinged with hostility and contempt. The Lazarene protagonist is ambivalent: he feels a desire to speak out, yet knows that his words will contaminate and shock the listener. He considers himself "a messenger of the dead among the living" (243), described by Irving Halperin as "the silent, poisoned messenger, despised in his own eyes and disturbing in the eyes of the innocent."[28] The stranger without a name who has rejected the reflection of his own face in the mirror prefers to be seen by others rather than to see himself. By his presence alone, he will serve as the mirror-monument of society, blinding and terrorizing all those who can bear to look at his warped image.

Wiesel's protagonist seems to be a spokesman for the author himself when he aggressively asserts his role as messenger-storyteller and issues his defiant declaration, warning us that he intentionally wants to disturb the potential listener to his troubled tales: "I am a storyteller. My legends can only be told at dusk. Whoever listens questions his life. . . . The heroes of my legends are cruel and without pity. They are capable of strangling you" (271). The theme of the stifled voice is repeated here. The author-narrator threatens to cut off the reader's breath by relentlessly exposing him to the corruption of mankind. The speaker takes on the role of the oppressor and the listener is cast as the oppressed, recreating the torturer-victim relationship of the camps. However, the menacing assault is not to be physical but metaphysical: the listener is cautioned that his basic values will be called into question upon hearing stories of the Holocaust. Indeed, his entire life may undergo an upheaval, for he is part of the society that allowed the event to take place: whether or not he actually lived through it, he is collectively responsible.

The "I" of *The Accident* is well aware that the witness can evoke in the listener emotions ranging from fear, rage, and guilt to hostility and despair. These responses can cause a deep sense of alienation. The unknown Englishman whom he meets on a boat to South America, and who becomes his first listener, says several times after hearing the survivor's story that he is going to hate him. Before he shares the burden of history with Kathleen, he warns her of the risk she is taking. When she accepts the responsibility, he is certain that she will end up by hating this defiled messenger from the grave.

Nevertheless, the negative effects of bearing witness are counterbalanced by the presence of a sensitive and giving listener who has the power to combat the forces of destruction by simply *being there*. The deep and hoarse disembodied voice of the Englishman surges from the shadows of the ship's deck, and stops the young protagonist just as he is about to jump into the sea. At first, the stranger relates his own story, disclosing how, on his honeymoon, he too had an almost irresistible urge to plunge into the waves and end his life. And then, he tells how he conquered this impulse. The protagonist listens attentively to this tale and, in turn, lays bare his unimaginable account of atrocity before the unsuspecting spectator, who is quietly drawn into the kingdom of night. Speaking and listening become acts of salvation, for the youth finally does not commit suicide. The anonymous Englishman appears as the protagonist's double: he mirrors his attraction to death and, at the same time, is his protector. Along with Dr. Russel and Gyula, the Englishman in the novel embodies the "surviving" self pitted against the "dead" self. The need to save the life of another human being, manifest here, is a recurring Wieselean theme, fundamentally linked to the theme of the witness.

Although the Englishman—the nameless, faceless listener enveloped by darkness and silence—does save the protagonist's life, he finishes by hating him. In contrast to the Englishman, and contrary to the protagonist's expectations, Kathleen is a sympathetic and solicitous listener. Before he makes love to Kathleen, the narrator-protagonist kneels before the seated woman, stares into her eyes and relieves himself of his tainted memories by pouring forth his ugly tale:

> I wanted to get rid of all the filth that was in me and graft it into her pupils and her lips which were so pure, so innocent, so beautiful. I bared my soul. My most contemptible thoughts and desires, my most painful betrayals, my vaguest lies, I tore them from inside me and placed them in front of her, like an impure offering, so she could see them and smell their stench. [248]

The kneeling position suggests that of a religious figure praying and confessing his sins of survival. The past takes on a life of its own, as the survivor's nocturnal legacy—impure offering—is transmitted to the listener. But if the posture is pious, the tone is not. Unlike the detached manner in which he unmasked himself to the Englishman on the boat, his expression here is defiant. Forcefully emitting the poison that infects his insides, the narrator seeks aggressively to contaminate, to "dirty the hands" of the woman by emotionally and physically discharging his venomous words and sperm onto her moral virginity. Kathleen comes to represent that part of humanity untouched by the horrors of the concentrationary universe. The protagonist joins his evil, death-ridden self to her pure, life-giving one, thus insuring a bond between speaker and listener. While Kathleen remains a stranger to her lover's past, she wants to be united with him by participating in his suffering. Her encouraging voice is likened to that of a prostitute urging a man to continue making love:

> She was saying "more" in the eager voice of a woman who wants her pleasure to last, who asks the man she loves not to stop, not to leave her, not to disappoint her, not to abandon her half-way between ectasy and nothing. . . . From time to time, she insisted in the same eager voice that sounded so much like the old prostitute's, "More . . . More . . ." [247–48]

The analogy drawn between Kathleen's voice and that of a prostitute brings to mind Sarah, the young woman of the streets whom the narrator once encountered in Paris. While Kathleen exemplifies the human self struggling to come back to life, Sarah embodies the inhuman—the survivor's darker side. She is his twin sister of the Holocaust, his female counterpart, a mirror image of his self-hatred looming before him and staring him in the face. One has the impression that theirs is a meeting of two separate people who are in a fundamental way one and the same.

Like the protagonist, Sarah is a concentration camp survivor whose entire being is numbed, inaccessible, cut off from the world of the living. She has retreated into her own prison and presents a ghostlike appearance, speaking in a voice that seems to emanate from another world. Her eyes reflect "The God of chaos and impotence. The God who tortures twelve-year-old children" (209). Blessed and cursed, possessed and pure, this Lazarene heroine is a prostitute-madonna figure who has prolonged the degradation of her camp experience where, at the age of twelve, she was forced into becoming the "birthday present" of a drunken Nazi officer and subsequently the "special present" of the entire barracks. But this blond, blue-eyed woman bears the same name as the protagonist's mother, a name constantly repeated in the hospital room as he flashes back to his past, tossing and turning in a feverish state. Just as Kathleen is associated with the dead grandmother throughout the novel, Sarah is linked to the mother whose name the protagonist has vowed never to forget.

There are parallels and oppositions depicted in the main character's relationship with Kathleen and Sarah, the two principal women in *The Accident*. With Kathleen, he is the speaker, the subject of the testimony that he unloads onto her, the listener. The positions are reversed with Sarah: it is he who listens and becomes the recipient of her testimony. In sharp contrast to his desire to frighten Kathleen, he is terrified of Sarah. He remains outside of the young prostitute's universe in the same way that Kathleen is excluded from his. In *Dawn*, Wiesel showed how one man can be both victim and executioner. In *The Accident*, he describes the divided role of the witness as speaker and listener:

> To listen to a story under such circumstances is to play a part in it, to take sides, to say yes or no, to move one way or the other. From then on there is a before and an after. And even to forget becomes a cowardly acceptance. [228]

The listener, then, initiated into the realm of Holocaust darkness, assumes a responsibility to the witness by his presence alone. By choosing to listen to Sarah, the protagonist identifies and merges with her; he wants to join in her suffering, participate in her story, share her humiliation. One listens, one is anguished, and finally one must change after hearing the tale. To listen to a witness is to become one. The defiance of the witness who speaks out is applied to the listener as well. The narrator-protagonist calls for a refusal of the society that has led to the dissolution of moral values and demands the creation of another in its place. He condemns history itself:

> I curse history which has made us what we are: a source of malediction. History which deserves death, destruction. Whoever listens to Sarah and doesn't change, whoever enters Sarah's world and doesn't invent new gods and new religions, deserves death and destruction. [289]

The bold, assertive position of the narrator does not, however, make him less vulnerable to Sarah's nightmares.

Greatly disturbed by her account, he wants desperately to cry out in rage and shame, but fights to keep silent. Her tale stirs up painful memories of his own and he feels connected to her on a profound level. He is attracted to, and at the same time repelled by, this sick child whose inscrutable gaze pierces the walls. Mutely he listens, but with each word feels more and more suffocated, his voice stifled, his breath slowly leaving his body. Like a vise clenched around his neck, his fingers grow tighter with Sarah's every phrase and gesture. Her story smothers him mercilessly. He finally finds the confrontation with this sad deathlike shadow of himself too unbearable and takes to flight, escaping from the darkness of the prostitute's room. But even while running away, he realizes that his hands are still pressing against his throat.

We have been warned by the author-narrator that whoever listens to his legends puts his life in jeopardy and risks being strangled by the cruel heroes. This declaration of literary intention is illustrated within the text itself by the story of Sarah and the protagonist's reaction to it. Overpowered by the presence of death to which he is exposed as listener, the "I" of the novel chokes on the young prostitute's words, for in a sense her tale is his tale, her memories his, and her voice his own, detached from its source, yet strangely familiar. By fleeing from this saintly woman bearing the name of his mother, the Wieselean narrator demonstrates a need to distance himself from his own demonic past, which clutches at his neck in an attempt to strangle his very existence.

In *The Accident*, Elie Wiesel thus dramatizes the tensions between distance and involvement, separation and union. The Lazarene character has not yet resolved the struggle between the creative and destructive forces within himself. Drawn to the past, he constantly relives his death encounter, clinging to the dead who inhabit his conscious and unconscious life. Yet he wants to be relieved of the oppressive burden that weighs upon him. Taking to flight is perhaps a means of accepting the death of his family and friends—and of his mother, Sarah. It is a way of repudiating that part of himself that still dwells in the tomb.

The theme of flight also suggests that the author, like his characters, is too close to his subject at the time he is writing these early, highly autobiographical novels. He must first turn his back on the past in order to come to grips with it. A balance must be struck, between the descent into the domain of irrational forces within, and its rendering into literary form, a balance that does not appear to take shape until Wiesel's later novels.

The protagonists of *Dawn* and *The Accident*, fictional embodiments of their author's bleak state of mind, have not yet discovered this balance, nor have they found a justification for having been spared. They cannot distance themselves sufficiently from the past so as to live in the present. Messengers from the dead, their voices issuing from the grave are barely audible, their testimony scarcely articulated. These Lazarene witnesses are still in the process of running from the black night to the lifeless light of day. Repelled by the world of aftermath, embattled by an internal war that the "surviving" self wages against the "dead" self, they strain to distinguish between memory and reality, between the horrors of the Holocaust and the solitude of survival.

3

The Journey Homeward

Seul mon village existe, c'est son image que le monde me renvoie.
—Elie Wiesel

Eᴌɪᴇ ᴡɪᴇꜱᴇʟ's first three books describe the voyage away from his
origins, the long descent into the multiple layers of darkness that
dispossessed him of his identity, his traditions, his community. In the
novel that follows the trilogy, the survivor-protagonist embarks upon
the painful journey homeward in his search of his pre-Holocaust past.
Like a pilgrim, he sets forth upon a quest for a sacred place: a
Transylvanian kingdom lost somewhere between the Dnieper River
and the shadow of the Carpathian mountains. After the odyssey to the
end of night, *The Town Beyond the Wall*, Wiesel's first fictional account of
the return, marks a decisive phase in the author's literary-spiritual
itinerary.

Going back to one's beginnings is painful and complex. If the
Lazarene witness felt alienated in the world of the present, the
pilgrim-protagonist finds himself an intruder in the world of his past.
Filled with anguish, his homecoming confirms the traveler's worst
fears: the town as he knew it has died; his former life is irretrievable.
He recognizes that he is condemned to permanent exile, an exile
"without remedy since he is deprived of the memory of a lost home or
the hope of a promised land," as Albert Camus defines the absurd in
The Myth of Sisyphus.[1] This alienation characterizes the condition of
modern man in general, and the stateless Jewish refugee in particular,

who under extreme and abnormal circumstances was abruptly divested of what was most precious to him.

On the one hand, the return to one's birthplace is impossible and the theme of the "dead" town structures Wiesel's texts, both fiction and nonfiction, that deal with the journey homeward. On the other, the imaginative ability to go back to the source where "everything began, where the world lost its innocence and God his mask" (LT, 111) provides the uprooted stranger with a framework for reconstructing his shattered inner world. "The survivor cannot formulate from a void," Robert Jay Lifton points out. "He requires the psychological existence of a past as well as a present, of the dead as well as the living."[2] Retracing one's steps to one's native town can rekindle old feelings of security and nurturance. If in *The Town Beyond the Wall* the protagonist's trip to his once-cherished community ironically terminates in jail, from within the oppressive walls his memory is liberated. He grows aware of his powers to hear and to evoke those voices silenced by the forces of Night. The little *shtetl*, peopled with picturesque figures of the past, is brought back to life. Out of the ruins, a new town is built—with images and silence.

THE DEAD TOWN

Unlike other writers who have sought to return to their origins and recapture time past through their art, Wiesel's explorations are structured by the reality of the Holocaust. The author experienced the violent "death" of his town *before* he left it, and not within the ordinary course of events. At the age of fifteen, he was eyewitness to the brutal collapse of the Jewish community of Sighet—representative of so many other Eastern European *shtetls* devastated by the Nazi invaders. After the war Wiesel refused to be repatriated to Sighet, choosing instead to live in France. He became a journalist and travelled all over the world to such places as Africa, India, Israel. As he journeyed from one country to another, he obsessed more and more about his home town. In "The Last Return," a narrative description of the actual return to his birthplace in 1964 (two years after his fictional rendering of the journey homeward and in many ways similar),[3] the author reveals that he was unsure whether he travelled "in order to get away from Sighet, or to find it again. The town haunted me, I saw it everywhere, always the same as it had been. It invaded my dreams, it came between me and the world, between me and myself. By trying to free myself from it, I was becoming its prisoner" (LT, 112). The town is both imprisoned in his memory and imprisons him.

The compulsion to wander masks a longing to journey homeward. In an account about his former masters, Wiesel discloses: "I began to wander across the world, knowing all the while that to run away was useless: all roads lead home. It remains the only fixed point in this seething world" (LT, 9). The themes of exile and flight are linked, then, to that of the return. The further the nomad flees from his point of departure, the more it becomes an *idée fixe*. He is driven to the point of fantasizing that the entire world is an extension of his town: "Perhaps the whole universe is nothing but a phantasmagorical projection of Sighet; perhaps the whole universe is turning into Sighet," the author remarks in "The Last Return" (LT, 113). And in the parable recounted by Katriel in *A Beggar in Jerusalem*, the traveler in search of the big city returns unknowingly to his native town, realizing that "only my village exists, it is its image I see reflected in the world" (123). Azriel, the narrator of *The Oath*, is also haunted by his native town of Kolvillàg, destroyed by a pogrom: "I am still in my native town, I have left it only in my dreams, I have done nothing but change dreams" (49). Just as the liberated prisoner craves to visit the prison in order to know that he is free and the madman is propelled toward his madness, the survivor without a country is compelled to go home.

The prevailing mood of the journey homeward appears to be one of unreality, uncertainty, and fear. The pilgrim-protagonist is unclear as to the purpose of his undertaking; he is the messenger looking for a message, the storyteller in search of a story, the witness seeking the object of his testimony, the speaker who has not found his voice. As Frederick Garber observes, his is "a homecoming made by one who sees what he has come back to look at through a long tunnel filled with the thick smell of heavy smoke."[4] Despite its equivocal nature, three motives underlie the voyage to the past: curiosity to see what the town has become; the desire to relive one's childhood; and the need to overcome the anonymity of exile.

Like Elisha in *Dawn* and the narrator in *The Accident*, Michael, the protagonist of *The Town Beyond the Wall*, is a concentration camp survivor who has gone to Paris after the war. He has intentionally chosen not to return to his home town in Hungary but secretly longs to revisit it. A journalist for a Paris weekly, he is assigned to cover a story in Tangier, where he meets Pedro, the head of an international smuggling ring. Pedro finds out about Michael's wish to go home and decides to accompany him on a clandestine trip to his town of Szerencsevàros, ironically named the "city of luck"—which is the original title of the novel in French—*La Ville de la chance*. As Michael wanders aimlessly through the streets, now patrolled by the Hungarian police, he recalls Lot's wife, whose curiosity drove her to disobey the law by looking back at the destroyed city of Sodom and, consequently, to be punished by God:

> What have I come here to do? To what call had I responded? Of course, there was simple curiosity: to look back. Lot's wife was more human than her husband. She too had wanted to carry with her the image of a city that would live—that would die—without her. Doubtless there was something of that in my need to retrace my steps. [144]

The frozen prose of Lot's wife, transfixing the town forever in her memory, recurs throughout Wiesel's works. Instead of traditionally condemning the "don't look back" impulse embodied by the Biblical figure, the author depicts Lot's wife as sympathetic and humanly curious in her zeal to carry with her—and thus to perpetuate—the image of her birthplace. "Lot's wife, by glancing backward appears to us more human than her husband; . . . her gesture poses the problem not of justice but of *durée*," Wiesel states in the French version of his essay, "Rendez-vous avec la haine" ("Appointment with Hate"), in *Entre deux soleils* (96). He describes his trip to Germany after the war, reflecting upon the victim's feelings when he returns to the scene of the crime and, as a free man, confronts the enemy.

While the retrospective glance is a fundamental aspect of Wiesel's own thinking and writing, he points to the danger of retracing one's itinerary solely on the basis of intellectual curiosity. In the essay, "A Plea for the Dead," he notes:

> And Lot's apprehensive wife, was right to want to look back and not be afraid to carry the burning of doomed hope. "Know where you come from," the sages of Israel said. But everything depends on the inner attitude of whoever looks back to the beginning: if he does so purely out of intellectual curiosity, his vision will make of him a statue in some salon. Unfortunately, we do not lack statues these days: and what is worse, they speak, as if from the top of a mountain. [LT, 180]

By rejecting the grandiose and intellectual motives for bearing witness, the author here is perhaps expressing his own fear of transforming the retrospective glance into a sterile vision. He may also be responding to those contemporary critics who denounce testimony to the past as empty words proclaimed by false prophets.

Wiesel himself has been compared to Lot's wife in a positive way.[5] Indeed, as he makes his final departure from Sighet in 1964, he turns his head for a prolonged last look at the town—source of fear and fascination, of innocence and atrocity: "Sighet had long sunk below the horizon and I still kept my head turned toward it, as though it were possible for me to carry it away in my gaze" (LT, 130). He is glancing back to a world which is no longer his, but which confirms his realization that *he* is now the link between the past and the present, between the dead and the living.

The retrospective glance joins the themes of continuity and rupture: it is both a recognition of the ties to the past and an acknowledgment that those ties have been cut off. In a circular motion, it brings the past into the present and binds the beginning to the end. "A man's last vision of what was his beginning is like no other, for like that beginning, it becomes part of him, irrevocably and unalterably," Wiesel observes (OGA, 12). Yet, if the look to the past is an attempt to make a circle of history, it is also a way of lending a new dimension to the present and, in a sense, moving forward. Going backward in time is for Wiesel the expression of an aspiration towards continuity and connectedness that is important both in the psychology of survivors and in Jewish thought:

> I stress the word "return", so basic in our tradition. *"Teshuva"* to me signifies return, not repentance. Whoever returns to the source does not remove himself from the present. On the contrary; he lends it a new dimension. For he then realizes that in Jewish thought, everything is connected.[6]

If the retrospective glance joins the end to the beginning, the return to one's origins is also for Wiesel—as for other authors such as Nerval and Proust—the search for the lost idyllic world of childhood. "To become a child again" is a key expression in the Wieselean vocabulary, suggesting the recovery of innocence and amazement, and the desire to see the town through a child's perspective as a kind of Eden, a golden age.[7] "Szerencsevàros, that blasted Paradise where all had once seemed so simple," Michael recollects with nostalgia in *The Town Beyond the Wall* (78). The returning wanderer is like a child looking for a reunion with the mother, source of nourishment: "this town which gave me everything" (LT, 113); "my own city where I first saw my mother" (TBW, 139). The pilgrimage to his beginnings reactivates profound feelings of being part of someone and something that exists beyond himself, a past, a tradition, a family. "The joy of not being alone, of belonging, of being bound to someone, to someone who had lived before me and was living outside me," Michael thinks as he recalls the image of himself in the arms of his mother, together in front of a mirror for the first time (TBW, 139). At the same instant, however, he reminds himself that this attachment has been severed. The town which gave him everything took it all away. Paradise has been followed by the Fall. "And here I am alone. Mother is no more" (139). The child, expelled from Paradise, has died in Hell along with his mother, father, little sister, and the rest of the Jewish community. The theme of the dead child dominates the mood of the journey homeward as it did the voyage into Night.[8]

The pilgrim-protagonist is ambivalent toward the dead child within. He is aware of the wide abyss that separates his present self from his former self. Michael tells Milika, a survivor from his home town whom he meets in Paris after the war: "He [the little boy] didn't survive. He's dead. I deny him. Never saw him, never knew him. A stranger. An unidentified corpse. I have nothing in common with him" (TBW, 80). But Michael also knows that the lost being who dwells at the center of his psychic universe evokes a past that continues to haunt his present life; the cadaver buried inside of him cries out to be resurrected. "I know he's dead," Michael says to Milika, "but I also know that he won't leave me. He follows my trail; he walks in my footsteps. . . . When I run, he runs along behind me" (80). It is ultimately through the dead child in himself that the expatriate can be guided back to his town, encounter the characters who inhabited his little *shtetl*, and infuse them with life. As David, the narrator of *A Beggar in Jerusalem*, affirms: "there was a child waiting for me in my past and I was afraid to follow him; I knew one of us was dead. I also knew that he alone could lead me to our teachers. . . ." (20).

The conflicted attitude with regard to the dead-resuscitated child is related to the theme of the town. The pilgrim-protagonist is afraid of seeing the town again and afraid of not seeing it. He fears a vision of ruins but also dreads the sight of a reconstructed town that bears no resemblance to the town he once knew.

> What would be waiting for me when I arrived? The dead past or the past revived? Total desolation or a city rebuilt again and a life once more normal? For me, in either case, there would be despair. One cannot dig up a grave with impunity. [LT, 111]

The dispossessed voyager wants to be reunited with the dead child in himself and to reclaim that child's lost dominion, but, at the same time, painfully perceives that the town, like the child, no longer exists. He experiences what Proust calls "the contradiction brought about by searching in reality for images from the memory."[9]

The confrontation of past and present, of memory and reality,

create continuous tension in the Wieselean protagonist, often leading
him to the brink of insanity. Like Shakespeare's King Lear, a character
who obsesses Michael, the exiled survivor struggles against madness
because he too has been disinherited of his kingdom.[10] He is no longer
sure what is real and what is imagined; the town is simultaneously there
and not there for him. "Your town still exists, your town no longer
exists. It survives only in the twisted imagination of faceless and ageless
village fools," David tells the young madman in *A Beggar in Jerusalem*,
who questions his own perceptions of reality and who believes he is
losing his reason because he thinks that his town has been rid of all Jews
(128). In *The Oath*, Azriel tells the young man: "Kolvillàg does not exist
any more. I am Kolvillàg and I am going mad" (66).

The author, like his protagonists, also comes to doubt not only that
the town endures in its present state but that it ever had a life of its own.
In the retrospective narrative "Journey's Beginning," he observes:
"That town. I see it still, I see it everywhere. I see it with such clarity that
I often mock and admonish myself: continue and you'll go mad; the
town no longer exists, it never did" (OGA, 12–13). "The Last Return"
concludes with the paradoxical statement: "My journey to the source of
all events had been merely a journey to nothingness. For it had never
existed—this town that had once been mine" (LT, 130). Wiesel thus
questions the validity of his own memory and his own identity, as he
slowly discovers that the Eden of his childhood is "not the lost paradise
but the paradise which never existed."[11] This contradictory recognition
of the town's existence and nonexistence recalls certain aspects of the
French *Nouveau Roman* and novels by Samuel Beckett. Nevertheless,
while the result may be similar, for Wiesel it is not a question of
experimenting with literary techniques that contest and interrogate
the nature of reality, but rather of expressing the anguish caused by the
inconsistencies inherent in the Holocaust experience itself.

Despite the risk of madness, the pilgrim-protagonist seeks to
overcome his self-imposed exile and to rediscover the source of his
heritage, the third motive for the journey homeward. We have seen
that the Wieselean protagonist has chosen the life of a wanderer living
in what Lothar Kahn calls "the tradition of exile and flight."[12] The
figure of the Diasporic Jew, familiar in Wiesel's works, is represented
by the traveler, the vagabond, the refugee—all those who fall into the
class of statelessness—travelling about without attachments and living
in anonymity. An entire narrative devoted to "The Wandering Jew"[13]
in *Legends of Our Time* portrays one of the author's former masters, a
kind of "vagabond-clown" of unknown origins who spoke about thirty

languages and who inspired both fear and admiration because of his supernatural abilities. The Wandering Jew is also depicted by such itinerant characters as Moshe the madman and Elie the prophet, who reappear in various guises throughout most of the texts. In *The Town Beyond the Wall*, the collective image of the Jew as nomad is evoked on the day of deportation, when old men and children, rabbis and invalids parade through town, their heads bowed, sacks on their backs, as they unknowingly head toward the final solution.

The figure of the Diasporic Jew clearly embodies the condition of modern man as stranger, representing what Cioran, in his essay "A People of Solitaries," calls "the alienated existence *par excellence* or, to utilize an expression by which the theologians describe God, the *wholly other*."[14] The state of estrangement is epitomized by the pilgrim-protagonist, whose eventual homecoming makes him more than ever aware of his homelessness. He feels unwelcome in the town that was once his. Like Moses, he is unable to enter the inaccessible and forbidden Promised Land:

> I felt myself a stranger, if not an intruder, in this sinister town which was stripped of all vigor, of any life of its own. I searched for the people out of my past, I searched for my past and I did not find them. [LT, 125]

The plight of the undesirable other, driven out of his own past, is echoed in *The Town Beyond the Wall:*

> This is my city, I was born here. Here, I became a part of time, here I was launched upon the river, here is my source, here burrow my roots: and yet here I am an unwanted stranger; just as my own memories deny me. [84]

Two important motifs related to the theme of the town are suggested here: the bewitched or forbidden town; and expulsion from time. In the first case, the expatriate returns to find the town of his childhood *Judenrein*—menacing and sinister because its former Jewish inhabitants have been condemned, expelled, and forgotten. Possessed by forces of the demonic, the accursed land is the counterpart of the town as Paradise. The Holocaust has left the bewitched town scorched, arid, devoid of all life. "My pilgrimages kept leading me back to a source run dry. The life of the town, by continuing, had thrust me out," says the madman in *A Beggar in Jerusalem* (28).

This leads us to the second motif: expulsion from time. Once a part of a harmonious community, the returning survivor is met with the indifference of the townspeople. As he roams the streets in a dreamlike trance, desperately hoping to be acknowledged, he realizes

that he lives in a time different from that of the passersby. For them, he is a thing long dead and forgotten; his return is of no consequence. Just as in the concentration camp he was reduced to a number, a nonentity, so, too, in post-Holocaust times he has become a discarded object whose past and present existence remains unacknowledged. The apathetic inhabitants of the town have not only erased the deported victims from their memory, but, what is worse, they have no place in their consciousness for the survivors. Michael feels like a corpse among the living, a Lazarus returned but unrecognized: "The people come and go, not stopping before him. They do not see him. Perhaps they are pretending. For them he is already dead. For them he has never existed" (TBW, 84). The victims have not only been uprooted from the town, but ejected from time itself. "More than anywhere else, it was at Sighet that I understood that the Jews had lost the war," Wiesel tells us (LT, 123).

In addition to being ignored by the passerby, the pilgrim-protagonist's estrangement is intensified by his discovery that the sites of his former world have been replaced. On the one hand, the town has remained intact except for the disappearance of its Jewish population, but on the other, the once-familiar landscape has undergone significant changes. Michael runs to the public square where the old synagogue used to stand, and, to his dismay, is struck with the absence of all traces of what was the pillar of the Jewish community. In its place stands a modern four-story edifice. The sanctuary had been razed to the ground by the Germans, who by destroying the "Temple" followed in the footsteps of the Romans centuries ago in Jerusalem. Here, then, is a literal example of a pilgrimage to a holy place which, first desanctified, was then supplanted.

While the theme of substitution can be applied to the physical structure of the Jewish town that has been demolished and rebuilt, the idea of being replaced by others is even more painful than the discovery of torn-down or abandoned buildings. Michael makes his way back to 17 Kamàr Street where his house and his father's store still stand, unchanged from the outside. When he enters the store and sees a man of about fifty appear before him, he momentarily entertains the illusion that it is his father. Dream and reality, past and present, merge as Michael is torn between the desire to resuscitate his father and the recognition that his father is dead:

> Was this my father? Was that my father's voice? No, a strange face, a strange voice. And yet I wasn't convinced, not absolutely sure and convinced. My father might have changed; I might have changed; my eyes and ears might have changed. [142]

The theme of substitution is related here to the motif of the strange voice, that which has replaced the familiar one. Michael cannot accept that his father has died and that another man now walks in his steps, yet he needs to confirm his father's death in his own mind. He reveals this ambivalence to Pedro: "My father is dead, Pedro. I saw him die. I was with him right to the end. Or almost. As far as the threshold. But just the same: if it was only a dream? If he had just pretended to die? To leave? If he were dead only in my dreams?" (141–42).

Although Michael eventually acknowledges that the storekeeper is not his father, he has a sudden longing to reclaim his stolen territory, to announce his identity, to shout to the merchant, "I am Michael. This is my store, this is my house. You're living off my store and in my house" (143). But this desire to cry out is only a fantasy: the sounds stick in his throat. He remains a silent anonymous stranger, unable to bring back his father just as he is incapable of recapturing the cherished town of his origins. The juxtaposition of the here and now with what once was makes the survivor more than ever aware of his impotence and the impossibility of his mission.

This impotence is especially evident when the author in "The Last Return" dramatically describes the nocturnal visit[15] to his old house, now inhabited by strangers. He feels like a thief as he encircles the domicile, gazes at its closed shutters and prepares to penetrate its inner sanctum. As he reaches the courtyard, a dog ("friends of the enemy, all demons, all anti-Semitic . . . the true victor in this war" [LT, 121]) suddenly barks and frightens him away, thus preventing him from completing his exploration of the past. His longing to regain possession, "total, irrevocable possession," of his belongings has been frustrated: he has not dared to awaken the person sleeping in his bed. Instead, he flees through the dark streets, having discovered in despair that it is not the others usurping his domain who are the intruders but it is *he*, the stranger—the eternal *déraciné*, exiled in his own kingdom. Just as he had, minutes before, bolted toward the house, almost flown like some Chagall-like figure ("I no longer run, I fly, I am the angel who soars above the roof-tops" [*Le Chant des morts*, 157]), he now retreats in a state of rage and shame, banished a second time from his homeland.[16]

Having unsuccessfully attempted to embrace his lost childhood, the pilgrim-protagonist once again is forced to take to flight, a recurring theme in Wiesel's works. As in *The Accident*, where the narrator's confrontation with Sarah resulted in the need to escape and repudiate the prostitute who embodied his inhuman past, the pilgrim turns his back on the forbidden town, the shrine that for him has been transformed into an oppressive graveyard. He realizes that it is impossible to reestablish a sense of connection with the town. Like the precious Bar-Mitzvah watch unearthed by the author-narrator in the tale "The Watch" (OGA), concealed in its tomblike box, the memory of the past cannot be excavated and left exposed. The rusty and worm-ridden watch is a relic of time lost, and if putting it back in its native soil is in some way indicative of the survivor's desire to leave a trace behind—a reflection of his presence which might some day be dug up by an unsuspecting child who would learn that there had been Jewish inhabitants in the town—the survivor knows he must bury the past, bury the town itself. Condemned to remember all alone, he vainly calls out in the middle of the night. No one listens, for the witness is mute: "I shouted but no sound came out. The town went on sleeping with no fear of the silence" (LT, 119).

The voice of the survivor, like the voice of the town, has been extinguished by the night. Similar to the once animated Jewish community now enveloped by the quiet of a grave, the pilgrim-protagonist is incapable of making himself heard. His attempt to communicate is futile, his cries drowned out by the forces of darkness. Instead of becoming a defiant spokesman for the victims and the survivors, he is the taciturn spectator. His return to the town is a second death, since it confirms his worst suspicions: the outer structure of the town remains unimpaired but the Holocaust has turned the *shtetl* of his youth into black ashes.

Nevertheless, the Wieselean protagonist, imprisoned by the apathy of the town to which he has returned, yearns to bear witness to the stilled landscape embedded in his memory and to give a voice to its vanished inhabitants. He understands that he is the living connection between the town he once knew and the night that surrounds him: "Here I am alone in the town, alone in the night. I am their link. I say aloud to myself: 'My town, my night'. . . . the town, the night and I who am their *point de rencontre*" (*Le Chant des morts*, 152). The tension between the assertion of the voice and the retreat into silence is at the core of the journey homeward. If death is silent exile, the regaining of lost speech is an attempt to bring back to life that which has died. The dead town is resurrected when the survivor refuses his anonymity and speaks out as a messenger of the deported community. Language has the power to restore. Michael's verbal confrontation with the indifferent bystander in *The Town Beyond the Wall* demonstrates how the spoken word liberates him from his internal prison and brings him closer to a reconciliation with the past.

THE RESURRECTED TOWN

As Michael roams about the streets of Szerencsevàros, uncertain of what has compelled him to go back to his birthplace, he finds himself at the site where the old synagogue once stood. As he tours the modern building that has taken its place, an image surges suddenly from the depths of his memory: a face impassively staring out of a window above the public square where the Jews were being rounded up for deportation. The violent impact of this recollection enlightens Michael as to the real purpose for his journey homeward. He has come back to confront, accuse, humiliate, and perhaps to understand the unconcerned, uninvolved spectator who observed the entire procedure without reacting.

The bystander, representative of all those neutrals indifferent to the fate of the Jewish people and depicted by the grotesque puffed-up face in the window, has been designated in the French text as *"le Témoin"* (the Witness). Although the author does not define *"le Témoin"* as compared to *"le témoin,"* a term more commonly used in his later works, it is necessary to differentiate the meanings. The witness is the survivor, whose mission is to testify to what he has seen and experienced, a notion not yet fully developed in *The Town Beyond the Wall*. The Witness, by contrast, is the apathetic onlooker, whose presence is explored in that novel. The use of the capital *T* (the only time in Wiesel's works the word is written this way) suggests an abstract and archetypal figure. In the Wieselean thematic network, the concept of the *witness* implies the Self in a positive sense while the *Witness* is the Other in a negative one: "The others—the Other—those who watched us depart for the unknown; those who observed us without emotion, while we became objects—living sticks of wood—and carefully numbered victims" (TBW, 148).

The spectator comes to personify the average man, the townspeople, and the world itself, all those who refused to take sides and who participated in what Lothar Kahn calls "the witness psychology, the policy of non-involvement in the injustices done to others, the pursuit of self and safety."[17] Moreover, Kahn suggests, the silent witness is also the Witness-God, "the silent, unconcerned God who also watched and allowed things to happen."[18] The spectator is like God in hiding *(hester panim)*: "The spectator is entirely beyond us. He sees without being seen. He is there but unnoticed. . . . his presence is evasive and commits him less than his absence might. . . . He says nothing. He is there, but acts as if he were not" (TBW, 151).

In a broad sense, the indifferent bystander symbolizes all of humanity and above all *the reader*, implied by the fact that when Michael finally confronts the spectator in his apartment, he is in the midst of reading a book. "We have all become the faceless ones in the windows," says Norman Friedman, who characterizes the Witness as the docile, conforming, obedient, twentieth-century "Bureaucratic Cipher," systematically depersonalized and dehumanized in a technological society.[19] The faceless face, indeed, allows us to fill in our own. Wiesel has intentionally presented us with an emblem of apathy, an allegorical figure rather than a truly developed character, recalling the conclusion of Franz Kafka's *The Trial*.

When K is about to be killed in the quarry, the window of a nearby house is suddenly flung open and someone leans forward, stretching out both arms. K wonders: "Who was it? A friend? A good man? Someone who sympathized? Someone who wanted to help? Was it one person only? Or was it mankind? Was help at hand?"[20] Despite the futility of the gesture, the human being with extended arms in Kafka's novel conveys a feeling of hope, reaching out to offer possible assistance or at least some sign of communication to the helpless victim. By contrast, Wiesel's figure in the window is reduced to a blank face with an empty stare. These onlookers nevertheless do resemble each other. Passive and silent, they look down at the persecuted from above, a posture suggesting a sense of superiority and detachment as well as the stance of a spectator viewing a theatrical performance.[21]

The confrontation between Michael and the bystander which did not occur either on the day of the deportation or during the author's actual return to Sighet, is enacted through the fictional narrative. The protagonist quietly walks into the apartment of the man and makes it clear that he has come to humiliate this insensitive individual who did nothing as the Jews were being sent to their death. Michael exchanges some hostile words with him and flings a glass of wine in his face. The latter continues to calmly, coldly, and silently glare at the unwelcomed visitor without flinching. His attitude reflects a total absence of emotion and a refusal of any feeling of guilt or shame. Michael does not succeed in humiliating the impassive Other.

Nonetheless, the encounter reveals to Michael that the neutral bystander is the third point of the mysterious triangle that links executioners, victims, and spectators and that one man can be all three at the same time. By interrogating the spectator, Michael takes a risk: "For the game can be played indefinitely: who observes the spectator becomes one. In his turn, he will question me" (152). In effect, the protagonist's attitude of contempt toward the onlooker and his accusations of cowardice and passivity are counteracted by the spectator's own charges that the victims let themselves be led docilely to the slaughterhouse without resisting: "You were afraid, you preferred the illusion to the bite of conscience and the game to a show of courage," he tells Michael (160). On the whole the dialectic of survivor and spectator denotes a common meeting ground, which the author underlines, if not on a manifest level then on an unconscious one.

A comparison of Michael and the bystander reveals similar characteristics, albeit from different points of view. First of all, both dwell in a state of anonymity. Walking through the streets twenty years after his banishment, Michael feels like a nonperson, a forgotten object, a dead man in the eyes of the townspeople. He, in turn, perceives the spectator as a debased object, something less than human:

> The spectator has nothing of the human in him: he is a stone in the street, the cadaver of an animal, a pile of dead wood. He is there, he survives us, he is immobile. The spectator reduces himself to the level of an object. He is no longer he, you, or I: he is "it". [160]

Michael's view of the spectator reflects the most negative and inhuman aspect of his own sense of self. The expressions used to transform man into a thing—stone, piece of dead wood, animal's cadaver—recall the language of the concentration camp universe where, according to Nazi ideology, the Jew was considered outside of the human race. We see here a link between the victim, survivor, and spectator, who come to represent the dehumanized, faceless, nameless citizens caught up in the evils of society.

A second characteristic that Michael shares with the spectator is the loss of the voice. Both are soundless onlookers—Michael, as he roams the streets of his town without being seen and without uttering a sound, and the spectator, as the observer behind the window, omnipresent but invisible and mute. When Michael returns to his father's store, he is unable to proclaim his identity and reclaim his family's appropriated belongings. The spectator likewise abstains from protest as he sits wordlessly by the window. Whereas Michael's voice is choked, the spectator's is absent; Michael has been coerced into speechlessness, his voice rendered impotent by the violence of Night, while the spectator has chosen the evasive silence of noncommitment, which Wiesel believes is the ultimate betrayal. "The cruelty of the enemy would have been incapable of breaking the prisoner; it was the silence of those he believed to be his friends—cruelty more cowardly, more subtle—which broke his heart" (LT, 189).

Even if the deadened voices of the survivor and the spectator stem from divergent points on the triangle and have different implications, they converge in its silent center: their muteness implies a resignation to society such as it is. However, underlying this submission is a movement from the absence of the word to its undeniable presence, from inarticulation to expression, from noninvolvement to *engagement.* The pilgrim-protagonist and the Witness follow a parallel course: by speaking out, the former to humiliate, and the latter to protect himself, each undergoes a kind of transformation.

Michael changes from a reticent stranger to a spokesman for his people. His verbal assault upon the man who encapsulates the indifferent world is a cry of defiance that releases him from exile and anonymity. By returning to the onlooker's apartment—to the so-called scene of the crime—the survivor has gathered up "the courage to vomit the collective poison, to spit the bitter taste of the world into the faces of all those who want to turn away from it."[22] "The witness of the night becomes a fighter," says Emmanuel Haymann about Wiesel,[23] and, for the first time in Wiesel's fiction, this judgment is applicable to his protagonist as well.

Michael's indictment of the unconcerned bystander whose "opaque eyes reflected an inner winter, sheathed in ice, impenetrable, stiff" (155) is an expression of personal and collective rage, an attempt to avenge the dead who paraded in front of the onlooker's eyes and were then erased from his memory. Most important, the survivor's final outburst is a positive assertion of his identity and purpose. It is a *prise de conscience* of his role as *messenger of the dead,* a function first asserted by the narrator of *The Accident* and subsequently assumed by most of Wiesel's protagonists. Here his position is declared in a challenging, vindictive manner: "The dead Jews, the women gone mad, the mute children—I'm their messenger. And I tell you they haven't forgotten you. Someday they'll come marching, trampling you, spitting in your face. And at their shouts of contempt you'll pray God to deafen you" (162).

Once uttered, Michael's message alleviates the tension built up throughout the years. As Thomas Idinopulos points out: "Honoring the memory of the dead, he has begun to earn the right to live. And for the first time in his stories, Wiesel has his character speak as a healed man."[24] Michael liberates himself through language, and the cycle is completed:

> I had come, I had seen, I had delivered the message: the wheel had come full circle. The act was consummated. Now I shall go. I shall return to the life they call normal. The past will have been exorcised. I'll live, I'll work, I'll love. . . . No more double life, lived on two levels. Now I am whole. [162]

This verbal discharge is similar to the venomous flow of words issued forth by the narrator of *The Accident* as he kneels in front of Kathleen. Words bring relief but at the same time incur contamination. Kathleen, however, is a pure and innocent recipient of the message in *The Accident,* while the spectator in *The Town Beyond the Wall* is the intended object of scorn and humiliation. The verbalization of things for a long time unsaid is an appeal for a modification in attitude, an acceptance of moral responsibility. Michael deliberately exposes this average man— "symbol of anonymity"—to the evil of indifference and demands that he leave his refuge of neutrality. After an event like the Holocaust, which drastically altered mankind's consciousness, the individual can no longer shield himself from the circumstances surrounding him: he is implicated by his detachment alone. Michael's call for a response from the bystander is comparable to the narrator's proclamation in *The Accident:* "Whoever listens to Sarah and doesn't change, whoever enters Sarah's world and doesn't invent new gods and new religions, deserves death and destruction" (289).

Michael's shift from silence to speaking out, from passivity to action, thrusts the spectator, too, into a more active role. He responds to the protagonist's accusations by instantly denouncing him to the Hungarian police. When Michael is picked up at the street corner by the police car, his eyes for an instant dramatically meet those of his informer in the car mirror. Although their final encounter in the glass is unspoken, the eyes of the man, so long without feeling, now reflect "defiance, an anticipation of victory, saying, 'Now you'll *have* to hate me!' " (164). Michael's words have given a voice to the spectator, albeit a negative one. In contrast to betrayal through lack of speech, the survivor is victimized this time by the word. The stand taken by the "neutral" in the postwar police state may not be that dissimilar to his position twenty years before: he collaborated then by taking refuge in silent anonymity, and now becomes an accomplice by deferring to the authority in power. But, for Wiesel, involvement of any kind seems to be preferable to indifference, a motif stressed in the last section of *The Town Beyond the Wall* and directly linked to the theme of the witness. By taking action and showing some expression of emotion, the onlooker has in some way left the realm of the inhuman:

> To be indifferent—for whatever reason—is to deny not only the validity of existence, but also its beauty. Betray, and you are a man; torture your neighbor, you're still a man. Evil is human, weakness is human; indifference is not. [177]

If Michael's visit to the land of his birth results in the "contamination" of the spectator, who leaves the security of his window seat to jump out onto the stage, it also brings about the protagonist's own condemnation. Ironically, the survivor—who has returned to his home town to accuse—once again becomes the accused. Michael is charged by the Hungarian police with being a spy because he has entered the country without identity papers, and is consequently forced to spend three days standing in a prison cell called the "Temple," where he is interrogated. This method of torture, reminiscent of Nazi techniques, is called the "prayer." Facing a wall, the prisoner is kept on his feet until he passes out or "talks." Under these conditions Michael comes close to insanity but remains silent in order to give his friend, Pedro, time to leave the country without danger.

The former victim, seeking to testify to the injustice he has endured and to indict the world, is himself punished a second time. According to Irving Halperin, Michael's incarceration satisfies "an involuntary inclination to self-victimization" in that he *"sacrificially"* becomes a prisoner again out of a sense of survivor guilt.[25] While the Holocaust survivor may often be motivated by his guilt, the theme of prison in *The Town Beyond the Wall* has more profound and far-reaching implications. A sinister place of torture and degradation, the jail represents the regimes of modern political tyranny and the abuse of power, in general, illustrated in the novel by the Hungarian police state. The confinement within an oppressive space can also be considered a paradigm for the circumscribed limits of the ghetto walls, the sealed cattle cars, the concentration camps fenced off by barbed wires, and, ultimately, death by asphyxiation in the tightly shut gas chambers. If the extremity of the Holocaust experience extends far beyond the traditional concept of prison, where there still remains some hope of life and some consolation in solitude, the image of jail in the novel nevertheless suggests those more massive enclosures of the ghettos and camps.

The walls of sequestration and lamentation isolate man from the rest of humanity. Paradoxically, while they entrap, they also liberate. "Only here, in 'the temple,' in the heart of the prison can I feel secure and free," (128) Michael's warden confides to him, explaining that he once dreamed of becoming a poet, but because the government needs jailers and torturers, the jailer can speak his true mind solely within the fortified walls. Cut off from the outer world, the prisoner, too, unhampered by the imperatives of time and space, is able to explore his inner landscape. The jail in *The Town Beyond the Wall* ironically serves as a sanctuary, a haven for contemplation and recollection, which enables the captive to escape the shackles of the present by evoking images of the past.[26]

The motif of the prison is used by the author as a fictional device for the retrospective glance—the reordering and reconstitution of memories that permit his character to mentally reconstruct the town of his childhood. In prison, time is suspended, thus giving a dimension of freedom to the narrative itself, which consists of flashbacks to the protagonist's childhood in Hungary (First Prayer), his adolescence in Paris (Second Prayer), and adult life as a journalist in Tangier (Third Prayer). After the three prayers that correspond to the three days of forced silence in front of the "Temple" wall, Michael loses consciousness and finds himself in a cell with three prisoners, characterized as the Religious One, the Impatient One, and the Silent One. The "Last Prayer," which takes place in this cell, is a detailed account of the journey homeward, focusing on the encounter with the spectator.

The past narrative joins the present moment in this final section, showing Michael's interaction with the other inmates, who are eventually transferred to different cells. The only one who remains with Michael is the Silent One, a catatonic youth who brings the protagonist face to face with his own madness. Michael's attempt to communicate with the boy designates an important stage in his own personal growth.

Rather than reject the mindless, speechless young man, who, like Sarah in *The Accident*, reflects the dehumanized part of himself, Michael strives to restore the dead self to life, the mad self to sanity. He tries to pierce the impenetrable walls of the boy's guarded fortress by teaching him how to respond to another human being. He offers him food, tells him stories, sings to him, and even pulls at his jaws in an effort to make him open his mouth and speak. Because of Michael's concentrated endeavors the sensibility of the demented deaf-mute is gradually awakened. He begins to show signs that he is slowly leaving his prison of silence; he extends his hand for a bowl of food. The narrative ends when the boy is at the threshold of life. The act of reaching out to another person and helping him *return* to the world of the living not only stops Michael from succumbing to madness but by the thrust of its moral purity redeems all of humanity, an important Wieselean theme. The salvation of one soul makes the protagonist feel that he is "suddenly responsible for a life that was an inseparable part of the life of mankind. He would fight. He would resume the creation of the world from the void" (172). Michael gives a name (Eliezer) to the nameless. This gesture establishes for him a new mode of being based on dialogue, friendship, and human contact.

The theme of the return within the prison walls is linked then to the theme of re-creation. In contrast to the alienation of the Lazarene messenger, frozen like a pillar of salt into a death-dominated backward glance, the pilgrim-protagonist clearly aspires to restore a dynamic connection to the outside world. As a result, *The Town Beyond the Wall* is a pivotal work in Wiesel's literary journey: for the first time, the protagonist affirms his sense of self and his responsibility toward others. By doing so, he gathers the strength to rebuild his own shattered universe.

The silence of the cell has given a voice to the inner self. Michael's retreat into the concentrated space allows him to descend into the recesses of the unconscious and endows him with certain creative powers. His captivity prepares him for a spiritual rebirth. He learns that God, too, is imprisoned and man must emancipate him (10). The cell becomes a kind of womb, a place of incubation, calling to mind initiation rituals that involve a return or *regressus ad uterum* which, according to Mircea Eliade in *Myth and Reality,* corresponds to the state of "prenatal darkness" or the "Night before Creation."[27]

One might say that the *rites de passage* in the sanctity of the Temple are represented by the "prayers" imposed upon the prisoner, which equip him for his exit. As the organizing structural principle of the narrative, the prayer is linked to suffering, but at the same time gives sustenance. It is both a device of torture and a metaphor for the creative act, which takes on religious and sacred proportions. "I would say prayer envelops every form of creation," Wiesel declares, quoting Kafka's statement that "Writing is a form of prayer."[28] This pronouncement calls to mind the Israeli poet Abba Kovner, who once said: "When I write I am like a man praying."[29]

If prayer in its infinite variety is a means of participating in creation and reaching beyond the self, it is also an act of atonement through which the survivor can rid himself of his guilt by restituting the objects he has lost. Fixed by the bounds of his dark chamber, Michael closes his eyes and becomes aware of his heightened perception. He discovers his ability to listen, to visualize, and subsequently to reproduce the multiplicity of images and sounds reverberating in his memory. From another time zone, he summons visions that bring to life figures woven into the fabric of his past:

> Upright, facing the wall, he finds himself able to hear a thousand voices at a time, each distinct, to see a thousand paths, to weigh a thousand destinies. . . . His sensibilities sharpen, his being opens: as to the Rabbi of Nicholsburg, all the sounds and echoes of land and sea come to him. He senses even the ultra-sounds that certain creatures, and certain destinies, give off. [97–98]

In the Temple, shrine of terror and house of worship, the protagonist recognizes that he cannot recover any meaning in the town as it exists. The pilgrimage has confirmed the dissolution of his kingdom, and his return is thus impossible. The real town is now a cemetery: immobile, empty, silent, and abandoned. Yet it remains a source of myths and images, names and faces. Michael seeks to transform this ash-filled graveyard into a living monument by resurrecting the town in himself. He becomes the link between the reality of the *dead* town and the legend of the *resuscitated* one. The quest shifts from the outer to the inner, from disintegration to creation, from dispersion to unity. The protagonist has mythicized, fantasized, and internalized the town so that ultimately he *is* the town, the lost Paradise, the Promised Land, his mother, father, and little sister, who are brought to life as he perceives and remembers them. Writing for Elie Wiesel is "an invisible tombstone, erected to the memory of the dead unburied" (LL, 8), and the book, therefore, is the author's means of constructing a memorial designed to commemorate his community.

The town of Sighet comes to embody historically all those towns of Eastern Europe destroyed by the Nazi regime and serves as a model for the fictional villages and cities that play a central role in Wiesel's works. Transposed into fiction, the town becomes the Town, transcending the real to take on legendary and universal significance as Szerencsevàros, ironically named the "city of luck" in *The Town Beyond the Wall (La Ville de la chance)*, as the reconquered and triumphant city of Jerusalem in *A Beggar in Jerusalem*, and as the annihilated community of Kolvillàg (translated as "all the world" in Hungarian) in *The Oath* (which in French is entitled *Le Serment de Kolvillàg*). The Town assumes a character of its own that structures the texts, as demonstrated by the importance given to the name in each of these titles.[30]

Just as the boundaries of the town extend beyond the immediate and the particular, the self of the protagonist expands to the Self—*le moi-somme*. The pilgrim in search of his past claims kinship with all those who have preceded him and those who will follow. For Wiesel, to be Jewish is to be "Sum, synthesis, vessel. Someone who feels every blow that ever struck his ancestors" (MG, xii). "To be a Jew is to work for the survival of a people—your own—whose legacy is its collective memory in its entirety. . . . Time is a link, your 'I' a sum total" *["votre Moi une somme"]* (OGA, 167–68). If in *The Town Beyond the Wall* the main character has not fully grasped the implications of his role as the voice of the victims and the survivors, the reconstitution of his personal history is an important step in his development as witness. Unlike the ghostlike Lazarene messenger who turns his back on the distant past, the returning traveller comes closer to establishing his own voice and vocation as spokesman of the deported community. The child of the

Night, severed from his origins, goes back to his beginnings in order to "regain possession of his spiritual patrimony"[31] and thus restore a sense of continuity to his life. By discovering within his own memory the historical memory of his town and of the Jewish people as a whole, the exiled wanderer finally reaches his point of departure. The true journey homeward occurs when the author, through his characters, leaves the solitude of his inner prison to return to a self rooted in tradition, thereby rebuilding a new town out of the scattered ashes, a town that becomes the meeting ground of the living and the dead.

The odyssey to the source terminates in the silent seclusion of jail. Yet, the imprisoned voice of the pilgrim-protagonist is liberated when he beholds the town beyond, which is to say *the town within.* As he digs like an archeologist through the multilayered ruins of his inner landscape, he defies the passage of time and brings the past into the present. The act of memory becomes an act of survival in the face of the tormentors. The survivor grows aware of the need to reach out and extend himself beyond his own limits, a theme that is developed in the later novels. The town cannot die, because the witness is still alive, and by remembering and speaking out he can resurrect people and places destroyed by the executioner. The *shtetl* has been swallowed up by smoke, disappeared forever, erased from geography, Elie Wiesel tells us, but "it has survived in words alone."[32] And as Pedro says to Michael in *The Town Beyond the Wall:* "Man may not have the last word but he has the last cry. That moment marks the birth of art" (96).

4

The Witness and His Double

Je suis l'oeil qui regarde l'oeil qui regarde.

—Elie Wiesel

T HE ACT OF reaching out to save another human being, depicted in
The Town Beyond the Wall, becomes increasingly important in Wiesel's
two succeeding novels, *The Gates of the Forest* and *A Beggar in Jerusalem,*
and is expressed principally through the theme of the double. In
Wiesel's early works the survivor-protagonist constantly experiences a
sense of *dédoublement,* or division of the self shattered by the Holocaust
and exiled from its own being. He is torn between the attachment to his
"dead" self—former world, family, community, traditions that have
been destroyed—and his "surviving" self, which endures but bears the
burden of life in the aftermath. Consumed by an intense guilt for
having remained alive while others died, the protagonist exists in a
death-in-life state, cut off from his fellow men, a stranger to himself.[1]

While this extreme alienation is most apparent in the Lazarene
witness, most of Wiesel's characters live in inner turmoil. They are
confused as to who they are, and are incessantly drawn to that
corpselike part of themselves still belonging to the kingdom of Night.
Yet, as the protagonist emerges from his death encounter and rediscovers the residue of humanness within, the shadow of the past begins
to relinquish its hold. He grows more aware of a need to connect to
others: "Whoever says 'I' creates the 'you'. . . . The 'I' signifies both
solitude and rejection of solitude," observes the narrator of *The Oath*

(9), one of Wiesel's later novels. This statement points to the contradiction in the survivor's state of mind, but also suggests a progression in
the author's own thinking from the individual to others, from isolation
to communication, from resignation to regeneration. The movement
toward dialogue and friendship is portrayed through the presence of
the double.

Throughout Wiesel's literary universe, the benevolent *Other* manifests himself in various ways—messenger, teacher, prophet, savior,
protector, and friend. He seems to possess knowledge that the protagonist lacks and serves as his spiritual guide, helping him to break
through the anguish of his isolation and reestablish his identity in the
present. Despite his mysterious origins and the mystical aura that
surrounds him, the figure is portrayed for the most part as an external
reality, independent of the main character. It is not until the later
fictional works that the affinity between the protagonist and the Other
deepens to the extent that the two seem to share a selfhood that is at
once separate and the same.

The author has created for his characters a second self who is
simultaneously unknown and familiar, inaccessible and intimate, "unmistakably outside but just as inescapably inside"; "the strange, expanded version of what and who one is . . . the Other who is also the I."[2]
For Wiesel, "*l'autre, c'est celui qui vit en nous et nous échappe*" ("the other is
the one who dwells within us and evades us").[3] He notes that in his
novels "all the tensions, all the relationships are always 'I and thou', the
dialogue of two persons who are one."[4] We often have the impression
that the author is listening to the multiple and sometimes contradictory
parts of himself speak through the voices of his invented characters.
"Isn't he present everywhere? Could we suspect him of *panwieselisme?*"
one critic asks.[5] And Lawrence Langer points out: "Wiesel's literary
work is a sustained dramatization of counterpositions, a long monologue disguised as a series of dialogues, revealing his own divided self."[6]
Clearly, the unresolved question of duality and unity preoccupies
Wiesel and resonates throughout his work, for he asks:

> The question of all questions is. . . . "Who am I?" Who is the "I" in
> me? The "I" that speaks? The "I" that is spoken to? This dialogue,
> this quest of the real "I", which can never be solved, I try to transmit
> in my novels. . . .[7]

The uncertainty in the search for the self is translated into the
fiction by the meaningful yet ambiguous relationship that the double
establishes with the protagonist. In a somewhat unexpected manner he
enters the life of the main character, offers him insights that help shape

his destiny, then vanishes without a trace. At important intervals throughout the narrative, and under different disguises, this enigmatic messenger makes his deeply felt absence a presence; rarely does he manifest himself in his original form. As if carrying out the orders of an awesome power from above, he reveals and hides himself, changes his face, gives life, and takes it away. What he leaves behind is the everlasting doubt about his existence. Not knowing if the double is dead or alive, the protagonist refuses to accept his departure as final, and persists in his quest to restitute the elusive Other whose sacrifice appears to be the condition for his own survival.

According to the Otto Rank, the notion of the double as assurance of survival originates in primitive man's conviction that man's shadow was the equivalent of his soul, a spiritual yet real second self that lived on after the body died.[8] The invention of the double was a way of defending oneself against separation and loss, a denial of death, or, as Freud, in agreement with Rank, put it, "a preservation against extinction."[9] In his essay "The Double as Immortal Self," Rank traces the evolution of the ancient belief in the double as symbol of eternal life to what he considers the modern concept:

> Originally conceived of as a guardian angel, assuring immortal survival to the self, the double appears as precisely the opposite, as a reminder of the individual's mortality, indeed the announcer of death itself.[10]

The Wieselean double embodies these contradictory roles: he is both a harbinger of death, signaling the triumph of the exterminating angel, and a protector of life, a guardian angel who sacrifices himself in order that the protagonist may live. His presence in the text signifies destruction at the same time that it represents the indestructible, thus fusing in one figure the mortal and immortal. His alliance with the main character is often confusing, as boundaries break down, names and roles are interchanged, and identities merge. While the knowledge of death he imparts is threatening, curiously, death seems not to have a hold on him. In general, he points the way to endurance and the will to survive.

For Wiesel, the fictionalization of the double is related to the loss of identity and fragmentation of the self suffered during and after the Holocaust. However, in contrast to Rank's theory of the change in attitude towards the double, the theme in Wiesel's work progresses in the reverse direction—from disintegration to reintegration and expansion. The self confronts itself, dialogues with itself, and seeks to recover its wholeness by binding the past to the present. Extending beyond its solitary and mortal limits, it aspires to unite the dead and living in order to become *le moi-somme,* the collective self. The first step in this restorative process is to establish contact with one human being, to save him, bear witness for him, and, indeed, to "become" him.

The theme of saving a life governs the relationship between the protagonist and his double, who save and are saved by each other. "If I have any moral message this is it: Try to save one person," Wiesel has stated.[11] In *The Gates of the Forest,* the same command is uttered: "No good deed equals in meaning and importance that of saving a human life—any human life" (46). And in *The Oath* the main character declares: "To save a man, one must think like him, feel what he feels, see what he sees and what he refuses to see. To save him, one must want to die like him. One must be he." (26). If one is to redeem another, one must take on his identity, incorporate him into one's being, and assume his voice. On his last night with Gavriel in the forest, Gregor vows to "become him in order to understand him better, to understand and love him, or to love him without understanding" (GF, 40). The imperative to save a life is ultimately linked to the theme of the witness: one needs the other to be rescued from oblivion, and if the other should die, one keeps his memory alive by transmitting his story. The doubles in Wiesel's literary world serve as witnesses for each other, assuring each other as well as themselves protection against death through their reciprocal testimony.

THE OTHER WHO IS ALSO THE I

Wiesel's early works are thematically structured by the haunted memory of the dead, which manifests itself in various modes as the ever-present and divisive "dead" self. Yet, figures in these texts prepare the way for a more positive realization of the double. In *Night,* Eliezer's father serves as a form of double, the Other who mirrors his son's torments but whose presence helps the narrator withstand the atrocities of the death camps. He acts as a kind of guardian angel, assuring survival to his son at his own sacrifice. Father and son become one in suffering, but do not share a psychical identity as do the later doubles. Although the young boy often identifies with the old man, the boundaries that separate the two are generally defined: the father possesses an external reality independent of his son's. It is only at the end of the book when Eliezer looks into the mirror that the corpselike image can be seen as the reflection of the dead father, personifying the Other who is also the I.

The father lost in the kingdom of Night reappears in different guises as a spiritual guide in the novels that follow.[12] In *Dawn,* Gad is the mysterious messianic warrior whose mission is to bring Elisha to the Promised Land by telling him tales of the Palestinian struggle for independence. In *The Accident,* it is Gyula who protests the narrator's death wish by affirming life. Both Gad and Gyula—whose names mean *good fortune* and *redemption,* respectively—are messengers or mentors. Presenting themselves in a somewhat problematical manner to the main characters, they attempt to show the way. These figures, along with Pedro in *The Town Beyond the Wall,* have been characterized as "teacher-philosophers" by Robert Alter, who observes that the figure of the teacher "derives from the Hasidic spiritual guide—more particularly, from a kabbalistic master of his own childhood whose message was one of redemption, involving the secret knowledge through which man could learn to loose the chains in which the Messiah is bound."[13] The teacher, according to Alter, first appears as Kalman the Mystic, but later returns in the form of a painter, smuggler, partisan, and terrorist. Josephine Knopp also discusses the role of the "teacher-philosophers" as emissaries of the Hasidic tradition that pits life against death. She stresses their growing influence upon the protagonists in Wiesel's later works, and describes their appeal to the ethical code of *"mentshlekhkayt"*—the belief in man's basic goodness, in action as the path toward moral redemption, and in man's responsibility to his fellow men.[14]

While such figures as Gad and Gyula try to turn the protagonist-survivor away from his post-Holocaust despair, they are not truly his doubles; they basically remain strangers who exist outside of his psychical reality. Profoundly close on one level, they are inaccessible on another. It is not until *The Town Beyond the Wall* that the main character finds a friend, Pedro, with whom he can profoundly communicate and who understands his suffering. This novel is, in effect, a transitional work from the thematic viewpoint of the double. Just as Michael realizes in prison that he has incorporated the town into his entire being—that he *is* the town—so, too, he internalizes Pedro by carrying on an imaginary dialogue with this humanist smuggler whose voice penetrates the prison walls. Pedro surpasses the role of teacher-philosopher; he is the Other who is also the I, the speaker and at the same time the listener. He teaches Michael that "silence is not an emptiness but a presence" (115), and his own presence becomes an integral part of Michael's reality. It is the Pedro in Michael who rediscovers how to be human, how to create instead of destroy, and how to keep from losing his sanity. Pedro also compels the protagonist to save the mad youth in the prison cell, thereby "re-creating" the universe by reaching out to another human being.

At the end of the novel, Michael "becomes" Pedro by adopting his name and, in turn, passes on his own name to the anonymous young madman as proof that man is able to survive and transmit his heritage. Pedro's Spanish name and origin place him outside of the protagonist's own Jewish tradition, and in that sense, he is the stranger, the unfamiliar second self who belongs to a different order of reality. Yet, it is he who assures the continuity of succession by leading Michael back to his home town—to his source and his patrimony. Pedro's important position in the novel suggests that he is a kind of paternal figure, the father who saves and is saved. In contrast to Elisha, the death-inflicting young terrorist in *Dawn*—who was not able to stop the execution of John Dawson (the father figure)—Michael does succeed in preventing Pedro from being imprisoned by the Hungarian police. The protagonist has broken out of the role of the guilt-ridden son who feels he is a passive witness to and responsible for his father's death. In *The Town Beyond the Wall*, Michael actively sacrifices himself by submitting to torture in prison in order that his close friend and spiritual father go free. Reciprocally, the inner presence of Pedro saves the protagonist from going mad. Thus, father and son save each other; the self saves the self; Pedro and Michael comprise two selves that are one.

Despite Pedro's significant function in the narrative, he is not fully developed as a character nor as a double; he is more a disembodied voice. His role in the novel has been criticized as "a fictional device added on . . . a purely literary strategy" designed to make Michael's resistance in the torture chamber seen more plausible.[15] Nonetheless, Pedro is a "transitional" double, marking a change from the teacher-philosopher who remains outside the protagonist's identity in the early books to the more intimate figure who forms a symbiotic relationship with the protagonist in the later novels. In *The Town Beyond the Wall* Wiesel appears to be in the process of working out the alliance between the "dead" self and the "surviving" one, between the dead father and the living son. The creation of a Pedro represents a positive step in the reintegration of the protagonist himself. This strange existential protector, humanitarian, and resurrected father figure with whom Michael shares his selfhood, helps him to put together the pieces of his fragmented life and, consequently, points to the more evolved and dominant role of the double in *The Gates of the Forest* and *A Beggar in Jerusalem*.

THE GATES OF THE FOREST

The simultaneous sameness and separateness that characterizes the theme of the double is dramatized in *The Gates of the Forest* through the encounters of Gregor, the protagonist, and Gavriel, the mysterious figure who appears early in the novel, disappears, and then reappears in various modes. Just as Pedro's voice penetrated the prison cell in *The Town Beyond the Wall*, Gavriel's laughter resounds in the forest and makes its way to the cave where the seventeen-year-old Gregor is hiding from the Nazis. The boy's father had led him to this spot in the Transylvanian mountains from the town ghetto below, and promised to come back in three days.

It is springtime, and Gregor has become acquainted with the secret voices of the forest, whose miraculous beauty and simplicity represent the security and freedom of life untouched by war: the world "before creation, before the liberation of the word" (GF, 120). But this forest is also a prison for the youth. For days and nights he crouches in the cold dark cave, awaiting his father's return. Suddenly he hears the sounds of footsteps and betrays the oath of silence he made to his father. Out of desperation, he calls out: "Who are you? What do you want?" All he hears is "the laughter not of one man but of a hundred, of seven times seven hundreds" (7). Thus, Gavriel enters Gregor's consciousness.

From their first meeting, Gavriel's presence dominates the text, and his manifestation at significant crossroads in Gregor's life structures the narrative in a more intentional and more integrated manner than did the characterization of Pedro in *The Town*. Gavriel is more complex and contradictory but also more credible as a second self than was the Spaniard from North Africa. His role in *The Gates* is multifaceted. A wanderer in exile, a storyteller, a madman who has lost his name, a kind of visionary, he seems to come from another world and to be the messenger of God or of the Messiah. This mystifying creature blends past and present into future and becomes Gregor's double, a part of, and at the same time apart from, the young boy's existence.

By his name alone, Gavriel represents an angelic being. *Gavriel* is a variation of the Biblical name *Gabriel*, which means *man of God*. In Jewish and Christian tradition, Gabriel is one of the principal angels who minister comfort and sympathy to man, praying and interceding on his behalf before God. According to Jewish legend, it was also Gabriel who dealt death and destruction to the sinful cities of the plain; and it was he who was identified as the "man-God-angel" or "the dark antagonist" who wrestled with Jacob in Genesis (32:22). Gabriel has been described as "the angel of annunciation, resurrection, mercy, vengeance, death, revelation."[16] Furthermore, the word for angel in the Old Testament is *malakh* and in the New Testament is *angelos*, both of which mean *messenger* and derive from the belief that God used angels as messengers, agents, and envoys in an arrangement similar to that of human potentates. Like a prophet, an angel is therefore an intermediary between the human and the divine, a messenger of God on earth.

The fictionalized Gavriel in *The Gates of the Forest* takes on many characteristics of his Biblical namesake: he is both the angel of death and of resurrection. He reports news of the "dead" town emptied of its Jews who were deported to destinations unknown. He tells Gregor of the chaotic madness that has invaded Europe and how Jewish communities are being massacred everywhere. As Gavriel recounts these incredible tales, Gregor feels a great weight bearing down upon him. His heart beats faster and he experiences a choking sensation in his throat. The message grows clearer: "His father was not coming back. No one was coming back. His family was gone, leaving no trace, gone with no hope of return" (17). Uttered with a sense of finality, Gavriel's words plunge Gregor into despair. The appearance of this messenger early in the novel corresponds to Rank's notion of the double as "a reminder of the individual's mortality, indeed, the announcer of death itself." Gavriel seems to embody Gregor's nocturnal self, the shadow of his deceased family, and the spirit of his lost father.

The theme of the double as omen of death is linked to the motifs of night and shadow. From his first apparition in the timelessness and blackness of the cave, Gavriel gives the impression of having come from the dim world of the dead. "Where do you come from?" Gregor asks. " 'Over there' *['là-bas']*. . . . Everywhere. On the other side," replies the stranger (9). The boy can barely distinguish the features of this "Jewish ghost" whose form merges with the darkness. Like the angel who wrestled with Jacob, described by Wiesel in *Messengers of God* as "a mysterious nameless and faceless fugitive" (104), he belongs to another order of reality, his being marked not by physical characteristics but by defiant laughter—"the laugh of a man who has known total fear and is no longer afraid of anyone or anything" (18)[17]—and by his voice.

The theme of the voice is connected to that of night: the voice of Gavriel "vibrated in the night and the night vibrated within it" (39). The secrets Gavriel possesses are disclosed only in the dark, which stimulates him and which he peoples with images and memories. He teaches Gregor how to listen, and fills him with stories of death and annihilation, describing events totally incomprehensible to the boy. Gregor learns of the Messiah, who will not come to save the Jews because he has already come and the world has remained an immense slaughterhouse. He hears of the imprisoned Messiah who has come too late, of the Messiah killed every day by man and God, of the corpses of Jewish townspeople piled up in ditches. Listening in amazement to the poisoned words of the messenger, Gregor is unable to grasp their significance. All he knows is that a cruel and foreign universe exists outside of the cave "in which things and events must have a secret meaning, a secret bond, impossible to understand, a warped meaning, a warped bond" (28).[18] Beyond the forest, things are falling apart.

Gavriel's unfathomable tales are told in a shadowy voice with a soft, curious accent that originates in another time, another era. His speech is at once strange and familiar to Gregor, who feels he has heard it before. The theme of the double is conveyed here by the motif of the strangely familiar voice. Gavriel is the Other who is also the Self, "the unbidden interloper who is also the bidden guest."[19] Struck by the differences between himself and this mad wanderer from another land, Gregor experiences a certain affinity with him that cannot be explained logically. Their encounter seems to be a reunion of two persons who have met in the past, perhaps in another life. There is something almost sacred about their coming together, as if ordered by a power higher than both of them, beyond their control. But for their meeting to reveal its significance and to open up a "gate," the two selves must give it a meaning in the present. The one who is innocent must learn from the one who knows.

Gavriel, "announcer of death," brings Gregor messages of the devastated Jewish towns haunted by the "orphaned names" of their former inhabitants who hover over them like ghosts, but, at the same time, makes it clear that he will assuredly be the friend and protector of the boy in the cave ("the guardian angel, assuring immortal survival to the self"). When the protagonist is unable to distinguish his own shadow among the evening shadows that invade the cave, he fears this as a sign of death's imminence. "Where I come from they say that if your shadow leaves you, you're going to die within thirty days,"[20] he tells Gavriel, who repeatedly offers to be his shadow and take care of him. The notion of the shadow as protective spirit becomes a leitmotif throughout their short time together. Gavriel commits himself to his friend's survival: "Look around you. Your shadow hasn't left you. You'll live. I promise" (40). Filled with confidence, hope, and certainty, his words point the way toward deliverance. "I want you to value your life. I demand that to win this war. I want you strong and victorious" (20). The mission of this messianic messenger is clearly to save the protagonist. An example of positive *dédoublement*, Gavriel thus acts as an "insurance against destruction,"[21] embodying that aspect of the self which refuses to believe in its own mortality, and confirming Freud's idea that "at bottom no one believes in his own death, or to put the same thing in another way, in the unconscious every one of us is convinced of his own immortality."[22]

If Gavriel's presence in the novel evokes the triumph of the spirit over death, Gregor's attempt to come to grips with the odd figure who saves his life is filled with uncertainty. His long night in the cave recalls Jacob's night wrestling with the angel at Peniel. The Biblical story recounted in Genesis surely underlies *The Gates of the Forest*: "Imagine a life-and-death struggle between two angels, the angel of love and the angel of wrath, the angel of promise and the angel of evil," is one of the opening passages of the novel (3). And at the end of the novel, Gregor asks the Hasidic Rabbi in Brooklyn: "Which one of us is Jacob? And which the angel?" (200). Wiesel focuses here on the idea of duality. By confronting the enemy within, one aspires to overcome one's unworthiness and achieve a victory over oneself. But *The Gates of the Forest* reverses the Biblical tale. In Genesis Jacob defeats his adversary and wins from him a name, "Israel," which means, "he who has fought with God and has vanquished him." By contrast, in the novel Gregor gives his Hebrew name away—"Gavriel" or "man of God"—to the stranger deprived of his own. The protagonist then adopts a false name so that he may survive but throughout the book struggles to keep "Gavriel," his Jewish self, alive. Wiesel thus links Biblical traditions to modern catastrophe by developing the theme of the name with its infinite variations.

In times of war, the name takes on an especially vital significance as the embodiment of man's identity and heritage. One of the first things the Germans tried to obliterate were the names of their victims, a fact often stressed by Wiesel: "When they reduced man to a number, they took away his name. When they reduced him to an object, they took away his name. . . . I think nothing can be more denigrating, nothing can be more humiliating, than to take a name away."[23] In *The Gates of the Forest* the theme of the "dead" name is accentuated by Gavriel's anonymity: "My name left me. You might say that it's dead. It went away one day, without reason, without excuse. . . .I looked for it, but without success" (9). The loss of name here dramatizes the state of exile that characterized Jews and other refugees during the war. Certain Jews, whom Albert Memmi calls *"les mutilés du nom"* ("those whose names have been mutilated"),[24] tried to disguise themselves before the Nazis could reduce them to non-beings. Gregor typifies these Jews, camouflaged in an effort to survive. "Your name left you," he tells his guest, "and mine has gone into hiding, like myself" (13). The motifs of the false and dead names thus symbolize the widespread destruction of human identity that characterized the Nazi period.

While Wiesel thematically demonstrates the highly organized assault on Jewish names, he also affirms his faith in their permanence, an essential part of Jewish history and Jewish conscience.[25] Gavriel tells Gregor:

> A dying man takes his soul with him but leaves his name to the survivors. The Germans don't know to what extent they are branded by their stupidity: they kill off the Jews but can't find a way of erasing their names. The Talmud teaches us that the deliverance will come because Israel has not changed its name. It is not by chance that God is known as the Everlasting; every name has something immortal and eternal about it which defies time. [16]

The motif of the transmitted name conveys the idea of its indestructibility. One of the obligations of Jewish lore is to render a name immortal by passing it on to a newborn. In this way, the chain is not broken. After Gregor is finally persuaded to reveal his true Jewish name, "Gavriel," the name of his father's father, he subsequently offers it to the unknown messenger. The protagonist recognizes that during wartime, when the laws of normal, everday life are no longer needed, one has the right to give one's name away when still alive, and he feels lucky to be able to present his as a gift to his newly found friend. This transmission is not only basic to Judaic beliefs and to the survival of the Jewish presence in the world but serves as a focal point in the development of the theme of the double.

In *The Town Beyond the Wall* Michael adopts Pedro's name, and at the end of the novel, he offers his own to the young prisoner in his cell. *The Gates of the Forest* begins where *The Town* leaves off with the protagonist presenting his name to a stranger, a madman. The giving of a name, as Thomas Idinopulos indicates, is "a symbol of human communion"[26] but it is also a way of simultaneously retaining one's identity and sharing it, of being oneself and, at the same time, becoming another. When one person gives another person his name, Wiesel observes, "he gives him his destiny. He gives him the most precious thing that he has received."[27] The power of naming is a fundamental part of creation, for to give someone his destiny is to give him his life. "Adam named creation to become the master of creation," states the author,[28] and Gavriel explains to Gregor in *The Gates:* "It was by naming things that God made them" (10). By offering Gavriel his name, Gregor, like Adam and God, is creating or re-creating a successor, a double, a *witness* for himself. However, the act of naming-creating is fraught with ambiguities for the protagonist, for the author, and ultimately for the reader because the boundaries between the real and the imaginary are no longer distinguishable.

In effect, we are never quite sure who Gavriel is and if he really exists outside of Gregor's imagination. "Does the man of God really exist, wonders the hero who now takes the Gentile name Gregor, or has Gavriel been only a creature of his own naming, his own creation?" asks Robert Alter.[29] Is Gavriel a manifestation of the divine being, a messenger of God who has come to initiate and sustain a dialogue with man? Is he the Messiah come to deliver the boy from the cave? Is he a Just Man who takes the world's suffering upon his shoulders? Or is he, as Joseph Bertrand wonders: "a prophet come back, an hallucination, a visionary. We will never know, but the character resonates throughout the book like a calling, a provocation, a reproach, the face of conscience."[30] science."[30]

Like a ghost from the past or a supernatural being, Gavriel departs as he arrived, uttering his absurd laughter, which echoes far beyond the trees of the forest. At the end of the long night, just when the sun is beginning to warm the earth, the Hungarian soldiers with their barking dogs approach the cave. Gavriel pushes aside the rock blocking its entrance, slips through the small passage and surrenders himself. The gate is closed but he has bequeathed his stories and secrets to his successor ("What Gavriel left to him was beyond sorrow, beyond justice" [61]). Having inherited this fearful legacy, Gregor is now obliged to transmit it. If Jacob was transformed into a warrior by his encounter with the angel, Gregor is transformed into a messenger-storyteller. A totally different person, he now knows things he did not know before.

Blinded by the presence of this man of God who swiftly came into his existence, Gregor is haunted by his sudden absence. He spends the remainder of the novel searching for his lost double, the Other who bears his name and who chose to sacrifice himself in order that Gregor might live. Gregor's obsession to find the man who saved his life seems partially motivated by the guilt and betrayal he feels at having had his life preserved at the expense of another's, a disturbing yet common occurrence in the Holocaust universe. This guilt is intensified because he does not know for certain if Gavriel has been killed or if he remains alive in prison. The author appears to intentionally create this doubt in the mind of the protagonist and consequently in that of the reader, as a means of developing the dialectical tension between the "dead" self and the "surviving" self. The equivocal nature of Gavriel's appearance and disappearance—and the quest to find him—is one of the generating principles of *The Gates of the Forest* designed to serve a major function in the structure of the narrative.

In each of the three sections which follow the first; "Spring," and which correspond to the seasons, "Summer," "Fall," and "Winter," the voice of Gavriel makes itself heard. On one level, Gavriel's captivity—or his possible death—liberates Gregor from his hiding place and compels him to leave the cave in order to look for the elusive Other. After his friend's arrest, in the summer episode, the youth leaves the cloistered universe of the forest and in a dreamlike trance makes his way through night and fog, through fields and woods to the village of his family's servant, Maria. When he knocks on the door of her hut in the middle of the night, a familiar hoarse, warm voice welcomes the fugitive but also reminds him of what no longer is:

> Everything that remains of the past is in your voice, *is* your voice. It opens up to me like a house, my house, for me to live in and find rest. You don't know it, but your voice is my house, my childhood, my memory. . . . But your voice, it's exhausted, a crumbling house, a house in ruins. And I am only a ghost without the strength to walk or shout. [54]

The familiar voice of Maria is contrasted to the strange voice of Gregor. Once he has found refuge in the home of "divine old" Maria, the sole remnant of his decimated past, the boy bursts forth with a flow of words describing what he has heard, what man is doing to man in a world where everything is now possible. Dismembered and mutilated, Gregor's words and images crowd the tiny space of Maria's hut. As he keeps talking: "The past became present, everything became confused with everything else: beings lost their identity, objects their proper weight. His own identity merged with that of all mankind, which did whatever it wanted to whomever it wanted in obedience to any law it chose" (58). Maria no longer recognizes the Gregor she once knew. Possessed by a demonic presence, inhabited by an *other,* the boy has radically changed. "A stranger speaks from your lips. I don't want to know him," Maria whispers softly but suspiciously (59).

Gregor has internalized Gavriel, and "becomes" him, not only by assuming his voice and telling his tales but, ultimately, by giving up the power of speech. Silence is turned into a weapon of survival. In order to live with Maria without being denounced by the townspeople, Gregor pretends to be the deaf-mute son of Maria's sister, Ileana, a passionate woman who seduced many men in the village and who, because of her immoral behavior, was forced to leave town. Gregor

spends much time with the village characters—Milhai, the carpenter;
Constantine Stefan, the old schoolteacher; Stan, the blind man; and
the town priest—all of whom confide in him since it is safe. The silent
witness acts as a communal repository, a custodian of their darkest
secrets, fantasies, and obsessions. The townspeople unburden their
guilt, shame, and hatred, their sorrows and joys upon this mute
receptacle who can neither hear nor speak. And Gregor, the perfect
listener, listens with a faith and courage bestowed upon him by the
Gavriel dwelling deep inside:

> Without realizing it Gregor had been transfigured. The voice of
> Gavriel vibrated within him, regulating his breathing and giving
> depth to his silence. He hid himself behind Gavriel's face, beneath
> Gavriel's star and this was why he was able, almost without effort, to
> keep silent. [83]

Despite the strength of Gavriel's internal voice, which helps him to
endure, Gregor is unable to sustain his mask of silence. The need to cry
out and declare himself erupts when he is selected to play the role of
Judas in the annual school Passion Play. During the last act, as he
appears on stage, the audience, in a fit of rage and hysteria, attacks him
as the symbol of Christ's betrayer. In the middle of a scene that takes on
the unreal aspects of a nightmare, Gregor stupifies the spectators by
asking the spectators in a loud voice to forgive Judas, whom he sees as
the crucified victim, the persecuted Jew. The protagonist faces death
defiantly by making the audience aware that he, as Judas, is their
scapegoat; he confesses his true identity—he is a Jew and his real name
is not Gregor but Gavriel. Once again he has incorporated Gavriel's
courage into his own being, this time not by maintaining silence but by
speaking out.

Incurring another violent assault by the crazed onlookers, he is
saved at the last moment by Count Petruskanu, a character not fully
developed by the author. Portrayed as the mysterious and venerated
mayor of the village "in league with some celestial or diabolical power"
(71), he seems to emanate from another realm of being. Petruskanu is
the only one to silently communicate with Gregor during the entire
theatrical episode. When he sees that the protagonist's life is in danger,
he unexpectedly jumps onto the stage and leads him outside, where a
carriage takes them to a group of Jewish partisans in the forest. Like
Gavriel, Petruskanu represents the enigmatic guardian angel—the
savior—repeating the theme of rescue. Also like Gavriel, he disappears
into the darkness as abruptly as he came onto the stage. In effect, after
Gregor heroically speaks out and accepts the possibility of his own

death, he hears a strange voice whispering to him: "You are to die but your death has a meaning; Gavriel and Petruskanu are not two persons; they are one. . . . I am going to die and I am not afraid. I shall make my death a gate" (112).

In the third section of the novel, "Autumn," Gregor encounters another protector, Leib the Lion, a childhood comrade who defended him and taught him to defend himself from the gang that attacked Jewish children on their way to Hebrew school. Leib is now the leader of a group of Jewish resistance fighters hiding in a bunker in the forest. Just as Gavriel was Gregor's messenger, the protagonist transmits to Leib the "message" of the Nazi massacres. Silently listening in horror as they walk through the forest, Leib finally asks in disbelief: "Are you sure that Gavriel exists? That he ever existed?" And Gregor responds with certitude: "Sometimes I doubt the existence of Gregor, but never that of Gavriel" (130). The Other—the witness with the terrible secret about the collective Jewish destiny—must be saved. "Gavriel knows things that we don't know," Leib declares. "We ought to try to free him."

A complicated scheme involving Gregor, Leib, Clara, Leib's girlfriend and Janos, the town jailer, backfires. Leib is picked up by the police, imprisoned, tortured, and eventually deported. Gregor's fixation on finding his double has led to the loss of his friend, an event that signifies not only the enormous sacrifice of the strong heroic fighter and "king of the jungle" but also punctuates the death of his childhood and of the child in himself.

Gregor believes that he is the instrument of Leib's destruction, repeating the Judas motif of betrayal. Once again the theme of substitution, of one man dying in another's place, is dramatized in the text and linked to a sense of culpability: Leib sacrificed himself for Gavriel just as Gavriel surrendered himself to save Gregor. The protagonist, the tie between them, feels responsible for having caused their deaths and for having remained alive, "for not being in Leib's place. Or Gavriel's" (169). "To live is to betray the dead," he states (172), as he gravely attempts to grasp the shameful implications of his own role as survivor: "He who is not among the victims is with the executioner. This was the meaning of the holocaust: it implicated not only Abraham or his son but their God as well" (166). Our generation is worse than that of Sodom and Gomorrah, Gregor claims, for ours is "the generation of the guilty" and "we all have a share in the crime even if we combat it" (129).

Gregor assumes the burden of his complicity by bearing witness for Leib. In a strong, clear voice, he gives a coherent account of the events leading to his friend's capture: how Janos had been warned by

Clara and Gregor to look out for a Jew who had changed his name (Gavriel) and how instead Leib had been arrested. Without omitting a detail, the protagonist repeats the story four times to the silent, suspicious group of Leib's followers in the murky, airless bunker. As he journeys back in time and relives the experience, Gregor's thoughts wander. His voice carries him far away and places him outside of himself: "He was there and elsewhere" (162). Disassociated from the sounds he is uttering, he listens to himself speak and becomes another *["il devenait autre"]*. His voice no longer belongs to him and seems false; the more he talks, the more he empties himself of the truth and misrepresents it. The hurtful phrases separate him from his listeners. The voice here is a thematic expression of self-alienation and incrimination, erecting walls and prisons that set men and women against each other.[31]

Gregor's throat burns feverishly, his tongue is scorched, and his lungs are bursting, as he persists in recounting the narrative over and over again. He desperately wishes to undo the ending—to inform the partisans that their chief was miraculously saved. But because of his knowledge he is unable to authentically reverse the story's grotesque *dénouement* and to complete it as he would like. Several times, he deliberately distorts the conclusion, blaming himself for what occurred and falsely confessing that he betrayed Leib to free his own parents. Gregor uses words to relieve himself of guilt and awaits, without fear, a deserved death sentence from his comrades. He seeks punishment yet is condemned to live, not to die, for Clara tells the members of the resistance to listen not to what Gregor is saying but to "that which is unspoken" (174). The obligation of the messenger is to keep alive the *Other* or *Others*—Leib, the Lion, and Gavriel, the man of God—not by the invention of miracles or lies but by repeating the veritable tale of courage and faith, by becoming their undying witness.

Gregor acts not only as Leib's witness but as his substitute in the final section of the book, "Winter." He has emigrated to America after the war and is married to Clara. The protagonist visits a Hasidic synagogue in Brooklyn and enters into a dialogue with a rabbi who contends that Auschwitz has proved that nothing has changed; man is capable of murder and of sacrifice, he is both Abraham and Isaac, but God has remained the same. Although Gregor is troubled by his unanswered questions about belief in God after the Holocaust, his contact with the songs and dances of the joyous Hasids draws him closer to the faith of his origins and to the teachings of his old masters. He begins to realize how much he craves the Hasidic fervor and how he wants to fight the night inside of him. He confesses to the rabbi a need to reach out and help at least one individual: "I'm no longer intent upon measuring myself against fate and saving humanity. I'm content with little; to help a single human being is enough for me" (196). Gregor is reiterating Gavriel's command, pronounced in the cave, and one of Wiesel's central concerns: "No good deed equals in meaning and importance that of saving a human life—any human life" (46).

During this winter episode Gavriel once again appears, this time as a bearded middle-aged stranger with a mocking, somewhat cruel, smile. Gregor hears his unforgettable laugh in the synagogue and tearfully whispers to him in hopes of being reconciled with his double and reunited with himself. The man does not respond, as Gregor assails him with questions and implores: "Gavriel, give me back what I gave you. I'm alone and leading a false life. I want to change, to become again what I was. Give me back my name" (205). Gregor feels rejected by this person with the strangely familiar voice, this person whom he has seen and heard before and yet who does not seem to recognize him. He becomes poignantly aware that "this man who resembles Gavriel and now strangely recalls his father is neither" (208).

When the stranger finally speaks to Gregor, it is not clear to us whether he has ever met the protagonist, and if he is real or simply an illusion. Nonetheless, he encourages Gregor to recount his adventures, starting with his experience in Maria's village. Whereas in the cave Gavriel was the speaker who taught Gregor how to listen, their positions are now reversed: this problematic figure representing Gavriel becomes the listener. It is now Gregor who talks, who relates the story within a story, bringing his listener up to the present time and thereby unifying the narrative. Yet curiously, at the end of the tale told by the protagonist, the so-called Gavriel expresses annoyance at Gregor's preoccupation with his double, and, just as Leib before him, questions Gavriel's very existence: "What's this obsession of yours? Are you sure that he really existed?" he asks, and Gregor replies: "You may be right. Perhaps Gavriel never did exist. Or I myself either. And you. Yes, you exist. You've existed forever" (210).

There is no resolution, therefore, of the uncertainty as to Gavriel's being, who he is, what he symbolizes, and in what form he continues to survive. This incertitude has been the principal element of drama in the text. *The Gates* centers on Gregor's quest for his double, the Other who is also the I, manifesting himself under different identities, possessing the ability to break down boundaries between the living and the dead, past and present, the real and the imaginary. He seems to emanate from a force higher than himself with the faculty to change his face and expand his self into a multiplicity of selves. When the last

apparition of Gavriel leaves the Hasidic synagogue, the novel comes to
an end. As Gregor recites *Kaddish*—the Jewish prayer for the dead—
for his father, for God and for Leib, he realizes that the strength to
survive lies in his ability to establish contact with his fellow Jews and to
become a part of the vast spiritual community. His experience in the
Hasidic synagogue of Brooklyn inspires him with renewed faith and
affirms his sense of Jewish identity.

Furthermore, in the final pages of *The Gates*, Gregor takes back his
Jewish name, *Gavriel*, thereby becoming one with his double. The
fragmented self is united as it was in the harmonious and simple
atmosphere of the forest before the external forces of disintegration
tore things apart. In existential terms, Gregor proclaims his intention:
"I am what I choose to be; I am in my choice, in my will to choose. There
is no divorce between the self and its image, between act and being. I
am this image, I am this act. I am one and indivisible" (221). The
encounter with Gavriel has compelled Gregor to relinquish his name,
give it to another and then regain it, recalling Jacob's struggle with the
angel: "He had to cross night, go to the end of the confrontation—face
solitude and anguish—to become worthy of his name" (MG, 130). The
protagonist who survives the long night journey in *The Gates* is
transformed from a seventeen-year-old boy abandoned in a cave by his
father into a man who has painfully gained an awareness of himself
and his relationship to the Holocaust victims and executioners. He has
thus earned the right to his heritage—the name of his father's father.

The importance assigned to the transmission of the name establishes the bond between father and son. On one hand, by giving Gavriel
his name, Gregor defies time and assures the continuity of his own
succession as a father who bequeaths his legacy to his heir. On the
other, Gavriel is a type of father-surrogate for Gregor; it is he who
comes to the cave after Gregor's father has disappeared and replaces
the void in the boy's life. Messenger of the dead, Gavriel also represents
the "surviving" self who encourages the protagonist to speak of his
father: "As long as you go on, he is still alive" (24). A kind of spiritual
parent to Gregor, this man of God becomes *the witness of the witness* as he
listens to Gregor's stories about his dead father and his attempt to
resurrect him through the spoken word. Gavriel's presence helps to
combat the loss of the paternal figure and, in a sense, to bring him back
to life. He therefore embodies both father and son. And as Elie Wiesel
says of his own son who bears his father's name: "I discover gestures of
my father in him and in a way, he's my son and my father. Through
him, my father will come to life again or at least his name will come
back. . . ."[32]

At the end of Part I, when Gavriel is about to surrender to the Hungarian police, Gregor is anguished by the fear of separation: "He was afraid, not of death, but of being separated from his companion. If at least he could be assured that they would die together" (40). This wish to be united, even in death, recalls Eliezer's obsession to hold on to his father in *l'univers concentrationnaire*. Yet just as father and son are destined to part in *Night*, so, too, are Gregor and Gavriel forced to take leave of each other in *The Gates of the Forest*. Both Eliezer and Gregor never actually witness the death of their fellow sufferers and consequently continue to question the possibility of their survival. Michael in *The Town Beyond the Wall* also keeps wondering if his father really is dead. The Wieselean characters are not ready to accept the permanence and reality of death. At the same time, a part of them has ceased to live with the passing of the Other. "When my father died, I died. At leat, something in me died," Wiesel tells us.[33] But if one "I" dies, another must stay alive to tell the tale in order to assure immortality to that dead self whose name must be transmitted—even if his story is condemned to remain unfinished.

A BEGGAR IN JERUSALEM

If *The Gates of the Forest* concludes with the equivocal disappearance of Gavriel and the death of Leib, *A Beggar in Jerusalem* commences with the absence of Katriel, the mysterious double of David, the novel's narrator-beggar. At the end of *The Gates* Gregor, slowly and with a great deal of concentration, recites the last *Kaddish* for his childhood friend, Leib, "in order that the fighter might find peace" (GF, 226). The prayer for the dead is a "solemn affirmation filled with grandeur and serenity, by which man returns God his *crown* and his scepter" (GF, 225; my emphasis). The figure of Katriel combines the traits of Leib and Gavriel: he is both a soldier who fights to defend his country, Israel, in the 1967 Six Days War, and a student of the Talmud whose name in Hebrew means "the crown of God."[34] As with the names of the main characters in Wiesel's other works, Michael (who is like God) in *The Town*, Gavriel (man of God) in *The Gates*, Azriel (whom God helps) in *The Oath*, and Paltiel (God is my refuge) in *The Testament*, the "*El*" refers to the part of God—the mystical part—in each character.[35] Katriel in *A Beggar in Jerusalem* thus embodies the man of God and the Jewish warrior who in his struggle for the survival of the Jewish nation becomes "the bridge between the Babylonian sages and the generations to come" (BJ, 96).

Just as Gavriel's presence-absence dominates the narrative in *The Gates of the Forest*, Katriel's problematic existence-nonexistence becomes the focal point of *A Beggar in Jerusalem.*[36] Unlike Gavriel, however, Katriel has a name from the outset and it is only at the end of the novel that David questions this name:

> Katriel: was that even his name? Yes or no, it hardly matters: that was the name he flaunted to exorcise a threat, to ingratiate himself with that which is present but unseen. Sometimes, contented, he would enunciate it slowly, solemnly probing it, savoring it. Other times he would angrily, bitterly blurt it out as though to dispose of it. [205]

The name here takes on a magical life of its own; it evokes a hidden force issuing from a different order of reality and suggests Katriel's association with the uncanny, the unknown, and the God-like Other. Moreover, the wide gamut of emotional responses and of ambiguity surrounding Katriel's name characterizes the narrator's confusion with regard to this second self, who is present through his absence. Throughout the timeless night at the foot of the Wailing Wall in Jerusalem, David is obsessed with Katriel. He shares his stories with the other beggars near the wall—Shlomo, Dan, Menashe, Yakov, Moshe, and Zalmen. He speaks to them of his childhood, of his experiences in the death camps, of life as a survivor in postwar Europe and of his return to his native town. Accounts of the Holocaust are interwoven with tales of triumph, as David steadfastly thinks of his companion, who has disappeared during the attack on the Old City of Jerusalem. Like Gregor in *The Gates*, the protagonist lives in constant uncertainty as to his friend's possible return. This element of doubt creates the dramatic tension of the novel.

The theme of the return manifests itself at the beginning of the text. In a style that uses techniques similar to those of the *Nouveau Roman*, a statement is made, then contradicted. The narrator announces to his readers that he is looking for Katriel in the crowd, at the same time that he assures us we will neither see him nor become acquainted with him. The reader is caught up in David's dilemma and is perplexed by his conflicting expression of hope that Katriel will come back and despair that he has slipped away without a trace. "I invoke the face of Katriel: where is he? will he return? is he still alive?" (15), David asks himself as the sun goes down behind the purple veil of Jerusalem's treetops.

These key questions are later echoed by the beggars who, like a chorus in a Greek tragedy, cry out as they witness the meeting of David and Katriel's wife, Malka (whose Hebrew name means "the Queen"):

"Katriel? Who is he? What does he do? Why isn't he here with us?" (91–92). When Malka poignantly asks: "Who is Katriel?", David tells her that Katriel may still return and that he is the one who will respond: it is her duty to wait for his answers. Throughout the book and even at its conclusion David reiterates his belief that Katriel will come back, perhaps under another guise: "One day he will have had enough and will reappear, with another name or without a name, more mysterious and more invincible too, and he will tell Katriel the adventures of Katriel" (206).

The motif of the anticipated return thus structures *A Beggar in Jerusalem* as it did *The Gates of the Forest*. Torn by doubts as to whether the Other is living or dead, the protagonists in both novels nevertheless are sustained by faith in his resurgence. David's refusal to accept Katriel's departure as final is not unlike Gregor's desire to behold Gavriel. The same inconclusive story is governed by the quest and the wait. But in contrast to Gregor, who never admits that Gavriel might be his own creation (it is the others who doubt), David expresses his fear that Katriel may be only a figment of his imagination, a creature of his own naming. He confesses to the beggar, Moshe: "Katriel is my obsession, my private madness. I may even have invented him. I would need proof, but no one can provide that now that the war is over" (34).

Katriel is for David the person he cannot be and yet is, different and the same, strange and familiar, "unmistakably outside but just as inescapably inside." He is the evasive Other, described by Wiesel as "the one who lives within us and escapes us." Katriel is the self David might have been or wished to be, and the narrator reveals that he is jealous of this self.[37] He envies his friend's innocence, simplicity, sense of vulnerability, his overwhelming need to love and to magnify the human element in an inhuman universe. He respects his ability to observe, listen, and be silent; he admires his knowledge of how and when to use words, even though Katriel believes that words are suspect and that they destroy what they aim to portray. David discloses to Moshe that his strong feeling of envy causes him to doubt Katriel's existence.

Not only does Katriel represent the narrator's idealized self but also his "dead" self, what Manès Sperber describes as "the shadow he lost while wandering along the endless path of an impossible return to the past. . . . that part of himself which is a Lazarus resurrected but unreconciled with life, neither his own nor others."[38] Robert Misrahi sees Katriel as the Talmudic student, whose death the day Jerusalem was taken back by Israel signifies the man of the spirit giving way to "the new man of war and violence, the man of history. . . . It is Katriel in David who has died: and perhaps it is God."[39] Dominique Baux asks if

David himself has perished in order to save Katriel, "the most beautiful part of his being," or, she ponders, "has Katriel died, as Katriel, the day that war forced him to kill his fellow-men?"[40]

Katriel's disappearance at the culmination of Israel's triumph and his ambiguous relationship with the protagonist clearly pose more questions than answers. Wiesel deliberately creates an unresolved tension between the "dead" and "surviving" selves. As identities merge and fall apart, and the boundaries between life and death break down, David wonders if his counterpart is still alive or *ever was*. Unsure as to who is the victor and who the victim, he has "this thought which keeps coming back, chilling my blood: What if I am dead and he is the survivor?" (207). What David is certain of is this: "Someone died inside me. I still don't know who?" (209).

Despite the irretrievable loss of the Other that is also the I, the quest for the double is sustained throughout the novel and evolves as the protagonist strives to keep the dead self alive through memory. Two key events exemplify the theme of *dédoublement* and stand in opposition to each other: the parable and the pact. The parable, recounted by Katriel to David in the army camp the night before the battle of Jerusalem, stresses the dichotomy of the double, whereas the *"pacte de témoignage"* established by the two men underlines the more positive need to bear witness as a means of unifying the splintered self.

The parable is the story of a man who leaves his native town in search of adventure in the big city. He spends the night under a tree, takes his shoes off, and points them in the direction of the city. At midnight, a practical joker turns the shoes around with the result that, in the morning, the wayfarer unknowingly follows the road back to his village. The mysterious and promised city looks strangely familiar (motif of the town as double) to the surprised traveler, who roams through the streets, finally coming upon a house that resembles his own. A whining voice similar to his wife's invites him to enter. He sits down at the table with children who smile at him; the youngest one plays with his beard and asks him to stay. Sadly, with the realization that he is trapped because he has been mistaken for the master of the house, who must be his double, the stranger caresses the child's blond hair and promises not to leave.

David asks Katriel to finish the tale but Katriel merely repeats the last line, for he has nothing more to add. David is troubled by the warning signal that the parable touches off in him. The story resonates in his memory and consciousness. He is disturbed by the actions of this strangely familiar character whose real wife and children, abandoned in their village, suffer as they await in vain the return of their husband and father. He is upset that the traveler is untrue to himself by assuming another's identity and yet willfully persists in the deception. The protagonist resents Katriel for having told him the parable and angrily accuses him of lying:

> I also dislike your main character. He lies. As a result, he makes you lie. It is inconceivable to me that a man could shed his "I" as he might an attachment or a memory. That "I" sticks to him and belongs to him and only to him; it is he. One does not exchange one's "I" for another, even a more refined or truer one. . . . The "I" is comparable to death. Your traveler can live and even die for you, but not in your place. [125–26]

In a soft but wounded voice, Katriel tells David that he knows he does not have the authority to speak in the name of the traveler: "It may be his fate to live a lie and submit to it freely and deliberately, out of excess or lack of pride. Perhaps all he wants is to lie to death so he may finally be allowed to die. . . . But a tale is only a tale after all, isn't it. It is made to be lived then passed on" (126).

The metaphysical discussion that takes place between David and Katriel questions the duplicity of existence in the world to which the alienated survivor has returned, and corresponds, in effect, to what Wiesel has termed "the dialogue of two persons who are one." Like Gavriel in *The Gates of the Forest*, Katriel is the possessor of secrets which the first self (David) has difficulty comprehending but which are not totally unknown to him. Like Gavriel, Katriel is a storyteller and transmits the parable recounted by his blind father. David has the feeling that he knows Katriel's father, but Katriel indicates that this is highly improbable. Nonetheless, the narrator insists that at another moment in time he has met him and has heard the tale of the traveler.

We have the impression that David is in the process of discovering his shared identity with Katriel. The two men seem to have met before and share the same father, just as they will share the same wife. The "basic oneness divided into a simultaneous twoness"[41] mirrors itself endlessly: Katriel, David's second self, tells a story that David thinks he has already heard (motif of the story *dédoublé*), and, in this tale about a man and his double, David identifies with the main character as his double.

In a flash of insight, David understands that the traveler in the parable is himself and that the story is his own. Like the stranger, merely a shadow of his former self,[42] he is only going through the motions of living. His life in the present is a kind of death:

> "I" ["*le vrai moi*"] had remained over there, in the kingdom of night, a prisoner of the dead. The living person I was, the one I thought myself to be, had been living a lie. I was nothing more than an echo of

voices long since extinguished, nothing more than a shadow stumbling against other shadows. . . . I thought I was living my own life, I
was only inventing it. I thought I had escaped the ghosts. I was only
extending their power. [133]

These words characterize the death-in-life state of the Wieselean
protagonist-survivor, especially evident in the early works but also
apparent throughout the later ones. David's identification with the
outsider in the unrecognizable town parallels his own feeling of
alienation in the post-Holocaust universe, where the familiar has
become strange. The forces of Night have exiled the self from itself.
Moreover, David recalls a beggar from his childhood who proclaimed
that the day the story of your life is told to you, you will not have much
longer to live. He realizes with terror that by telling the tale Katriel has
inadvertently become the messenger of impending doom, "a reminder
of the individual's mortality, indeed the announcer of death itself."

The narrator-protagonist struggles against the threat of finality
by forming a pact with his double. For the first time in Wiesel's novels,
the theme of *the witness* is directly enunciated: David is conscious of an
overwhelming need to have a witness to assure his survival after death.
When he first meets Katriel, he instinctively feels: "He will testify for
me" (104). If, by warning the narrator of his imminent end, Katriel is
the instrument of death, he also assumes the role of guardian angel, the
protector of life. David proposes a pact in which he would help conquer
Katriel's fear of war in exchange for the latter's commitment to be his
witness. Katriel would prepare himself for the task by listening to
David carefully, staying by his side, even in combat, and inscribing in
his memory his friend's every word, his every gesture. David promises
Katriel that the arrangement will be reciprocal: the one who survives
will serve as witness for the one who dies. By insinuating, however, that
Katriel will outlive him, the narrator causes his companion to tremble
in bewilderment at the offer, and is deeply moved by his response:

How vulnerable, how innocent is the face of a man at night, the face
of a man whom you choose as your ally, your heir. . . . how pure, how
sad is the trembling of a man who, foreseeing his role as witness,
suddenly glimpses the mutilation or end of a life other than his own.
. . . how profoundly human and how wounded is the voice of a
friend who senses in you and in the night surrounding you, the
shame inherent in survival. [134]

The situation of a man facing another man and presaging the
termination of that man's life brings to mind the scene at the conclusion
of *Night*, when the son is forced to watch his father slowly die. In "The

Death of My Father" (LT) the author also describes in detail the last moments spent witnessing his father pass away in the stifling barracks of the concentration camp. It is not surprising, then, that the father figure is evoked as death hovers over the warriors in *A Beggar in Jerusalem*. Katriel's first reaction to the pact is to wonder what his father would say about it. David assures him that his father would advise him to accept the agreement because he has probably agreed to a similar one with God: "Let's say He also needs witnesses. In the beginning there was the word; the word is the tale of man; and man is the tale of God" (135). David's wish to have Katriel ("crown of God") as his witness is thus linked to man's covenant with God: a binding agreement of mutual testimony.

In the quiet darkness outside of his tent on the eve of battle, David thinks of his own father. When Katriel discloses his plans for the future, the narrator realizes that he has none. "I know that tomorrow I shall die," he predicts, and begins to visualize his own death. The word "tomorrow" suddenly brings to mind an image of the last night in the ghetto. David remembers the gathering in the courtyard where family, friends, and neighbors anxiously awaited the return of his father, who had gone to seek information about the deportation. He recalls how a few hours later his father came back with a defeated spirit, repeating over and over the same words: "It's for tomorrow, it's for tomorrow." As David relives this event in his memory (BJ, 167), a scene described vividly in *Night*, he starts to whisper the identical phrase. This incantation, uttered with a sacred and decisive tone, identifies the narrator with his father and with all those whose life stories were destined to be aborted "tomorrow."

David's preparations and premonitions mask a strong death wish. "Why tomorrow and why in this land?" he asks himself. "Because I am forty and Jewish? Because the survivor is tired of running after the dead," he speculates (163). The protagonist here seems to be expressing not only a desire to join the dead, but also an unconscious wish to substitute himself for his father, for Katriel, and for all his lost companions. Convinced he will be the first to perish, David is condemned to survive. The son cannot die in his father's place. Instead, he becomes his successor, bearing witness for him and thus continuing the heritage. Like Gavriel, it is Katriel, the mysterious double, friend, and father surrogate who vanishes without a word.

Katriel's abrupt exit from the world causes a conflict in David essentially related to the notion of survival guilt and the theme of the witness. At the end of the novel, the narrator admits that he is incapable of imagining Katriel's death and, therefore, of completing his story. "I can't see Katriel other than alive. His disappearance proves nothing, except that certain stories don't have an ending. Or a beginning" (207). If, in fact, he could accept for certain that Katriel had been killed, he would know what to do: he would bring him back to life by telling his tale. However, if there is the slightest possibility that Katriel is still among the living, David wonders if he is justified "to act as though he were not and speak and live in his stead" (207).

The protagonist's fear of betrayal through substitution resumes one of the basic issues posited by the parable: does one have the right to exchange one's identity for someone else's; can one live or die in another's place? The difficulties of the survivor-as-witness are brought to light by David's dilemma. He is torn by the promise to preserve Katriel's memory, on the one hand, and the fear of misrepresenting him, on the other. How to speak of and for the dead, how not to speak of them? The duty to remember conflicts with the compulsion to remain silent. No conclusion is reached by the protagonist, nor by the author, for in the final pages of *A Beggar in Jerusalem*, David continues to ponder this unresolved matter: "How can one work for the living without by that very act betraying those who are absent? The question remains open, and no new fact can change it" (210).

However, if feelings of guilt and ambivalence toward replacing the lost object are part of the burden of survival, the imperative to testify prevails. "And the way to fight death is to create life," Katriel's father teaches him (99), echoing Albert Camus' declaration: "l'homme devait affirmer la justice pour protester contre l'injustice éternelle, créer du bonheur pour protester contre l'univers du malheur" ("man must affirm justice in order to protest against eternal injustice, create happiness in order to protest against a universe of unhappiness").[43] The way for the survivor to protest injustice and to create—or re-create—life is by bearing witness. David is aware that he cannot save Katriel from death but vows to keep his pledge "to say what he [Katriel] could not say, to save him and his tale from distortion and oblivion" (17). Like Eliezer in *Night*, who commits himself to recounting his father's unfinished story, David too keeps his friend and double alive by telling his tale—even if it has no ending. "His trace? I am his trace" (7), David informs us at the beginning of the text, implying that to be a witness signifies a fusion of "the two separate selves, the mortal and immortal, in one and the same personality."[44]

The merging of two selves into one ("How can I convince myself that it is his wish, not mine that drives me to speak of his memories and his obsessions, which I find difficult to distinguish from my own?"

[207]) is a thematic expression of unity, and counteracts the threat of separation. In spite of Katriel's sacrifice during an atmosphere of war and death, his final departure occurs at a time of conquest, suggesting the contradictory nature of his being: a state of death-in-triumph. For the first time in Wiesel's novels, a spirit of victory awakens the city of Jerusalem to new dimensions. A vast assembly of exiled Jews is mobilized. Rabbis and soldiers, madmen and beggars, kings and prophets throng the streets:

> all the dead of the town, all the dead towns of the cemetery that was Europe. Here they are, at the timeless twilight hour, pilgrims all. . . . they have now come back from far, very far, beyond the roofs and stars, from another time and other homes, wanting to live the beginning and the end of their tale. [201]

Spanning time and space, the tumultuous crowd of more than six million joins the Israeli army in a march through Jerusalem, happy to come home finally to a place where they are taken in instead of being expelled. As in a dream, past and present flow together and all faces blend into one: an old man lifting his arms to the sky is at once King David, Abraham, the Messiah, and Katriel. A delirious shout brings together Jewish pilgrims from every century as the Wailing Wall is liberated. In a moment of miraculous exultation, the Old and New Cities of Jerusalem are reconciled, connected by the Wall, which is "not a wall of separation but a wall of union, the mystical wall of Jerusalem regained across time and space."[45] The Wall comes to be a symbol of the beginning and end of Jewish history, a paradigm of the Jewish and human condition representing with its defeats and conquests the union and reunion of an ancient people with the young Israeli nation, the survivor with his past, and the protagonist with his double.

Heart and spirit of Jerusalem, the Wall occupies the dominant position in the narrative, serving as the source from which the collective memory of the Jewish people emanates; it is the "witness to the unity of the past, and promise of that of tomorrow."[46] Events of the Holocaust, interspersed with Hasidic legends and Talmudic parables, commence at the Wall and spiral out to encompass different epochs in history. The Wall is the gathering place for all the characters from Wiesel's previous works, as the author states in his introduction to the original French edition of the novel (which has been omitted in its English translation): "tous les personnages de tous mes livres, eh oui, ils m'avaient suivi ici pour faire acte de présence et témoigner comme moi, à travers moi" ("all the characters of all my books, yes, they followed me here to be present and bear witness, like me, and through me") (*Le Mendiant de Jérusalem*, 11). Wiesel affirms that *A Beggar in Jerusalem* is a culmination of his other works—*"un livre-somme"*:

> As this book is a total sum, I imagined a meeting of all my characters, all those who I invented in the past from different places and under different circumstances; and they came with me to the Wall of Jerusalem. They were judges and witnesses; they asked me: "what did you do with us and with yourself?" That became the novel.[17]

In front of the Wall, the author thus convokes the dispersed witnesses who have peopled his real and imaginary worlds in order that they, too, may share in the mystical experience of reclaiming Jerusalem. As a writer, Wiesel feels responsible for allowing his characters to participate in one of the decisive moments of Jewish history. "The writer must assume the totality of his being," he claims. "I wanted here to assume the totality of my characters and to add this ultimate episode to their incomplete destinies."[48]

In the course of these historical circumstances, the thoughts of Wiesel's beggar-narrator reflect the author's own awareness of an identity that has grown larger than itself. "Spectator, he turns witness. Visionary, he now becomes all those characters to whom long ago, he imported a heartbeat, a glimmer of life" (116). Just as Jerusalem in its moment of jubilation transcends its earthly bounds to become a universal meeting place—*une ville-somme*—the individual swells into the expanded self—*le moi-somme*—stretched far beyond its mortal limits to include all those who are part of its tradition and its creation. At the time of the Israeli victory, the author, through his protagonist, discovers the depth of his Jewish solidarity. He listens to the multitude of voices vibrating both within and without, and realizes that his is a collective voice:

> I understood then that in time of trial man is more than himself, he represents more than his own person. When his roots are at stake, he becomes the sum of his experiences, given or acquired, a combination of intertwined destinies, a subterranean network of friendships and alliances. He becomes *conscience*. [115; my emphasis]

The realization of *le moi-somme* as *conscience* is an integral part of the theme of the witness and reaches its climax in *A Beggar in Jerusalem*. David perceives that by his survival alone and his will to speak for both the living and the dead, he is a crucial link in the endless but fragile chain joining the generations of the past to the present and uniting the Diaspora with its homeland. David the protagonist is inseparable from Wiesel the writer, when he tells us: "He who says 'I' has said everything.

Just as every man contains all men, this word contains all words" (7). "When I say 'I', I speak for all men who say 'I'," Wiesel declares.[49] Surely the "I" denotes the "we" for, as Terrence Des Pres has pointed out: "almost all survivors say 'we' rather than 'I'," making it evident that "survival is an act whose value extends beyond the individual who survives."[50] If every man contains all men, then we are all responsible for the collective survival of mankind and for transcending the unconditional reality of death by bearing witness. It is thus each person's task to keep the universal memory alive by testifying for the other and others who have been slaughtered in the night.

For the first time in Wiesel's novels, the main character, despite feelings of guilt and ambiguity, asserts his position as witness and attempts to come to grips with the necessity of saving the Other who is also the I, the I who has died and must be resurrected. By recognizing his mission to transmit Katriel's story to his fellow beggars, the protagonist integrates the two selves into one—*le moi-somme*—which transcends the particular to become part of a larger force, both historical and mythical.

The beggar's memory is a strange one; it encompasses several eras, never ceasing to expand its dimensions as it accumulates more and more events, faces, and figures, and eventually loses its ability to differentiate between the past of others and its own. The beggar, a figure endowed in Jewish lore with hidden magical qualities, is a seer of sorts: "because he is from nowhere, he is from everywhere."[51] A messenger, wanderer, holy wise man, he is Everyman just as all of us are beggars waiting at the Wall of Jerusalem, and participating in the triumphant liberation of the City. As we endlessly partake of the legends of our times we, too, become witnesses, for to listen to a tale is to heighten its meaning, as Katriel has taught David: "Do you know that it is given to us to enrich a legend simply by listening to it? It belongs as much to the listener as to the teller. You listen to a tale, and all of a sudden it is no longer the same tale" (107).

The beggar of Jerusalem is above all the author, who as principal witness, observes, absorbs, listens, and then re-creates, bringing back to life those who have perished before their time. Like the beggar-narrator, he identifies with the many characters who are creatures of his own naming—*witnesses of the witness*—and by "becoming" them often loses his sense of boundaries, merging his own existence with theirs. Wiesel seeks in his vast testimony to preserve the presence of all those beggars, visionaries, madmen, and prophets who have informed him. He believes that the role of the writer is "to bear witness for his epoch, his generation, his brothers, his dead" and also for "the heroes who won the war and saved the lives of many of their fellow men."[52] Through the power of the word, be it oral or written, they must be remembered. The book then, like the vast spiritual community itself, becomes an extension of the author, which is to say, his double or mirror image: "the eye that looks at the eye that is looking" (196). The creation of a literary universe grants permanence to the survivor and to his multiple selves, both living and dead.

Katriel's final words to David occur, significantly, at the Wailing Wall, where he advises his friend to follow the customary tradition of scribbling a wish on a piece of paper and inserting it between the cracks: "You must write something new," he insists (195), as he hands David some paper and a pencil, thus passing on the legacy from father to son, from victim to survivor. Katriel vanishes into the turbulent crowd, but his own crumpled scrap of paper becomes as immutable and indestructible as the stones of the Wall, rendered immortal by his heir and witness in an enduring work of art, a book—collective monument to the survival of himself and his people.

5
Chronicle of Memory

. . . la volonté du juif de survivre était dans son entêtement à
recommencer le livre
—Edmonds Jabès

In *A Beggar in Jerusalem* all of the Wieselean characters are convoked to
bear witness to a momentous and triumphant event in Jewish history.
Gathering place for a multitude of victims and survivors, the book as
total sum becomes the organizing principle of Wiesel's following novel,
The Oath. The authority of the written word as testimony is established
but, at the same time, its validity is questioned. From the narrative
point of view, the novel describes the total destruction of an Eastern
European town in the early part of the twentieth century by a massive
pogrom that ends in fire, a fierce prefiguration of the Holocaust and
emblem of catastrophe in general. At the core of the text, however, lies
the story of a Book—the *Pinkas*[1]—communal archive of Kolvillàg
(which in Hungarian means "all the world"). Revered object to be
passed on from generation to generation, this Book assumes legendary
proportions as sacred monument and collective witness of the Jewish
community. Destined like the town itself to be consumed in the
burning ruins, the chronicle miraculously survives. Yet this repository
of history is sealed by an oath of silence.

The account of life in the Jewish *shtetl* is registered daily by
Shmuel, a character totally committed to the vocation of scribe. Before
he perishes along with the other inhabitants of Kolvillàg, he transmits

the records to his son, Azriel, who turns out to be the sole survivor, and narrator of the novel. Azriel inherits the responsibility of keeping alive the Book, the only document testifying to the community's existence. This task, which appears to be a privilege and blessing, is a curse and burden as well. Before the pogrom, Azriel takes a vow of silence prescribed by Moshe, the mad seer of Kolvillàg, and pledges never to tell the tale of the once flourishing town, nor of its flaming annihilation. Consequently, the volume that accompanies the exiled Azriel throughout his wanderings cannot be opened: the word is forbidden, absent, dead.

The supreme value accorded the written word in Jewish tradition, solidified by the stone tablets handed down to Moses at Mount Sinai, is contested in *The Oath* by Moshe, the contemporary Moses of post-pogrom (or post-Holocaust) times. This latter-day prophet sets forth a new commandment—the law of silence. It is the tension between this law and the compulsion to speak out that underlies the text, revealing the basic conflict of the survivor-as-witness.

THE SANCTITY OF THE BOOK

The imperative to keep the Book alive is the focal point for a thematic series in the text which stress the importance of bearing witness through the written word. Motifs related to writing and the writer characterize the Book as sanctuary, monument, and total sum, pointing to the decisive role of language as a means of survival.

When Azriel is confronted with the possibility of breaking the oath of silence in order to save the life of a young man, he cries out in frustration to his master, long dead: "Open the sanctuary, open the *Pinkas*. Speak, Moshe, speak" (O, 84). Gaining entrance to the hallowed pages of the chronicle is analogous to penetrating the walls of a Temple, for, like the Bible or Talmud, the scripture is a holy place, its words surrounded by a sacred aura. The veneration of the Book in *The Oath* indeed reflects Wiesel's esteem for words, which he believes constitute the foundation of Judaism: "Judaism is words. . . . Judaism is not buildings, Jewish building is in words, we build words. The only way for us to communicate what happened in the past is through words, whether of past glory or of past disaster. Only words."[2]

Words have not only enabled the Jewish people to forge and articulate their history, but they have also been influential in altering destinies. Moshe acknowledges their power when he offers himself as a scapegoat to appease the authorities who accuse the Jews of the ritual murder of Yansci, a disreputable Christian youth who mysteriously disappears.[3] "Three words and it would all be over. . . . *I did it.* One brief sentence, and the destiny of a Jewish community somewhere between the Dnieper and the Carpathian Mountains would be changed" (O, 152), Moshe thinks as he presents himself to the local police. He believes that by falsely confessing to the killing of the boy he will assume the burden of communal guilt, and imminent disaster will be averted.

Instrument of life, language is utilized here to fight the enemy. When later on, Moshe dramatically addresses the public, he declares: "Words have been our weapon, our shield; the tale, our lifeboat. And we wanted those words strong, stronger than our foes, stronger than death" (O, 238). The sanctity of the tools granted to the speaker—and to the writer—obliges him to solemnly respect their authority and to handle them with care as Wiesel points out:

> The only power we have had is the word, and with it we managed not only to influence history but to stay alive. No other people has had such an impact on events. Therefore the writer has a frightening, a gratifying but awesome task: words and their use. Because God created the world with a word, Jews view that word as holy. We are the only people that picks up a sacred book and kisses it: we believe our tradition to be the only revered tradition, handed down by God, not by man.[4]

Language is thus revered because of its divine source. "In the beginning there was the word; the word is the tale of man; and man is the tale of God," David tells Katriel in *A Beggar in Jerusalem* (135).

If words bind man to God, they also join the living and the dead. Writing is a means of commemorating those who have been destroyed and left unburied.[5] Letters sculpted into tablets solidify and petrify, rendering permanent that which has disappeared, replacing and immortalizing lost objects. Shmuel, the official chronicler of Kolvillàg, carves his entries into the *Pinkas,* and thus builds a monument for the community: "He chiseled his words and fitted them like stones into a gigantic tower, until they burst apart, like so many dismembered bodies tumbling into the precipice" (O, 79). The analogy made between stones and dismembered bodies suggests the indestructibility of words and their dissolution. The Book is simultaneously a tombstone bearing eternal witness to the dead and a reminder that beneath the monument lie the ruins of a people. There exists, says Wiesel, "a link between words and the ashes they cover" (OGA, 14).

In contrast to the imperishability of stones, ashes signify death and disintegration, not only of words but of the doomed civilization they embody. At the end of *The Oath*, the town, representative of other Eastern European Jewish communities, is engulfed by flame, ablaze in a "wedding by fire," reduced to a "handful of ashes under a glowing red sky." Only Azriel and the *Pinkas* survive the apocalyptic, hallucinatory, nightmarish scenes of this burnt-out universe, the last witnesses of a living town transformed into a cemetery of smoke and cinders.

Despite the underlying tension between stone and ashes, between the permanence and devastation of the word and world of Kolvillàg, the Book endures. Symbol of survival, relic, testament, and memorial consecrated to the dead town metamorphosed into a kingdom of fire, the *Pinkas* is granted the status of a principal character in the novel, as demonstrated by the title of the third section, "The Madman and the Book." Other main characters in *The Oath* are designated by the titles of the first two sections. The first, "The Old Man and the Child," refers to Azriel, the narrator, as the old man, and the child, the young man who listens to Azriel's tale several generations later. In the second section, "The Child and the Madman," a flashback describes Azriel in his youth interacting with his master, Moshe the madman—prophet of silence.

Significantly, the only other main character not cited in the titles, beside the town itself,[6] is Azriel's father, Shmuel, keeper of the Book. For the first time in Wiesel's novels, the father is portrayed as a writer. Although primarily a recorder of events, not unlike a creator of fiction Shmuel involves himself with the people parading through his pages. "His life? Total identification with the heroes and characters of the *Pinkas*, his only reading matter" (79). Similar to Michael in *The Town Beyond the Wall* and David in *A Beggar in Jerusalem* ("he becomes all those characters to whom, long ago he imparted a heart-beat, a glimmer of life," [BJ, 115]), Shmuel's total immersion in the Book is linked to the notion of *le moi-somme* and to the expanded identity of the writer-as-witness.

If Shmuel continues in the tradition of other Wieselean protagonists whose existence is bound up with the life of the community, his task as witness is defined in greater detail than in any of the other novels, indicating the author's need to share the complexities of his vocation with the reader. Unlike the other texts, *The Oath* depicts the actual process of writing; the story of the town is registered by the father-scribe as it unfolds before his eyes, thus allowing the reader to participate in the very act of bearing witness.

Clearly the author's spokesman for "the prominent role of the witness in Jewish tradition" (188), Shmuel observes, listens, and then describes what is happening in the purest form possible instead of imposing his own meaning upon it by creating legends. "It is my duty to record everything, to transmit everything. Even that which lies beyond my understanding," he tells Moshe when visiting him in prison (185). Closer to an historian than a storyteller, Shmuel's presence in the novel embodies that aspect of the witness devoted to transcribing what is seen and heard. He is the listener rather than the speaker; he does not make decisions but sets them down in writing.

Custodian of the *Pinkas*, Shmuel is intensely concerned with what Wiesel refers to throughout his work as "a veritable passion to testify for the future, against death and oblivion, a passion conveyed by every possible means of expression" (OGA, 39). The word is of supreme value to the town chronicler, for it enables him to pass on history to future generations. His aspiration is to protect the sacredness of the Book, as he firmly declares to Moshe in the dark, airless cell when asked by the prisoner why so determined to write down his personal testimony:

> To record and to safeguard. For the sake of history. Aren't we the people of memory? Is oblivion not the worst of curses? A deed transmitted is a victory snatched from death. A witness who refuses to testify is a false witness. As for me, I do not refuse; on the contrary, I do nothing else, I yearn to do nothing else. [187]

The overwhelming need to remember, to testify and to transmit, essential components of Wiesel's argument in favor of the witness, are reinforced later on in the text by Moshe himself:

> Jews felt that to forget constituted a crime against memory as well as against justice: whoever forgets becomes the executioner's accomplice. The executioner kills twice, the second time when he tries to erase the traces of his crimes, the evidence of his cruelty. [237]

Bearers of memory, the writer, the witness, and the Jew must thus persevere in their fight against the affliction of forgetfulness.

The force of memory as a weapon is related to another important function of the witness: the conscience of history. "I believe that the first task of the Jew and of the writer is to make people aware of their conscience," Wiesel states. "We have been the guilty conscience of the nations for 2,000 years."[7] Although Shmuel himself is not portrayed as an active agitator of conscience, he nonetheless envisages the chronicler as one who must disturb, arouse, challenge, and warn mankind: "The anguish of the witness facing history; his obsession not to depart without having scarred a single consciousness or ripped a single veil" (188). Moshe, too, affirms this position: "We must tell, awaken, alert and repeat over and over again without respite or pause, repeat to the very end, those stories that have no end . . ." (238).

The father-writer advocates many of the author's own views with regard to the role of the witness and serves as a vehicle through which the theme is developed to its fullest. However, Wiesel distances himself enough to show the limitations of his character's all-encompassing devotion to his vocation. Described as somewhat compulsive in his duties, Shmuel is seen by his son, Azriel, as stubborn and indiscreet, sometimes capable of irritating members of the community by his excessive desire to know every detail:

> He sometimes hurt people's feelings with his compulsion to find out everything, consign everything to paper. Never mind if people were annoyed, antagonized or hurt. Professional conscience pushed to the extreme? A sublimated outrageously magnified sense of duty? His zeal angered people or made them smile. [187–88]

Wiesel is perhaps smiling here at the intensity of his own preoccupation and is mocking its obsessive nature. Yet behind the smile, the ultimate validity of the struggle to bear witness is questioned, for, as Azriel observes, his father's task proves futile. Shmuel is the last writer of a book and tradition sentenced to silence: "his project, at this very moment, contained its own negation" (188).

Despite the imminent threat of violence, throughout the narrative the father-scribe maintains an unwavering faith in the act of writing and in the awesomeness of his vocation. He is perpetually taking notes. At the emergency meeting of the Jewish leaders, called to discuss the course of action necessary to stop the growing anti-Semitism that began with Yancsi's disappearance, Azriel is proudly conscious of his father's authority: "Above the voices I could hear a pen scratching the paper. Shmuel, the Chronicler, silently writing, omitting nothing of what was being said around the table. Each fulfilled his role and my father his" (118). While other members of the community are identified by their voices, Shmuel is associated with the sound of pen on paper.

Later on, Shmuel reports on a Jewish celebration held in the midst of the foreboding danger. No major incidents occur, but a sense of doom hangs over the festivities. Long after they are over, the father sits in the same position all night and records his observations: "Bent over the book, the Chronicler wrote: 'The Exterminating Angel has not yet entered the walls and I wonder to whom and to what we are beholden for it. Is it only a postponement? For the moment we are all survivors'" (229). The pose of leaning over the *Pinkas* calls to mind the motif of the Book as mirror: "Every page is a mirror of paper. Bent over it, you look at yourself," Edmond Jabès states in *Le Livre des ressemblances*.[8] The book reflects its keeper's image as *le moi-somme* of the community. Father, town, and Book merge into one, linking the witness and the object of his testimony, an important Wieselean concept. "Between the one who writes and the dramas and triumphs he describes, there is a connection of truth if not of cause and effect" (189). Shmuel's entire being is, indeed, immersed in the story he is relating. He identifies totally with the town; he *is* the town. "Whatever happens to the community I want to happen to myself as well," the recorder jots down in his thick black notebook (250).[9] As the menace draws closer, another Town Council is held. For a moment the scribe, sick with a migraine headache, stops writing. He feels his heart beating fast, and, curiously, hears a strange disembodied voice ordering him to note this phenomenon as well. The heartbeat of the Book thus becomes inseparable from that of its writer.

Toward the end of *The Oath*, as fear invades the air and the Jews huddle behind their barricaded doors, terrified of the approaching disaster, Shmuel stays in his own house, bends over the Book, and continues to record in semidarkness. His son stays by his side during the long hours of their final night ("This night was to be our last together" [249]), recalling the theme of the *last night* in the book *Night*. Together Shmuel and Azriel descend into the windowless cellar to take refuge from the enemy. In the constricted space and murky light the father persists in writing. Throughout the night he steadfastly bears witness, not knowing who will read his story or even if there will be any readers left. The fact that he is so often portrayed by his son as writing in obscurity demonstrates a capacity to withstand adverse circumstances. But the emphasis placed on the darkness also suggests the advancing Night, which ultimately silences the father and eclipses his story.

When Azriel's father lights a candle in the black cellar, he does so not for the purpose of writing, but rather to read to his son. Citing excerpts from the *Pinkas* that commence with the twelfth-century Crusaders, Shmuel shares with Azriel historical accounts of persecutions, pogroms, and attacks on the Jews of Kolvillàg. He stresses those stories which show how certain inhabitants of the town sacrificed their lives for the rest of the community. The scene of father and son reading aloud by candlelight takes on the aura of a holy act, similar to the incantation of a liturgy, a prayer—perhaps the *Kaddish*—recited in advance for the town about to be consumed by fire and for the Book itself, about to be closed. Above all, the act of reading from the sacred text ritualizes the act of transmission from father to son. The father has opened up the sanctuary to his son and bequeathes him the legacy of the word. The gesture itself becomes of utmost significance: "The chronicler handed the Book to his son: 'Will you remember?' 'Yes,

Father.' " (271). Azriel's acceptance represents a vow to assume his father's mission to preserve the collective memory. The Book unites father and son as they desperately struggle to hold on to a tradition and order threatened by annihilation: "Together we clasped the thick bound notebook; never had we been so close" (272).

If the Book serves as a meeting ground for the two generations, the transfer of the communal record also marks the end of one epoch in history and the beginning of another. As in most of Wiesel's works, the son and his father are forced to part. Urged by Shmuel to leave Kolvillàg before it is too late (" 'Go my son, the moment has come.' . . . it was now or never. The moment had come to leave, break out of the circle, slip outside. . . . the moment had come to choose life" [279]), Azriel clutches the *Pinkas* to his heart as he pushes his way out of the blazing inferno, looking back, like Lot's wife, to forever engrave on his memory the image of his father and the town.

Because Azriel has been able to save the document from destruction, it, in turn, saves him: "What helped me to stand fast was the Book, the *Pinkas* of Kolvillàg. If I used all my wits to stay alive, it was to save it, to protect it. A matter of duty. I had no right to die" (70). The son's obligation to stay alive in order to take care of the Book recalls Eliezer's sense of duty to his father in *Night:* "I had no right to let myself die. What would he do without me? I was his only support" (N, 99). The Book in *The Oath* becomes a substitute for the lost parent: it is both the father's testament and the testament to the father. Azriel's will to live is ultimately bound up with prolonging its existence: "By entrusting the Book to him, his father doomed him to survival" (33). And being destined as a survivor is, according to Wiesel, "both the privilege and the tragedy of the Jew. A privilege because it makes him into a witness. And a tragedy because he cannot die."[10]

Forced into a life of exile, Azriel carries the Book with him as he wanders from town to town. He refuses to be separated from his most treasured possession or allow anyone to touch it; it is the sole relic from his past and he respects its authority as one would a father, sometimes reversing positions and treating it like his own child. The large black volume is his loyal and constant companion. Nonetheless, Azriel finds himself in a difficult situation. Because he has taken Moshe's oath of silence, he is unable to share the contents of the text with anyone, nor can he contribute to its historical pages. The Book that the father was in the process of writing will not be completed, just as in *Night* the story that the father was in the midst of telling in the ghetto courtyard was so abruptly interrupted by news of the deportation. Before leaving Kolvillàg Azriel had anxiously asked his father: "And now—what will happen now? Who will write what is to follow? This night. This fear. This uncertainty. Who will record them?" (264). "Who will write the ending?" (271). "The ending will not be written," his father sadly answered, repeating the theme of *the unfinished story*. Inheritor of a story whose ending he knows but which cannot be told, Azriel is a messenger unable to deliver his message. He is torn between the conflicting legacies of his father, the witness obsessed with transmitting the word, and of Moshe, proponent of silence.

UNIVERSE OF SILENCE

If *The Oath* is Wiesel's first novel to reveal the construction of a book, a book in the process of being written, it is also the first to show its deconstruction. The glorification of the father's vocation as writer is counteracted by Moshe's rejection of the word. While the character of Moshe has appeared in different guises throughout Wiesel's works, in *The Oath* he achieves the status of a major protagonist. His principal function in the novel is to expose the author's views on silence as an alternative to speaking out. Moshe's position represents a break with the traditional reverence for the word in Jewish history and his proposal of the *Herem*—the oath of silence—is uttered with a sense of defiance and rejection of the past.

> We shall innovate, do what our ancestors and forebears could not or dared not do. We are going to impose the ultimate challenge, not by language but by absence of language, not by the word but by absence of language, not by the word but by abdication of the word. . . . we shall testify no more. [239]

Moshe's plan to defeat death through silence brings the theme to its culmination and reflects a turnabout in Wiesel's own spiritual-literary itinerary as witness.

In order to understand the full impact of Moshe's calling verbal testimony into question, let us briefly trace the author's post-Holocaust journey from one kind of silence to another. After his liberation from Buchenwald in 1945, the young Wiesel made a vow to wait ten years before speaking of his concentration camp experience. He needed time to reflect, read, and study so as to "learn to listen to the voices crying inside my own. . . . to unite the language of man with the silence of the dead" (JT, 15). Wiesel wanted desperately to understand what had happened to himself and to mankind but knew all along he never would.[11]

He admits that he did not bear witness because he lacked the tools of expression and was afraid of not living up to the task of "saying the wrong things, of saying too much or too little or becoming sentimental, or romantic, or too literary."[12] In his essay "One Generation After," the author gives reasons for the reticence of survivors immediately following the war. Although thousands published eyewitness accounts, journals, and memoirs, many remained silent. They were fearful of not being believed, of being told that they were asking for pity, or of being reproached for commercializing their suffering. Most of all, they did not want to desecrate the memory of the dead by freezing their recollections onto the printed page and "attempting to communicate with language what eludes language" (OGA, 8). Survivors found themselves in a predicament: how to transpose the experience of extremity into written evidence. The imperative to testify conflicted with the impossibility of finding vocabulary to describe the new reality that was Auschwitz. Words were dismembered during the Holocaust and in its aftermath could only deceive.

Clearly, no rational mode of expression can articulate the degree of bestiality that infected the world of the concentration camp. "Our language lacks words to express this offence, the demolition of a man," says Primo Levi in *Survival in Auschwitz*.[13] And Wiesel, too, points out that "the language of night was not human; it was primitive, almost animal—hoarse shouting, screams, muffled moaning, savage howling, the sound of beating. . . ."[14] How, he wonders, can you convey the cries of children being thrown alive into the flaming pits of Auschwitz?

The notion of the duplicity of language underlies Wiesel's fiction and his commentaries. "By saying things, one betrays them; by telling the story, one distorts it. Thus it would perhaps be better to remain silent," he declares.[15] In *A Beggar in Jerusalem* Katriel reflects the author's distrust of language when he announces to David: "I don't like words! They destroy what they aim to describe, they alter what they try to emphasize. By enveloping the truth, they end up taking its place" (135). Words cover up; they falsify, misinterpret, and diminish the intensity of the subject. In the face of radical evil, words are hollow, pale, lifeless. If as George Steiner puts it "the world of Auschwitz lies outside speech as it lies outside reason,"[16] and as Piotr Rawicz claims, in *Blood from the Sky,* words wilt and then like dead scales drop away because they have lost all meaning after such a catastrophe,[17] the logical response is a retreat from language, a closing off of speech, a holding of the breath—terminating in absolute and unconditional silence. Yet the paradox of the Holocaust is that while it imposes silence, it demands testimony.

In the course of time, survivors such as Wiesel were compelled to tell the world what had taken place. At first, their documents were accorded deep respect, for never had terror on such a massive scale been exposed. But as years passed, those who dared to speak out were criticized for being obsessed with the past, for putting salt in their wounds, and exaggerating the truth. Their stories were misunderstood, twisted, challenged; the witnesses were even accused of exploiting their situation. Ironically, it was the others who had not been in the camps who began to trivialize and desanctify the Holocaust, reducing it to the level of a spectacle, a fashionable topic of conversation, a gimmick for a sensational best-seller, or even a political instrument used by ambitious politicians.[18] The popularization of the event by the media and the explosion of interest in the subject led to a proliferation of publications, films, and theatrical productions. Moreover, the centrality of the Holocaust as a rallying point for raising consciousness and creating Jewish solidarity has provoked critical debates within the Jewish community itself.[19] The most extreme counterreaction in recent times has been the growth of a revisionist movement which denies that the Holocaust ever took place. Over one hundred books and pamphlets written and distributed by neo-Nazis and pseudo-scholars in countries around the world call the Holocaust a hoax, a myth, a lie.[20]

More than ten years ago Wiesel detected signs of abuse and warned against the cheapening of a topic which for him had to remain sacred. In his book *One Generation After* (1970), he called into question the act of writing itself and asked if it has not been a mistake to testify. Witnesses, he said, were disillusioned by the reaction to their experience and perceived their task as futile. They felt impotent for being unable to stir the conscience of an apathetic society and guilty because they had tried. Genocide was still taking place across the continents. "It means nothing to write today," Wiesel protested. "We had the puerile ambition to think that the world which wanted to destroy us could later be saved by us. Now I have the impression that nothing has changed and the world is still the same."[21]

If in 1967 Wiesel wrote the essay "Plea for the Dead" (LT), in which he defended the memory of the dead victims subjected to posthumous humiliation, in 1977 the author felt a need to plead for the dignity of the survivor. In "A Plea for the Survivors" (JT), he traces the journey of the survivor from postwar times to the present, showing the critical attitude of society toward survivors as well as the general debasement of the event. Forced into a position in which he had to justify his words, Wiesel once again gravitated toward silence as an altenative to written testimony. However, in contrast to the self-imposed, fearful reticence of early post-Holocaust times, this silence is essentially based on the disappointment and frustration of a man who chose to speak out and whose message was not heard. More than ever aware of the ineffectiveness of words in dealing with the Holocaust, Wiesel has realized that all the writer can hope for is "to communicate the impossibility of communication." How is this possible? Through silence— not an ascetic withdrawal from language but rather a silence that demands to be transmitted, the defiant and awesome muteness of a man who has much to say but is not going to speak. "My silence is meant to be a very eloquent silence, a screaming silence, a shouting silence. . . . a gesture, an act, a deed, a testimony against indifference, silence with a capital 'S'," Wiesel proclaims.[22]

If words structure Wiesel's literary universe, silence envelops it and lies at its deep center. Throughout his writings, the unspeakable reverberates in both negative and positive tones. Negative silence is isolation, exile, retreat. In theological terms, it is the hidden God who refused to speak out when his people suffered.[23] Politically, it is the criminal indifference of the neutral bystander—of the world itself— who stood by as the Jews were deported to destinations unknown; or the constraint imposed by totalitarian governments, such as the Soviet Union, where Jewish eyes mutely reflect the hopelessness of their people's condition[24] From the human point of view, the inexpressible is understood through the choked despair of thirsty children rounded up by the police, the unrelenting and unnatural quiet of crowds driven to the cattle cars: "The town had never known such a silence. Not a sigh, not a sound. Silence: the perfect setting for the last scene of the last act" (LT, 116). The noiseless departure reaches its crescendo in the soundless void of the gas chambers. Absolute stillness is what persists in the aftermath of stifled screams.

The witness seeks to make this legacy of unheard voices speak. He wants to transform the absence of the dead into a presence that transcends the finality of death. If words dissolve into darkness, the density of silence emanating from the extermination camps accumulates to the point of exploding, and it is just at this intersection of extremes, where language and silence are pushed to their limits, that the survivor-writer finds himself. This meeting place of words and non-words is what he tries to capture in his art. Wiesel knows that to truly convey the shattering cries of the night, he would have to publish a book with the pages left blank. Since this is not possible, he must choose his terms carefully, condensing hundreds into one, or what he calls *tzimtzum*, "condensation."[25] Writing, like sculpture, means taking away words: "With a painting what you add on the canvas is important. A sculpture is what you chip away. . . . It's what you don't say that is important."[26] The unutterable resonates through the selection of certain words and the exclusion of others. And these cautiously chosen expressions, chiseled into monuments, are imbued with a sacred stillness that takes form. "A mediocre man may surround silence with empty words," Wiesel observes, "but a poet surrounds his silence with words containing layers of silence, dramatic tension, visions of horror, acts of gratitude."[27] Like a sculptor and poet then, Wiesel coats and layers his language, displaying restraint and sobriety in transposing his inner landscape onto the printed page.

In *The Oath*, Moshe recalls Rabbi Levi Yitzhak's belief that when the Messiah comes, man will understand "not only the words but the blank spaces of the Torah. . . . Man is responsible not only for what he says, but also for what he does not say" (154). The blanks between the words evoke a subject so overwhelming in its nature that it assumes a presence, and if Wiesel insists that he writes and speaks *around* the Holocaust and not *about* it, the message is communicated through the truth left unsaid. By avoiding direct description of physical atrocities in his first book, *Night*, for example, he evokes a certain atmosphere through scenes and images that suggest rather than state. The clinical horrors of the event, omitted in his writing, underlie every page and form the core of his work. The Holocaust is the yardstick, the central and absolute point around which his tales are woven, and resides not only at the dark center of every word but, even more intensely, within the zones of silence. It is up to the reader to grasp the knowledge concealed between the lines in order to complete the narrative. The reader is the taciturn yet active recipient of the unfinished story.

While Wiesel as a writer is preoccupied with the purification of language through silence within an artistic context, he is also concerned with the literary dramatization of the theme in the texts themselves. Silence is rendered in a multiplicity of shades, as André Neher points out with precision in his book, *L'Exil de la parole*.[28] In contrast to the angry, hateful reticence which imprisons and divides, a shared solitude or *silence à deux* can be a source of friendship, a vehicle of human communion. At its most profound level the will to remain speechless transforms itself into an instrument of survival which saves the protagonists in Wiesel's novels and is critical to their very being. "It's when I'm silent that I live; in silence I define myself," Michael says in *The Town Beyond the Wall* (96), and his restraint in the face of torture allows his friend Pedro to go free. In *The Gates of the Forest* Gregor assumes the stance of a deaf-mute to save his own life. By his refusal to speak, Azriel in *The Oath* upholds his allegiance to the dead and keeps the Book of Kolvillàg alive.

If the muteness of the characters, on the one hand, is emblematic of their barren existence in the present, on the other, it offers them a sanctuary in which to remember the past. In the quiet recesses of their memory they dialogue with those who have disappeared, for it is these wordless spaces that the dead inhabit. The zones of emptiness turn into those of plenitude when the dead come back to the living. "Why are we silent? Because silence is not only our dwelling place but our very being as well. We are silence. And your silence is us. You carry us with you," the boy ghost of Elisha tells him in *Dawn* (183). The universe of silence quietly declares itself and emerges as a character in its own right in the writing of Elie Wiesel. "The hero of my story is neither fear nor hatred; it is silence," says Michael in *The Town* (110), as introduction to the tale of Mendele, the five-year-old hero whose body is savagely pierced by the long swords of the Hungarian police as he lies close-mouthed beside his mother at the bottom of a truck covered with hay. The crucified child who bravely dies without uttering a cry embodies the murdered six million and depicts what Terrence Des Pres calls "silence as the presence of the dead, of the camps, of evil so overwhelming and unspeakable that only silence, in its infinitude, can begin to represent it."[29]

Although Wiesel believes that no one has the right to speak for the dead nor the power to make them speak, he wants their stifled voices to be heard. At the end of *One Generation After,* he declares that his itinerary as a witness to the Holocaust has come to an end: he will no longer call upon *l'homme concentrationnaire* to testify at the stand. "The inventory is closed," he states with a certain finality (11). This proclamation marks a decisive point in the author's intellectual and spiritual odyssey as both sign of mastery over the trauma so central to his life, and admission of his disillusionment with the task of bearing witness. Nonetheless, he is continuously compelled to activate the memory of the dead. That is why he searches for modes of articulating their voicelessness as another kind of expression which eludes language, refuses it, and, at the same time, extends far beyond its grasp—a *silence after death:* "silence, more than language, remains the substance and the seal of what was once their universe, and . . . like language, it demands to be recognized and transmitted" (OGA, 198). The importance attributed to the transmission of silence in this last sentence of *One Generation After* evolves into the principal theme of *The Oath.* Moshe, the madman, is the author's advocate for a path as yet unexplored, a form of communication still untried—testimony without words.

In direct contrast to the father, emissary of the Book, Moshe admits the failure of language. He does not contest the authority of the text but doubts the efficacy of the word. The old order must be abdicated. The model of Jewish scripture and canon of Jewish law—the covenant of Sinai—is implicitly called into question by Moshe, the anti-Moses, anti-Messiah, and anti-witness of the novel.

When Moses brings the tablets down from the mountain, he establishes the basis of a new moral and religious legacy, as Wiesel observes in his study, "Moses: Portrait of a Leader," in *Messengers of God*: "Moses, the man who changed the course of history all by himself; his emergence became the decisive turning point. After him, nothing was the same again" (181). In *The Oath*, Moshe takes on some of the characteristics of the highly venerated biblical figure, but is basically the inversion of his namesake. Like the prophet, he, too, is a seer, a leader who passionately struggles to alter the fate of his community. The oath of silence that he proposes "marks a turnabout in the destiny and itinerary of our people" (O, 241). Like Moses, he is alone in his task, removed from the others yet committed to their survival, solitary yet awe-inspiring in his position. Unlike Moses, he is not concerned with transmitting the word but with transmitting silence. Whereas Moses embodies a certain sense of rationalism and order, Moshe, "king of clowns, the prophetic fool free to do anything" (LT, 82), transcends the boundaries of reason.

Moshe in *The Oath* is a composite of all the mad Moshes who have appeared throughout Wiesel's works. Mystical in his attachment to humanity, righteous in his attempt to redeem mankind, a martyr who sacrifices himself for the sake of the community, he is a "madman turned saint, or the saint gone mad" (O, 162). Oracle and inspiration, existing in a world apart, he belongs to no one and yet is everywhere. Moshe possesses the ability to see clearly to the essence of things. His painful journey to the dark kingdom of Night has propelled him beyond the bounds of history and, as a result, has bestowed upon him a special status, that of a visionary.

Moshe is Wiesel's original witness, "the first link in this dynasty of madmen" (LT, 81); "the first survivor of organized death: Moses—Moshe. We have received the legacy, not only of his Law but also of his name. And what goes with it" (*Le Chant des morts*, 112). In the book *Night*, Moché the Beadle is deported from Sighet because he is a foreigner. Wounded in the leg, he escapes from the death pits and returns to the town in order to tell his tale and to warn the Jews of their fate. But no one listens, and, weary of the disbelief and indifference of the townspeople, Moché lapses into silence. He is forced into the role of the mute and impotent witness, rejected by the world of the living just because he has penetrated into the realm of the dead. His presence disturbs the order of things and is dangerous to those unwilling to face the truth. As Frederick Garber points out:

> What he knows separates him from others, and his role as remnant separates him from what he has seen. . . . separated as the Prophets were separated, by special knowledge; but without the Prophets' full sense of where they were, who they were talking to and why.[30]

Moché, who serves as the model for Moshe in *The Oath*, is thus the anti-prophet of modern times, announcing an unprecedented era in history. During the reign of Night, the tale of exodus is indeed reversed, for the Jewish people advance toward their oppressors instead of being led away, and once again they are enslaved.[31] Biblical tradition radically shifts its course as Moshe comes to be the new Moses, revealing the message of a new Sinai—"a Sinai of darkness."

In effect, the Holocaust is for Wiesel equal in significance to the handing down of the Law on the mountain; it is "the other side of Sinai, the dark face of Sinai."[32] Just as the mystical dimension of Sinai remains unrevealed, so too the cosmic magnitude of the Holocaust can never be totally disclosed. These two major events are linked by the silence that shrouds them. The silence of Sinai, however, is healthy, fervent and profound—one of presence and plentitude—in contrast to the chaotic, soundless void which preceded the creation of the world and is related to the Holocaust annihilation.[33]

The purity of Sinai—the blanks between God's words—is what Moshe evokes when he proposes the abdication of language as an alternative to bearing witness:

> I don't believe in the written word; I never did. The words pronounced at Sinai are known. Perhaps even too well. They have been distorted, exploited. Not the silence, though it was communicated from atop that same mountain. As for me, I like that silence, transmitted only among the initiated like a secret tradition that eludes language. [187]

The *initiated* here imply the survivors, who, like mystics, communicate in a hermetic code which transcends language. Enveloped by silence, this code has the potential of mystically transforming reality and of deafening the world.[34]

Before Moshe addresses the townspeople from his pulpit in the ancient synagogue of Kolvillàg, the absolute and awesome stillness surrounding his presence recalls that of Sinai. A current of silence emanates from the source of his being and electrifies the audience: Moshe is a contemporary Moses about to forge another covenant for the Jewish people. His words, barely pronounced, are recited like a prayer, a litany, as he seeks to deliver the Jewish community from the approaching danger. Building up momentum, this twentieth-century prophet turns his prayer into a sermon prescribing the strategy for the enactment of an oath that would collectively bind all potential survivors of the pogrom to silence. He argues in favor of this pact by, first of all, demonstrating the importance of the witness in Jewish history. Examples are cited from texts and legends to show the persecutions of Jews throughout the centuries from ancient Judea to Central and Eastern Europe. Moshe points out, however, that despite the mass murder of Jewish communities, one person was always left to tell the tale—the last survivor, the last storyteller, the last witness, a recurring Wieselean theme:[35]

> Yet one man had always remained behind, miraculously unscathed, one man who saw and recorded everything; the sorrow and the fury on one side, the indifference on the other. . . . Since the executioner seemed to be immortal, the survivor-storyteller would be immortal too. [237]

As Wiesel's spokesman for the need to testify, Moshe claims that the persistence of the Jewish memory robbed the executioner of his final victory, and served as a warning to the rest of mankind. In the past, he declares, words have been weapons to combat death.

After summing up the argument in favor of the witness, which for generations has been the bulwark of Jewish tradition, Moshe then rejects this role as unsatisfactory. The fate of the Jewish people has not been altered by their protracted accounts of oppression and martyrdom. Consequently, the new spokesman proposes to the inhabitants of Kolvillàg that they change the course of history by refusing to speak, and thus take the story of their torture and destruction to the grave. His rationale is based on the notion that if suffering and the history of suffering are linked, silence as a method will prevent the executioner's memory from being perpetrated and will therefore rule out future possibilities of persecution. According to Moshe's reasoning, no story is to be saved from oblivion, because the rendering of the tale proclaims death's triumph as well as its defeat. Telling the story of suffering does not alleviate suffering. Only through the refusal to testify will atrocities be less likely to be committed, and fewer potential murderers will profit from the publicity of genocide.

While Moshe's cry for silence as a new weapon is tenable, the categorical denial of the importance of language is problematic in light of Wiesel's obsession with the theme of the witness and the need to speak out. Questions generated by Moshe's position remain: if no one tells of slaughter and mass murder, will the enemy cease to destroy? Can silence as a strategy be effective enough to stop violence? Is silence a practical solution or can it be considered mainly a theory, an ideology? If Moshe's plea for silence does not sufficiently answer these questions, it nevertheless raises them, indicating the author's disillusionment with the power of words to change the course of events. Silence is depicted above all in *The Oath* as a challenge to tradition, a means of breaking patterns of the past and confronting the dark burden of history. The pact of silence advocated by Moshe is surely an act of protest.

Moshe's ability to compel the entire community to adopt the sacred vow is not only audacious in the larger historical perspective, but marks a significant phase in Wiesel's own writing. The pledge of silence taken by the inhabitants of Kolvillàg at the insistence of the mad seer is a dramatic inversion of Eliezer's solemn declaration the night he arrives in the concentrationary universe. The fifteen-year-old boy stares into the flaming pits of Auschwitz and recites an incantation which takes the form of an oath. Repeating the word, "never," before each vow, he pledges never to forget the night, the smoke, the fire engulfing little children, and the black silence which has assassinated his God and devoured his soul. He concludes with "Never shall I forget these things, even if I am condemned to live as long as God Himself. Never" (N, 43). This awesome pronouncement affirms the author's intention to remember his entrance into the world of *Night* and to preserve this memory for the rest of his life. By contrast, the *Herem* enacted by the town of Kolvillàg is a repudiation of the will to bear witness through words. Collectively, the men, women, and children repeat after Moshe: "Never . . . shall I reveal . . . Never . . . How I survived . . . Never . . . Nor how the dead perished. Never" (242). The communal pact directly responds both in form and substance to Wiesel's commitment to testify uttered in *Night*.

Ritual plays a fundamental part in Kolvillàg's initiation into the universe of silence even more than it did in Eliezer's vow to bear witness. Deeply religious in its nature, the ceremony conducted by Moshe threatens excommunication to any potential heretics who transgress the holy *Herem*. The notables of Kolvillàg wrap themselves in their prayer shawls, black candles are lit, and Moshe slowly pronounces every word of the formulas of anathema as he gains absolute allegiance from the gathered assembly. The ceremony terminates with the blowing of the shofar and the invocation of the *Kaddish*, the prayer of mourning which not only prophesies the death of the town but also suggests the death of an epoch—and perhaps the beginning of another.

The covenant of silence, ushered in by a madman—"the herald of a new era" (242), "last prophet and first messiah of a mankind that is no more" (281)—designates a turning point in the theme of the witness. The imperative to speak out is surpassed by the resolution to remain silent; the memory of a people reduced to ashes will no longer be kept alive through the word. The sanctuary is not to be profaned by language incapable of penetrating its mystery, and the *Pinkas* maintained throughout the centuries by the chroniclers of Kolvillàg is condemned to be closed.

Reverence for the Book, and the faith in its endurance sustained by the father-scribe, is thus countered by the mad master's oath of silence. The tension resulting from these antithetical positions is never fully resolved in the novel. The conflict between the obligation to speak or not to speak, to write or not to write, to be silent or not to be silent is the ponderous legacy transmitted to Azriel, the only living survivor of Kolvillàg. His predicament epitomizes Wiesel's own dilemma as survivor-writer: "I should like to be able to speak without betraying myself, without lying. I should like to be able to live without self-reproach. I should like to remain silent without turning my very silence into a lie or a betrayal" (41). If the dialectics underlying the theme of the witness are clearly exposed by Azriel's double heritage, the author ventures, nonetheless, to reconcile the opposition between language and silence. The theme of the voice—instrument of life—emerges, as the will to survive prevails and the vow of silence is violated in order to save the life of one human being.

THE SURVIVING VOICE

Essentially a book about a refusal, *The Oath* begins with Azriel's resolution not to speak. As the sun sets one autumn afternoon, the protagonist, now a weary old man dwelling in permanent exile, meets a young adolescent boy about the same age he was when he forced his way out of the burning remnants of his town. "What I have seen, nobody will see, what I am keeping back, you will never hear. . . . For you see, I am not free. My voice is a prisoner," he tells the youth (7–8). Yet this homeless messenger, who has roamed from village to village for several decades as a *Na-venadnik* (which in Hebrew means "beggar" or "wanderer fated to a nomadic life") liberates his imprisoned voice precisely because of the young man. If the narrator-protagonist spends most of the first section of the novel ("The Old Man and the Child") explaining to the youth why he cannot relate the story of Kolvillàg and why the word is denied him, the remaining sections of the text are, in effect, consecrated to the tale of the town and its senseless devastation.

Azriel informs his young listener of a life spent in solitude and silence. Traveling from country to country, through cities and forests, he is the paradigm of the Jew as wanderer, "a stranger among strangers" (43), destined "de vivre sous un signe constant d'arrachement et de séparation" ("to live under a constant sign of uprootedness and separation") (*Le Serment*, 66). Because of his endless journeys, however, he becomes rich in experience, and his role as the bearer of news, the courier—"hyphen between countless communities" (47)—is respected by the inhabitants of the villages through which he passes. He belongs to all towns and yet to none. All of the Jewish hamlets come to resemble one another and, for Azriel, all resemble the place of his birth, situated somewhere between the Dnieper River and the Carpathian Mountains. The invisible kingdom of his childhood exists only within the confines of his internal landscape. The town that once nourished him has been transformed into a graveyard whose tombstones, engraved in his memory, drive him to the limits of reason: "Kolvillàg does not exist, not any more. I am Kolvillàg and I am going mad" (6).

Azriel discloses the reason for his madness to the nameless youth he encounters by chance: he is the sole survivor of an entire community convulsed in flames, the last messenger, who cannot die. The old man's loneliness has been doubly intensified because he cannot share his memories of the nightmarish universe from which he escaped. His only possession, the *Pinkas*—collective record of the once-flourishing *shtetl* gone up in smoke—is sealed, its voice, like that of its guardian, arrested within pages which will never be open. "What you have written, Father, nobody will read," Azriel sadly and quietly tells his dead father who was once the proud historian of these now con-demned archives (80). Moshe's oath has made of his devoted disciple the *last* and, more significantly, the *mute* witness who alone must listen to the soundless voices of the dead loudly reverberating in the depths of his being.

Like the author himself, who initiated a self-imposed vow to remain silent for ten years after the Holocaust, Azriel has kept still for several decades after the pogrom, bound by his allegiance to the decimated town and to the memory of Moshe. If by establishing a new covenant for his people, Moshe glorified the ideology of silence, his faithful follower has been subjected to the frustrating, often tormenting, consequences of his master's vision. Renunciation of the word has not changed the world, nor has it brought about the coming of the Messiah. There is no evidence to prove the effectiveness of silence as a strategy for social or spiritual transformation; suffering has not ceased and oppression continues to exist. Azriel's fidelity to Moshe's *Herem* has not provided a substantial alternative to bearing witness through spoken and written testimony. On the contrary, the protagonist is tortured by his pledge and even tries to be delivered of it by going to the eminent Rabbi Zusia of Kolomey. Azriel sits in front of the Rabbi, stares at him, and, without uttering a word, retraces his steps back to Kolvillàg, vividly reliving the events that led to the brutal annihilation of the town. The Rabbi listens intensely to this unspoken chronicle of terror: "He listened in silence, listened to the silence welling up inside me with every image as though to stifle it; ultimate total silence suffused with twilight, the deadly kind that rises from wilderness at dusk" (43). Here then is an example of the transmission of silence—a speechless tale, conveyed by a taciturn witness about the total and terrifying collapse of a community, forever stilled. The Rabbi grasps the significance of Azriel's gruesome account but instead of relieving him of his burden as voiceless messenger of the dead, endorses Moshe's covenant: Azriel is designated as a *Na-venadnik*, doomed to exile, but privileged because he is the sole guardian of a secret and holy text.

And yet, Azriel is not satisfied with holding the key to this universe of silence enclosed within his memory and his imagination. As he grows older and approaches death, he deeply interrogates the validity of the oath he took as a youth. How can the mute testimony that lies at the core of his innermost recesses take on meaning if he is no longer alive? When the witness dies, the knowledge of the past dies with him. The story of the town must be passed on or, as Azriel fears, the *Pinkas* will fall into obscurity, its scorched pages buried alongside the ashes of Kolvillàg and the corpse of the last survivor.

Azriel is thus confronted with a legacy at odds with itself: the continuity of the Book vis-à-vis its dissolution; reverence for the word mixed with fear and distrust of language; the imprisoned versus the liberated voice. How are these opposing themes reconciled? Through another and perhaps the most important character of the novel, the son of survivors, a child of the Holocaust, whose encounter with the old man links persecutions of the past to those of the present. Afflicted by the unrest of aftermath without understanding why, the boy has inherited the burden of the event without its mystery. He feels useless, left out, and in despair. He wants to die in order to repudiate a world that has nothing to offer him.

The youth, whose age is not explicit and whose portrait is intentionally vague, is characteristic of the post-Holocaust generation. "That young man is everyone," Wiesel tells us. "He arouses our pity because he doesn't even have the consolation of being a witness. He represents all my students and all the young people who are so perplexed today."[36] The boy is a survivor without a story, and, as a commentator points out: "Survivors without stories are witnesses without their historic mission. The boy is both—moreover he is a Jew without a sense of Jewish history."[37] Symbol of the younger generation, the youth also embodies the future; he is mankind capable of destroying itself through another genocide. Before all else, this child of survivors is the listener who, in turn, becomes the narrator—the person responsible for transmitting the Book. He is us, the reader, inheritor of the testimony.

For Azriel, the young man is a kind of surrogate son whom he wants to save from committing suicide. The theme of rescue is repeated here, with the father (or grandfather) figure seeking to save the life of the son, the older generation attempting to assure the survival of the younger one. Azriel wants to prevent death from one more victory by saving the life of this individual, for he strongly believes that all death is absurd and that life is sacred: "Triumph over death? Excellent. Begin by saving your brother" (22). "To turn a single human being back toward life is to prevent the destruction of the world, says the Talmud. . . . Let me succeed in diverting death from this boy and we shall win" (80). To save one person, then, is to save the world. Azriel's weapon is his story. If Moshe elevated silence to a form of protest, the voice for Azriel is a munition against self-destruction: "Speak, the old man thinks. The best way. Make him speak. Speak to him. As long as we keep speaking, he is in my power. One does not commit suicide while speaking or listening" (14).

The theme of the voice as an instrument of life reaches its culmination here. In order to galvanize the youth's will to survive, the narrator gives him what some French critics have called "un 'bouche à bouche' véritable . . . la cure psychanalytique (a true mouth to mouth resuscitation, a psychoanalytic treatment)."[38] As in the psychoanalytic process, forbidden thoughts are brought to the surface and verbalized. By being freed of destructive obsessions, one is thus better equipped to fight off one's death instincts. The spoken word saves the young man from himself.

If the concepts of psychoanalysis seem foreign to Wiesel's mode of thinking, the significance of the voice is nonetheless central to his thematic development, and particularly relevant to the notion of the witness. Despite its fragility, the voice restores, regenerates, heals. In the Wieselean literary universe, the faculty of speech is not only a vehicle of human communication and sharing, but is also an emblem of the creative act: the voice is endowed with the capacity to breathe life into a dead object and possesses the authority to defy death. Symbol of survival, the voice joins the past to the future, transcending time and space. The author listens to the multitude of sounds emitted by generations of Jewish scholars, rabbis, poets, and madmen, and then attempts to transmit the collective message that echoes in his ears. "What counts in my work," he states, "are the voices I hear. And those voices do not come from this world or from this time."[39] His emphasis on the oneness of the Jewish people is conveyed by the concept of the voice as repository of memory and the belief in its perseverance throughout history.[40]

For Wiesel, the act of speaking is sacred. His faith in the sanctity of the voice stems from the oral tradition, so fundamental to Judaism in general, and particularly important in the Hasidic movement. "The truth will never be written," he notes with regard to the Holocaust. "Like the Talmud, it will be transmitted from mouth to ear, from eye to eye" (OGA, 10). Committed to passing on a kind of "oral Law" in his works, Wiesel pursues the path of the *Maggid* or *Zaddik*, the religious leader of the Hasidic community whose oral teachings of the Torah took the form of storytelling. He admits that as a child, he was fascinated by those learned figures and today, follows somewhat in their tradition.[41] In effect, Wiesel sees himself more as a teller of tales than a novelist. In the postscript to *Souls on Fire*, a book about Hasidic figures and their legends, he defines his role as a writer. Disclaiming the roles of historian and philosopher, he embraces the more limited one of the storyteller, who "transmits what was given to him, as faithfully as possible, yet lending it his own voice and intonation and sometimes his wonder or simply: his fervor" (255). Wiesel's voice *is* the voice of a Jewish *Maggid* who expresses himself in French. He returns to the source to go beyond it, spinning modern myths, legends, and fables, blending fact and fiction, history and imagination in a way that rises above the tumultuous noises of the contemporary world. His words possess a prophetic resonance, surrounded by the inviolate mystery and despair of what he has experienced. His is a voice grimly illuminated by the nocturnal light and fire of the Holocaust.

Sometimes strained, his tone understated and austere, Wiesel persists in speaking, bent on delivering his message, for while the function of storyteller is basic to his craft, that of messenger is equally important: "I have received the words, and in combining them I am simply fulfilling the function of a messenger, which is to me as important as that of a storyteller. In fact, the storyteller is important only as a messenger; I am communicating what I have received; I'm passing it on."[42] Wiesel is indeed, obsessed with the messenger aspect of being a writer, that aspect which motivates him to relate tales of spiritual, moral, and social significance. The theme of transmission is an integral part of Jewish tradition and essential to the theme of bearing witness: "In Hebrew, the word *massora,* tradition, comes from the verb *limsor,* to transmit. In our history, this need to communicate, to share, comes closer to being an obsession" (SF, 257). Transmission means forming a link between author and reader, between man and God, bcween one generation and another, and for Wiesel, "the task of a writer is to create links, nothing else."[43] Above all, transmission affirms life: "The difference between death and life is life transmits, death stops," he tells us.[44]

In *The Oath,* Azriel is the fictional embodiment of the storyteller-messenger. When he decides to reopen the *Pinkas* and pass on the tale of Kolvillàg to the young man who wants to commit suicide, the protagonist openly acknowledges the gravity of his gesture: "I'll transmit my experience to him and he in turn, will be compelled to do the same. He in turn will become a messenger. And once a messenger, he has no alternative. He must stay alive until he has transmitted his message" (33). By bequeathing the Book to the youth, Azriel assures the continuity of the communal legacy; but his primary motivation is to save a life. He recalls the words of his father uttered in the darkness of Moshe's prison cell: "A deed transmitted is a victory snatched from death" (187). The violation of Moshe's oath of silence thus takes on larger dimensions rooted in the very act of survival itself. To be a witness-storyteller-messenger demands a moral and human commitment and an ethical thrust. Wiesel does not believe in art for art's sake. "To be a writer means to correct injustices," he states,[45] and this means reminding the world over and over again that entire communities were devastated, that a whole tradition in Jewish history and the history of mankind was wiped out. Correcting injustices also means preventing another catastrophe from occurring, both on a massive scale and on an individual one. Azriel's decision to deter his young acquaintance from self-destruction provides the ethical thrust vital to bearing witness.

Nonetheless, a poignant struggle takes place within the protagonist. His allegiance to the dead conflicts with his responsibility to the living. During the course of the entire first section of the novel, he implores Moshe to release him from his vow. In Moshe's eyes, speaking of Kolvillàg would be sacrilegious, the narrative act an *act of transgression*. But while Azriel reveres his master's memory, he also knows that Moshe failed in his attempt to deliver the Jewish community from the disastrous pogrom. Consequently, the mad seer's proclamation of silence as an alternative to verbal testimony may also be doomed. It is possible, as an Israeli critic, Dan Vogel, observes, that "with all his magic, mysticism and wisdom, Moshe is a false prophet."[46] Although we cannot call Moshe's position "false" for he appears to have followed the authentic dictates of his conscience, this anti-prophet of a new age has not pointed the way to a viable solution. Moshe seems to be overly ambitious in his effort to take on the collective guilt of the community by claiming to be the murderer of the Christian adolescent. In contrast, his successor, Azriel, aspires to save the life of *one* Jewish adolescent and succeeds in doing so.

If for Moshe the narrative act transgresses boundaries, for his disciple it becomes an *act of salvation*. Azriel undoes the law established by the dead congregation of Kolvillàg, but in doing so reaffirms his faith in the sacredness of life. Keeping silent in the face of someone else's pain is more blasphemous than speaking out, the author discloses:

> If someone suffers and I keep silent, then it's a destructive silence. If we envisage literature and human destiny as endeavors by man to redeem himself, then we must admit the obsession, the overall dominating theme of responsibility, that we are responsible for one another.[47]

The witness who speaks thus assumes a human and moral obligation. To save a life, the story must be told: words declare themselves as instruments of redemption.

As the youth listens to the account of Kolvillàg related by the "mysterious messenger from an imaginary city" (8), he repudiates the idea of suicide. He grows attached to the town, obsessed by it; Azriel's past becomes his own and endows him with a sense of history. He feels part of a tradition he never knew. "By allowing me to enter his life, he gave meaning to mine. I lived on two levels, dwelt in two places, claimed more than one role as my own. In one night he had me adopted by his entire community," the young man reveals (16). He accompanies his old companion on a pilgrimage to the forgotten—and forbidden—town, acquainting himself with the picturesque characters who peopled the once-animated streets of the *shtetl*—Moshe the Madman,

Kaiser the Mute, Leizer the Fat, Yiddel the Cripple, One-Eyed Simha. Through the voice of the last survivor, this dead universe is resurrected and the inhabitants of Kolvillàg are brought to life once again. An attentive listener, the boy is transported into the alluring spirit and pulsating rhythm of a community totally foreign to him. He grows involved in the town's joys and sorrows, and learns about its network of alliances and complicities. The precious gift offered to the youth by the intriguing old stranger four times his age is not only the legend of a kingdom lost somewhere between the Carpathian Mountains and the Dnieper River, but is also the active part he is urged to play in the transmission of the chronicle.

The act of listening transforms the young man into a co-narrator and, in a sense, co-author, for, who listens to the witness becomes one. "Both the listener and the reader are participants in the same story and both make it the story it is," Wiesel affirms.[48] Mutually nurtured by each other's presence, speaker and listener come to be partners in a story that transcends both of them. "Whoever says 'I' creates the 'you.' Such is the trap of every conscience. The 'I' signifies both solitude and rejection of solitude," claims the author in *The Oath* (9), reflecting simultaneously the isolation of the human condition and the yearning to overcome this isolation by sharing the burden. For Wiesel, writing is *"un acte de générosité"*[49] through which the author opens up and invites the reader to enter the private world he carries within. "The creative process is a strange one," he states; "it comes from solitude, it goes to solitude and yet it's a meeting between two solitudes. It is just like man's solitude faced with God's solitude."[50] *The Oath* is precisely an encounter between two alienated individuals who link their destinies, exchange their most intimate secrets, and together forge a common testimony. The entire text, indeed, is structured as a dialogue between two "solitudes."

The young man's participation in the account itself is particularly important in the first section of the novel, "The Old Man and the Child," where he assumes the position of co-narrator along with Azriel. His introductory commentaries are interspersed with those of the protagonist, resulting in a point of view that frequently shifts from first to third person, sometimes to the extent of confusing the reader. The author also interjects his own voice in order to bring the two characters together. The middle and last sections, "The Child and the Madman" and "The Madman and the Book," relate the tale of Kolvillàg itself as told by Azriel, its last survivor. On the final page, the young narrator's voice is heard once again, reminding us that he has taken over the function of storyteller-messenger: he is now *the last witness*. The basic structure of the tale within a tale stresses the theme of transmission, one of the generating principles of the theme of the witness. Azriel's concluding statement to the youth, "Because now, having received this story, you no longer have the right to die" (282), obliges him to survive so that he too may pass on the town's legacy and sustain its memory. In this respect, he takes over Azriel's own duty to remain alive in order to protect the Book.

Azriel's words have not only served to redeem another human being, they have given a new meaning to his own existence. Reopening the *Pinkas,* glancing at its darkened pages, reliving the incidents, anecdotes, and legends of this secret kingdom, has been a painful odyssey for the old man but one which has renewed his life. On the threshold of death, he has returned to his origins. Fraught with anguish, the journey homeward has permitted the protagonist to rediscover his roots and come to terms with a trauma long repressed. Azriel now feels free to die in peace; by going back to the past, he has fulfilled his mission to the future. Liberated from its guarded fortress, the voice of the messenger sanctifies the scripture as well as the life it preserves. Yet as Azriel reenters the fiery universe of Kolvillàg and recounts the end of the story, we realize that the story has no end. The apocalyptic image of the town ablaze violated by the demonic forces of the pogrom prophesies the Holocaust yet to take place. For Wiesel, all events in Jewish history are connected.

The author feels that it is the responsibility of every Jew to assume and share the decisive moments of his or her heritage: "Any Jew born before, during or after the Holocaust must enter it again in order to take it upon himself. We all stood at Sinai; we all shared the same vision there. . . . If this is true, then we are also linked to Auschwitz."[51] Despite the awesomeness of the event, speaking out is a means of remembering the past and integrating it into the present, of atoning for the dead victims by resurrecting them and immortalizing their memory. Bearing witness brings back to life a dead town, an entire historical era, and, most important, restores by re-creating. "We cannot create," Wiesel says, "we are too weak to create. But we can re-create."[52] "Perhaps it is impossible for man to begin his story but it is possible to begin it again."[53] The notion of re-creation and beginning again through the word is essential to survival and especially to Jewish survival. As Edmond Jabès reflects in *Le Livre des ressemblances:* "la volonté du juif de survivre était dans son entêtement à recommencer le livre" ("the will of the Jew to survive was in his stubbornness to begin the book again").[54]

Out of the night, a new Book is reborn, "a book in the death of the book"[55] which like the phoenix rises out of the ashes, literally, and testifies to the fact that for Elie Wiesel total silence is impossible. If the Book undergoes a kind of symbolic death in *The Oath,* it is ultimately resuscitated through the voice of *the witness.* When Azriel takes leave of the young man at the end of the novel, he carries with him the large volume bound in black containing the town archives: he never relinquishes possession of the precious *Pinkas.* However, if the written word vanishes from view, the tale of Kolvillàg will not die: the true Book endures insofar as the survivor is able to speak of it. The act of bearing witness and of transmitting the story and history of the town is left to the old man's heir, who has become the collective witness, and to us, the readers—*witnesses of the witness.* To keep the Book alive we must explore its contents, interpret its meaning, and add to its unfathomable dimensions. Thus infused into the lifeblood of the present, this tale without end will be permanently engraved in our communal memory and will continue to unfold.

6

My Father Is a Book

You who harmed a simple man,
Do not feel secure
For a poet remembers.
                          —Czeslaw Milosz

DURING the course of his wanderings throughout Eastern Europe,
Azriel, the *Na-venadnik* of *The Oath,* encounters Abrasha, an agent of
the Comintern, committed to recruiting young members into the
international revolutionary movement. Convinced by Abrasha's fervent dreams of universal justice and his burning desire to abolish
poverty, oppression, and suffering, Azriel joins him in his efforts to
change the world. Together they distribute pamphlets in numerous
villages. Azriel takes charge of the Talmudic schools, where he engages
pious students of the Bible in discussions about Communist ideology,
teaching them the theories of "messianism without God" (O, 62). His
activities come to an end late one winter night in a small town hidden in
the mountains. The rabbi bursts into the room where the cell meeting is
taking place, dismisses the students, and sharply warns the young
stranger that one cannot annihilate the Jew in man to save man, and
that there can be no salvation outside of the community (O, 67). Azriel
leaves the village with a sense of failure, only to learn that Abrasha has
been called to Moscow. He later finds out that his comrade has been
shot in the neck, a victim of the party's first purges.

The dialectic between Communism and Judaism structures the

narrative of Wiesel's next novel, *The Testament*, written in 1980, seven years after *The Oath*. In the interim, Wiesel published three other books—*Messengers of God* (1975), *A Jew Today* (1977), and *Four Hasidic Masters and Their Struggle Against Melancoly* (1978)—and a play—*The Trial of God (As it was held on February 25, 1649 in Shamgorod)* (1979). These works all revolve around Biblical portraits, Hasidic tales, and the role of the Jew in contemporary society. Traditional concepts are interpreted in the light of modern Jewish thought. For Wiesel, all events in Jewish history are organically linked by a collective consciousness, a memory that transcends time and space. "No man is ever alone in history; every man *is* history," he tells us (MG, 63). In *The Testament*, more than in any other novel Wiesel has written thus far, the main character, Paltiel Kossover—a Jewish poet who was born in 1910 in the Russian town of Barassy (renamed Krasnograd) and who grows up in Liyanov on the Rumanian border—willfully plunges into the battlefields of twentieth-century history.

Unlike Wiesel's other tales and novels, which are often situated in a timeless and geographically indeterminate realm permeated with myth and parable, *The Testament* places its protagonist in concrete locations and immerses him in a social and political reality. The young Paltiel leaves his religious beliefs behind in Liyanov to journey through the major countries of Europe—Germany, France, and Spain—as well as Palestine and Russia—where he engages directly in the ideological struggles of his time. The story of his life—his testament, written from the confines of a Soviet prison—reaches out to encompass the principal events of his epoch and, indeed, becomes the global *témoignage* of a poet who is an active witness to the destruction of European civilization, what Czeslaw Milosz has called a "profound disintegration of the existing order of things."[1]

Whereas most of Wiesel's survivor-protagonists are modeled after Eliezer in *Night*, the deeply religious boy wrenched from the security of his house of study in Sighet and propelled into a universe of death, Paltiel in *The Testament* voluntarily chooses to forsake the faith of his ancestors. Ironically, it is late one snowy evening as he is exploring the sacred texts of the Kabbala in the study room of Liyanov that another student of the Talmud enters and begins to talk to him about Communist ideals. Like Gad, the messenger-warrior of *Dawn* who visits Elisha in his room in Paris and enlists him to fight for a Jewish homeland in Palestine, Ephraim is a kind of messianic figure in the guise of a Communist agitator. As the candles slowly burn out, Ephraim explains to his pious friend that in order to save humanity, the primary path of action is "related not to God but to history, to the events that produce history, in short to man himself" (T, 75). If in the kingdom of Night, Eliezer turned away from a God who had abandoned His people, Paltiel leaves his God for what he considers to be a higher cause, "a secular, social messianism" (79) that will rid society of its evils.

The call to combat the forces of injustice in the name of the Communist revolution clearly runs counter to Paltiel's immersion in the traditional practices and learning of Orthodox Judaism. The tension between these opposing activities forms the basis for the novel and is exemplified by the two meanings of the name, Paltiel: "God is my refuge" and "I am a refugee from God." The family name, Kossover, brings to mind Kossof, the home of the Rebbe of Wiznitz, thus suggesting the theme of the return to one's faith, as Arnold Ages points out.[2]

In contrast to other Wieselean characters expelled from the place of their origins—banished from history itself—Paltiel makes a conscious decision to leave his town and to embrace the world in its larger dimensions. Unlike Lot's wife he refuses to look back as he departs from the house of his parents, aware of his father's burning glance behind his back. Yet during the course of the entire novel this Jewish poet, strongly committed to politics, spiritually turns to his father at important intervals in his life. The book is circular in motion: Paltiel's far-reaching quest for "messianism without God" leads him back to the town where he was born; and it is there that he dies, a victim of the movement to which he consecrated his existence. His is a journey homeward, a retracing of his steps to his Jewish roots, and above all, a return to his father—source of his religious patrimony and center of his literary universe.

Paltiel's sweeping itinerary begins in the noisy, decadent Berlin of the later 1920s, where Nazis and Communists are beginning to clash. Although the young man never officially joins the Party, he writes articles and tracts in Yiddish, attends meetings, and participates in mass demonstrations to support the Communists in the 1932 elections. Disillusioned after a decisive Nazi victory, the protagonist leaves Germany two years later for Paris. There, he continues his pursuit of Marxist ideals by writing a poetry column for *Dos Blättel*, an anti-Zionist Communist newspaper, and, in addition, undertakes secret missions to Germany and Palestine. His desire to eradicate fascism leads him to fight with the International Brigades in the Spanish Civil War in 1937.

In Spain, Paltiel is hurled into the madness and savagery of war, where he witnesses at first hand obscenely mangled corpses and mutilated limbs, tangible evidence of man's debasement of man. He also becomes aware of another war being fought—the NKVD arrests and executions of his Trotskyite and anarchist friends, members of factions threatening to the central Party. Upon his return to Paris, he learns that his close friend, Paul Hamburger, a Soviet agent, has also mysteriously disappeared. Paltiel later discovers that Paul has been arrested, tortured, and assassinated in the cellars of a Moscow jail. Yet even with this knowledge, the young man decides to go to the Soviet Union and join the Red Army in the struggle against the Nazi invaders.

Submerged in the hallucinatory universe of the dead and the dying, Paltiel's job as stretcher-bearer is to collect "the shattered, trampled, abandoned human debris" (287). Wounded in the battle of Kharkov and delirious with fever, he spends three days in a dark cellar and is finally taken to a hospital, where he recovers. The protagonist returns with the Russian troops to Liyanov, the city of his childhood, only to discover strangers in his house and a mass grave in the Jewish cemetery. Wounded again in Lublin, the poet withdraws from combat and becomes a member of the Party. He marries a Russian officer, Raissa, whom he has met at the military hospital.

In 1946, he publishes a volume of poetry, *I Saw My Father in a Dream*, and frequents the circles of Jewish writers and intellectuals, meeting such people as Peretz Markish, David Bergelson, Der Nister, Kvitko, and Mikhoels. These Jewish men of letters are all destined to be purged by Stalin in the early 1950s. When the campaign of anti-Semitism begins and the Jewish printing houses and theaters are closed down, Paltiel decides to move to Krasnograd, the town of his birth and scene of his first pogrom. The end joins the beginning: Paltiel has lived as a Communist but is condemned to die because he is a Jew. In the place of his origins, his wife gives birth to a son—named Gershon (Grisha) after his father—and Paltiel is thrown into prison. It is there, while waiting for death, that the story of his life unfolds before him and he composes his testament, the legacy that binds his father to his son.

Paltiel's journal of confession, extracted by the examining magistrate to hasten the prisoner's sentence, extends beyond one man's life story to become "a document of the times—in which the experiences of the past will serve as signs for the future" (T, 336). The writer-poet of this deeply felt chronicle is a spokesman for all those Russian Jewish writers, dedicated to Communist ideals, who on August 12, 1952, disappeared without a trace. By creating a composite character—Paltiel—and by thrusting him into a turbulent novel of ideas and action, revolution and religion, Elie Wiesel has given voice to a forgotten era. The author has transformed events into consciousness, an objective which he believes is the function of literature.

The Testament, Wiesel's most accomplished and complex fictional work, was begun in 1965, when his own conscience was awakened by a trip to the Soviet Union. In the streets of Moscow, in the synagogue of Kiev, he came face to face with the silent and eternal Jewish eyes that communicated in a language of their own the isolation and fear of living under political tyranny. Compelled to inform the world of their plight, Wiesel published an eyewitness account, *The Jews of Silence*, in 1966, and two years later a play, *Zalmen or the Madness of God* in which an old rabbi, urged on by a mad seer, cries out against the oppressiveness of the Soviet system on the eve of Yom Kippur, the Day of Atonement.

The Testament takes place simultaneously in a Soviet jail and in Israel on the eve of the 1973 Yom Kippur War; in a sense, it represents Wiesel's culminating monument to Russian Jews, dissidents, and poets—all those who refuse to yield to the dictates of totalitarianism. But more than that, the novel brings together major themes from many of Wiesel's works and weaves them into a larger context. The personal vision of a writer is linked to a historical moment in time, the destiny of an individual fused with the collective memory. As the strange professor-prophet and apocalyptic messenger, David Aboulesia, who mysteriously reappears in the course of Paltiel's travels, teaches the young protagonist: "The work of the poet and of the historian are identical. . . . Let's say that poetry is history's invisible dimension" (T, 159).

If the scripture of the testament, gravely etched by the poet onto the white pages in the dark cell guarded by the Russian secret police, is a vehicle of historical consciousness, it is also a declaration of literary intention and a profound expression of human emotion. More than any other Wieselean protagonist, Paltiel is the embodiment of the writer-as-witness. He is not in search of an identity, nor does he grope for the faculty of speech: he is in command of his language. For a poet "everything begins and ends with words" (T, 153), and these words, awesome in their authority, can condemn a person to death. "Poetry is power," the Russian poet, Osip Mandelstam, once told his compatriot, Anna Akhmatova, and if they killed people for poetry, that meant that it was feared and respected. Mandelstam himself was arrested, sent into exile, and eventually died, because he had committed a "terrorist act"—he wrote an anti-Stalin poem.[3] In *The Testament*, Paltiel's poems (which appear throughout the text) are somewhat mediocre, and do not inspire the fear and respect which might make of him an enemy of the state. Yet the prose of his testimony written in the face of death creates "a kind of primary, impenetrable silence" (30) that transcends his condition and bravely, poetically, exposes the story of his life.

For the prisoner, writing is a trap designed to incriminate him—he is forced to bear witness against himself—but it is also an act of resistance. "As long as I write, as long as I put ink on paper, death will be powerless against me," Paltiel notes in his journal. "You can destroy my notebooks; no doubt you'll burn them, but a voice within me tells me that the words of a condemned man have their own life, their own mystery" (30). This *voice within*, emanating from the deepest level of self, is the same that Eliezer hears as he watches the hanged child on the gallows of Auschwitz. Source of the will to survive and to testify, the inner voice is what enables the victim to endure the torture of his oppressors and ultimately to achieve sovereignty over death. Paltiel's words declare themselves in the dense silence of the prison "isolator" that serves as sanctuary and place of sacrifice—"temple and altar" (192)—similar to the jail in *The Town Beyond the Wall*. Transmuted into the voice of the book, the poet's phrases take on a life on their own as they are read over and over again by his mute son, after his father has been assassinated.

Whereas the theme of the voice predominates in other works of fiction by Wiesel, the written word takes precedence in *The Testament*. In *The Oath*, the acts of writing and of speaking are equally important. As Shmuel, the father-scribe, records the daily events of Kolvillàg into the historical archives, we behold the chronicle in the process of being written and hear the sound of pen on paper. If however, the devastating pogrom forces the book to be closed and sealed by an oath of silence, Azriel, its keeper, breaks his covenant with the dead to save the life of a child of survivors. "One does not commit suicide while speaking or listening," he declares (O, 14), and death is warded off because the old man speaks and the young man listens. Azriel thus verbally passes on the town's legacy but, in the end, takes the book with him.

By contrast, in *The Testament* the written document is wrested from the executioner by the anonymous, nearly invisible court stenographer, Zupanev—the ideal messenger whom no one suspects because he is so ordinary and blends into the landscape. The text is eventually placed in the hands of Paltiel's son, Grisha. Like Shmuel in *The Oath*, Zupanev is a scribe; he also comes to be a father surrogate. After leaving the court, he finds a job as a night watchman for the group of buildings in Krasnograd in which Grisha and his mother live. There, the slightly mad old man who does not know how to laugh encounters the young boy; they spend hours together, Zupanev, the storyteller, and Grisha, the listener. This strange emissary of a Jewish poet, who keeps watch over night's secrets, becomes Grisha's protector, teacher, and friend—the link between father and son. He shows the child unpublished poems that Paltiel wrote in jail, and soon presents him with the testament "snatched from a dead man, from death itself, in order to be repeated, transmitted and kept alive" (T, 202).

At the age of three, Grisha had already discovered a trace of his father's presence. One day in the apartment where he and his mother lived, a book fell from the highest shelf. Grisha caught a glimpse of a man's photograph on the cover and asked his mother who the man was. His mother anxiously grabbed the volume from him, reprimanding the boy. "He's your father," she finally told him after he began to sob. Forbidden and inaccessible, the text was put back in its hidden place, but when Grisha was alone in the apartment he secretly leafed through its pages, fingering the words and caressing the lines as if it were a living being. The truth revealed itself suddenly to the child: "My father is not dead. *My father is a book*, and books do not die" (T, 39; my emphasis).

This simple and innocent declaration is the key to *The Testament* and to Wiesel's writing in general. The transmitted chronicle replaces the vanished father and must be infused with life in order for the patrimony to survive. The Book is the sanctuary, the refuge, the meeting place: it is *home*. Shut tight in *The Oath*, and again destined to be forever locked away, this time in the dark files of the Russian judicial chambers, the Book is miraculously reopened. When Grisha leaves the Soviet Union for Israel, he takes with him to the Promised Land his most precious possessions—a collection of poems, *I Saw My Father in a Dream*, and the autobiographical testimony bequeathed to him. Before his departure he spends hours listening intensely to Zupanev read pages from Paltiel's journal. Every sentence, every comma, is committed to memory, for in a country whose political system is designed to suffocate the voices of its victims and leave behind no traces, memory is both a force and a substitute for love. "To memorize is to restore intimacy," Joseph Brodsky says of Nadezhda Mandelstam, who repeated day and night the verses composed by her dead husband.[4]

In Jerusalem, the act of listening gives way to the act of reading. Grisha passes his days reading and rereading, copying and recopying the sacred texts. The son is thus the reader of the father (the entire narrative is structured by Grisha's reading), and his writer. Registering every phrase, he assumes the role of his father's scribe, the custodian of his past. Like the other surviving sons in Wiesel's works, Grisha's task is to preserve the continuity of history and the autonomy of the Book.

However, if Grisha is a writer in place of his father, it is not by choice but by necessity: he has lost the faculty of speech. As a boy in Krasnograd, in a fit of rage he clenched his teeth hard and bit off his own tongue. His anger was directed against Dr. Mozliak, his mother's friend who, by his relentless interrogation about his father, seemed to be stealing the dead man from him. Condemned to be voiceless for the rest of his life, Grisha can communicate only through the written word.

At the center of Wiesel's literary universe lies the dialectic of silence and language: the fear of betraying the dead by speaking in their place conflicts with the need to tell the tale. In *The Testament* this tension is resolved through the creation of a fictional character—a child of the second generation—who cannot speak and thus, need not struggle against himself. Grisha is totally committed to the endurance of his father's legacy, and if he is unable to express himself aloud, the absence of his voice nonetheless declares its presence. The author has succeeded in transmitting the unspoken thoughts of one who has lost his tongue. He has made silence go beyond its limits and, from another level of reality, cry out.

Elie Wiesel has come full circle. The son who gives his father a voice in *Night* takes it from him in *The Testament*. While the other Wieselean protagonists tell the story of how their author became a witness, Grisha takes a pencil from Zupanev and adds his own chapter to the communal record—how he became mute. The act of speaking is clearly less important here than the vow to remember. The father's testimony is doomed to remain incomplete for the poet is executed before he concludes his confession. Yet, his heir keeps the never-ending tale alive. Taciturn guardian of the living book that he carries within, the son bears witness to his father's unfinished life through history's silent and invisible dimension—the language of memory.

Appendix

Chronology of the Life and Works of Elie Wiesel

Date

1928 — Born September 30 in Sighet, Transylvania (then a part of Rumania; in 1940 part of Hungary). Two older sisters and one younger sister. Son of Shlomo and Sarah (Feig). Father, shopkeeper (grocery store); encouraged son to study modern Hebrew language and literature. Mother, daughter of Dodye Feig, Hasid and farmer; encouraged son to study Torah, Talmud, Kabbala, and teachings of Hasidic masters.

Education: Yeshiva (Jewish Orthodox religious school) in Sighet; high school in Debreczen.

1944 (Spring) — Deported by Nazis to Auschwitz with family; mother and youngest sister died in Auschwitz; father died in Buchenwald.

1945 (Spring) — Liberated from Buchenwald and sent to Ecovis in Normandy, France.

1946 — Went to Paris; learned French; taught Bible, Yiddish, and Hebrew; reunion with two older sisters.

1947–1950 — Student at the Sorbonne, University of Paris.

1948 on — Foreign correspondent at various times for *Yediot Ahronot*, Tel Aviv; *L'Arche*, Paris; and *Jewish Daily Forward*, New York. Traveled to North Africa, Africa, South America, and India as correspondent.

1949 — Went to Israel to report on struggle for independence.

1954 — Interviewed François Mauriac for *Yediot Ahronot*.

1956	Publication of *Un di Velt Hot Geshvign* (in Yiddish) in Buenos Aires.
	Came to New York to report on United Nations for *Yediot Ahronot.* Struck by taxicab in Times Square; during recovery, persuaded to apply for U.S. citizenship
1958	Publication of *La Nuit,* (translated and condensed version of *Un di Velt Hot Geshvign*) in Paris (Editions de Minuit).
1960	Publication of *L'Aube* in Paris, by Les Editions du Seuil, which publish all subsequent works.
1961	Publication of *Le Jour.*
1962	Publication of *La Ville de la chance.*
1963	Naturalized as United States citizen.
1964	Received French Prix Rivarol for *La Ville de la chance;* publication of *Les Portes de la forêt.*
1965	Received National Jewish Book Council Literary Award, Remembrance Award, and Jewish Heritage Award.
1966	Publication of *Le Chant des morts;* publication of *Les Juifs du silence* (originally written as series of articles for *Yediot Ahronot,* a portion appearing in the *Saturday Evening Post*).
1967	Granted Degree of Doctor of Letters (Honorary), Jewish Theological Seminary.
1968	Granted Degree of Doctor of Humane Letters, Hebrew Union College; publication of *Zalmen ou la folie de Dieu* (drama; presented on French radio, "France-Culture").
	Publication of *Le Mendiant de Jérusalem;* received Prix Médicis.
1969	Married Marion E. Rose
1970	Publication of *Entre deux soleils.*
1972	Publication of *Célébration hassidique;* received Prix Bordin, French Academy; Eleanor Roosevelt Memorial Award, and American Liberties Medallion, American Jewish Committee; appointed Distinguished Professor, City College of the City University of New York, Department of Jewish Studies (member of faculty until 1976); granted Degree of Doctor of

Humane Letters, Manhattanville College; son, Shlomo Elisha, born.

1973   Wrote *Ani Maamin,* a cantata with music by Darius Milhaud, performed at Carnegie Hall, New York; publication of *Le Serment de Kolvillàg;* granted Degree of Doctor of Philosophy (Honorary), Bar-Ilan University, Israel; Degree of Doctor of Humane Letters, Yeshiva University; and Degree of Doctor of Humane Letters, Spertus College of Judaica, Chicago; received Martin Luther King Jr. Award, City College of New York.

1974   *The Madness of God* (translation of *Zalmen ou la folie de Dieu*) performed in Washington, D.C.; granted Degree of Doctor of Humane Letters, Boston University.

1975   Publication of *Célébration biblique;* granted Degree of Letters (Honorary) Marquette University; and Doctor of Laws (Honorary), Hofstra University.

1976   Appointed Andrew Mellon Professor in the Humanities, Boston University; granted Degree of Doctor of Literature (Honorary), Simmons College.

1977   Publication of *Un Juif, aujourd'hui.*

1979   Publication of *Four Hasidic Masters: And Their Struggle Against Melancholy;* appointed Chairman of the President's Commission on the Holocaust (later named the United States Holocaust Memorial Council); granted Degree of Humane Letters (Honorary), College of St. Scholastica.

1979   Publication of *Le Procès de Shamgorod (tel qu'il se déroula le 25 février 1649)* (drama); granted Degree of Doctor of Humane Letters (Honorary), Wesleyan University; and Doctor of Laws (Honorary), Talmudic University of Florida.

1980   Publication of *Le Testament d'un poète juif assassiné;* granted Degree of Doctor of Humane Letters (Honorary), Brandeis University; and Doctor of Letters (Honorary), Anna Maria College; and Doctor of Laws (Honorary), University of Notre Dame.

1981   Received Prix Inter for *Le Testament d'un poète juif assassiné;* appointed Honorary Chairman of the World Gathering of Jewish Holocaust Survivors, Jerusalem; publication of *Five Biblical Portraits;* and *Contre la mélancolie: Célébration hassidique II;* granted Degree of Doctor of Letters (Honorary), Yale University.

Notes

INTRODUCTION

1. The word *holocaust* comes from the Greek *holocauston*, signifying *burnt whole*. The Greek word is a translation of the Hebrew term *olah*, which literally means, *what is brought up*, and in English has come to mean, *a sacrificial offering consumed entirely by flames, total destruction by fire*. The use of the term *Holocaust* to signify the massacre of the Jews has been criticized because of the implication of sacrifice. The Hebrew word for the Nazi genocide, *Shoah*, and the Yiddish word, *hurbn*, do not connote sacrifice. See Sidra DeKoven Ezrahi, *By Words Alone: The Holocaust in Literature* (Chicago: Univ. of Chicago Press, 1980); and Wladimir Rabi, "Elie Wiesel: Un homme, une oeuvre, un public," *Esprit*, September, 1980, p. 87,

2. Elie Wiesel, "Why I Write," in *Confronting the Holocaust: The Impact of Elie Wiesel*, ed. Alvin Rosenfeld and Irving Greenberg (Bloomington: Indiana Univ. Press, 1978), p. 200.

3. Albert Camus, interview with Gabriel d'Aubarède, *Les Nouvelles Littéraires*, 10 May 1951; reprinted in Albert Camus, *Lyrical and Critical Essays*, trans. Ellen Conroy Kennedy, ed. Philip Thody (New York: Vintage Books, 1970), p. 353.

4. See Michael Berenbaum, *The Vision of the Void: Theological Reflections on the Works of Elie Wiesel* (Middleton: Conn.: Wesleyan Univ. Press, 1979); and John K. Roth, *A Consuming Fire: Encounters with Elie Wiesel and the Holocaust*, prologue by Elie Wiesel (Atlanta: John Knox Press, 1979).

5. Pierre Descargues, "Elie Wiesel, le polyglotte: pourquoi écrit-il en français?" *Tribune de Lausanne*, 9 June 1963.

6. *Harry James Cargas in Conversation with Elie Wiesel* (New York: Paulist Press, 1976), p. 91. This book is the best published source on Elie Wiesel's life.

7. Ibid., p. 62.

8. Pierre Descargues, *Tribune de Lausanne*, 9 June 1963. See also Gilles Lapouge, "Elie Wiesel, le témoin: Entretien," *La Quinzaine Littéraire*, 16–31 July 1970, p. 15.

9. *Entre deux soleils*. p. 9. This same incident is presented in abridged form in the introduction to *Legends of Our Time*.

10. Roland Barthes, in *The Pleasure of the Text,* trans. Richard Miller (New York: Hill & Wang, 1975), suggests that the son's search for the father is at the basis of all narrative forms: "every narrative (every unveiling of the truth) is a staging of the (absent, hidden or hypostatized) father" (p. 10); "Doesn't every narrative lead back to Oedipus? Isn't storytelling always a way of searching for one's origin. . . ." (p. 47).

11. See Rosette C. Lamont, "Elie Wiesel: In Search of a Tongue," in *Confronting the Holocaust,* pp. 80–81.

12. Wiesel often refers to Camus in his writing. One can see similarities between Camus' *Lettres à un ami allemand* (Paris: Gallimard, 1948) and Wiesel's own "letters" in *One Generation After* and *A Jew Today.* For a comparison of Wiesel and Camus, see Maurice Friedman, "The Dialogue with the Absurd: The Later Camus and Franz Kafka; Elie Wiesel and the Modern Job," in his *To Deny Our Nothingness* (New York: Delta, 1967); and Josephine Knopp, "Wiesel and the Absurd," in *Responses to Elie Wiesel: Critical Essays by Major Jewish and Christian Scholars,* ed. Harry James Cargas (New York: Persea Books, 1978).

13. *Harry James Cargas in Conversation* p. 65.

14. Gilles Lapouge, *La Quinzaine Littéraire,* 16–31 July 1970, p. 15. Wiesel says he dreams in French except when the dream is about prewar times, and then he dreams in Yiddish or Hungarian (Georges Bortoli, "Elie Wiesel a vu Dieu mourir à Buchenwald," *Le Figaro Littéraire,* 15 June 1963, p.2).

15. "Femina et Médicis sans surpris," *Combat,* 26 November 1968.

16. Piotr Rawicz, "Un enfant de genocide," *Le Monde,* 27 November 1968, p. 28.

17. See Lothar Kahn, "Elie Wiesel: Neo-Hasidism," *Mirrors of the Jewish Mind: A Gallery of Portraits of European Jewish Writers of Our Time* (New York: Thomas Yoseloff, 1968); and W. Rabi, "Vingt ans de littérature" in *D'Auschwitz à Israel: Vingt ans après la libération,* ed. Israel Schneersohn (Paris: Centre de Documentation Juive, 1968), p. 363.

18. See R. M. Albères, "Du côté de l'Orient," *Nouvelles Littéraires,* 24 October 1968, who speaks of Wiesel's "style de rêve éveillé, coulant et doucement poétique." See also F. Lovsky, "Elie Wiesel, Compagnon des morts d'Israel," *Foi et Vie,* 1 April 1968, p. 56. Victor Malka, in "Elie Wiesel et le destin juif," *Réforme,* 26 October 1968, says: "c'est la voix d'un poète qui parle, d'un poète authentique qui ne triche pas avec les mots."

19. *Harry James Cargas in Conversation,* pp. 88, 87.

20. Anna Langfus, *Le Sel et le soufre [The Whole Land Brimstone]* (Paris: Gallimard, 1965); Piotr Rawicz, *Le Sang du ciel [Blood from the Sky]* (Paris: Gallimard, 1961).

21. *Harry James Cargas in Conversation,* p. 87.

22. See Ernst Simon, "The Jews as God's Witnesses to the World," *Judaism* (1966): 306–18.

23. Elie Wiesel, in Michael Goulston and Anthony Rudolf, "Beyond Survival: Conversation between Elie Wiesel and Eugene Heimler," *European Judaism* 6 (Winter 1971–72): 4.

24. Elie Wiesel in "Jewish Values in the Post-Holocaust Future: A Symposium," *Judaism* 16 (1967): 285.

25. Ellen S. Fine, "Dialogue with Elie Wiesel," *Centerpoint: A Journal of Interdisciplinary Studies* (New York) 4 (Fall 1980): 22.

26. Albert Camus, "The Enigma," *Lyrical and Critical Essays*, p. 160.

27. Elie Wiesel, "The Fiery Shadow—Jewish Existence Out of the Holocaust," *Jewish Existence in an Open Society: A Convocation* (Los Angeles: Jewish Centers Association and Anderson, Ritchie & Simon, 1970), p. 39.

1. WITNESS OF THE NIGHT

1. *Night* was published in Yiddish under the title *Un di velt Hot Geshvign [And the World Has Remained Silent]* (Buenos Aires: Yel Mundo Callaba, Central Farbond Fun Poylishe Yidn in Argentina, 1956); in French as *La Nuit* (Paris: Les Editions de Minuit, 1958); in English as *Night*, trans. Stella Rodway (New York: Hill & Wang, 1960). All further references will be to the English edition, *Night, Dawn, The Accident: Three Tales* (New York: Hill & Wang, 1972).

2. Elie Wiesel, in Michael Goulston and Anthony Rudolf, "Beyond Survival: Conversation between Elie Wiesel and Eugene Heimler," *European Judaism* 6 (Winter 1971–72): 5.

3. François Mauriac, "Les Bloc-Notes de François Mauriac," *Figaro Littéraire*, 8 June 1963, p. 20.

4. Wiesel notes, in *Harry James Cargas in Conversation with Elie Wiesel* (New York: Paulist Press, 1976), p. 54: "Whenever I say 'night' I mean the Holocaust, that period. 'Night' has become a symbol of the Holocaust for obvious reasons. As we have said, a night has descended upon mankind, not only in Europe, but everywhere. Whoever was alive in those days has absorbed parts or fragments of that night. Night enveloped human destiny. Night is a symbol of that period, a frightening symbol. Whenever I try to speak of those nights, I simply say 'night.' " It should be pointed out that while Wiesel emphasizes the otherworldly aspect of the Holocaust, many historians and scholars stress the documented historical, political, social, and economic antecedents of this major catastrophe of our century. See Raul Hilberg, *The Destruction of the European Jews* (Chicago: Quadrangle Books, 1961); Lucy Dawidowicz, *The War Against the Jews: 1933–1945* (New York: Holt, Rinehart & Winston, 1975); Yehuda Bauer, *The Holocaust in Historical Perspective* (Seattle: Univ. of Washington, 1978).

5. *From Holocaust to Rebirth* (New York: The Council of Jewish Federations and Welfare Funds, 1970), pp. 3; 2.

6. Maurice Blanchot, *L'Espace littéraire* (Paris: Gallimard, Collection Idées; 1955); pp. 216, 221.

7. Frederick Garber, in "The Art of Elie Wiesel," *Judaism* 22 (1973): 301, speaks of Moché as Wiesel's first witness: "What he knows separates him from others and his role as remnant separates him from what he has seen. Moché is

Wiesel's paradigm for the survivor tossed out of moral time, loosed from all relations with value, or at least, shuddering at those relations that are left."

8. Nora Levin, *The Holocaust* (New York: Schocken Books, 1973), pp. 597–98. See chap. 29 for a detailed historical account of the Nazi deportations from Hungary. Dawidowicz, in *The War Against the Jews, 1933-1945* pp. 379–83, also discusses the prewar conditions of the Hungarian Jews. One of the first anti-Jewish laws was enacted on May 24, 1938, by the Horthy government, limiting employment of Jews in private business firms. A year later, a law was passed defining the status of Jews and barring them from positions in the media and from entrance to professions. The government was authorized to appropriate Jewish landed property. The first deportation of stateless Jews from Hungary took place in 1941. See also Hilberg, *The Destruction of the European Jews*, pp. 509–54; and Randolph L. Braham, *The Politics of Genocide: The Holocaust in Hungary*, Volume I and II (New York: Columbia Univ. Press, 1981).

9. Auschwitz was divided into three main camps: Auschwitz I for slave labor; Auschwitz II or Birkenau, designated as a killing center with gas chambers and crematoria; Auschwitz III or Buna-Monowitz, an industrial camp composed of a synthetic rubber plant and coal mines (constructed by I. G. Farben), where camp inmates were forced to work as slave laborers.

10. George Steiner observes, in *In Bluebeard's Castle* (New Haven, Conn.: Yale Univ. Press, 1971), pp. 53–54: "The camp embodies, often down to minutiae, the images and chronicles of Hell in European art and thought from the twelfth to the eighteenth centuries. . . . The concentration and death camps of the twentieth century, wherever they exist under whatever regime, are Hell *made immanent*. They are the transference of Hell from below the earth to its surface. They are the deliberate enactment of a long, precise imagining."

11. "Beyond Survival," p. 5.

12. Simone Weil's perceptions on delayed forms of killing are particularly relevant here: "From the power to transform him [man] into a thing by killing there proceeds another power, and much more prodigious, that which makes a thing of him while he still lives. He is living, he has a soul, yet he is a thing." "The *Iliad*, Poem of Might," in *The Simone Weil Reader*, ed. George A. Panichas (New York: David McKay, 1977), p. 155.

13. Wiesel states: "Le temps compte moins que le principe: l'homme est capable de se défaire de son Moi ("Time is not as important as man's capacity to obliterate himself") (*Entre deux soleils*, p. 245). See David Rousset, *L'Univers concentrationnaire* (Paris: Editions du Pavois, 1946): "L'homme se défaisait lentement chez le concentrationnaire" (p. 60). See also Robert Antelme, *L'Espèce humaine* (Paris: Gallimard, 1947); and Primo Levi, *Survival in Auschwitz: The Nazi Assault on Humanity*, trans. Stuart Woolf (New York: Collier, 1961).

14. For comments on the importance of the father-son relationship see Irene Paul, "The Night of Nazism," *Jewish Currents*, April 1961, p. 40. Frederick Garber also notes: "Sanctified by tradition, even more than by

instinct, the relationship of father and son was all that time's knowledge had left as a possibility for valuable action in the immediate present" ("The Art of Elie Wiesel," p. 302).

15. Wylie Sypher, *Loss of the Self in Modern Literature and Art* (New York: Random House, 1962), pp. 6–7.

16. André Neher, "Elie Wiesel: *La Nuit*," *Evidences*, March 1959, p. 48.

17. The childlike behavior of the father is manifested toward the end of the book when, dying from dysentery, he begins to lose control. Bruno Bettelheim describes the prisoners' "regression into child-like behavior" in *The Informed Heart* (Glencoe, Ill.: Free Press, 1960) and in his essay "Individual and Mass Behavior in Extreme Situations," *Surviving and Other Essays* (New York: Alfred Knopf, 1979). For a refutation of Bettelheim's ideas, see Terrence Des Pres, "The Bettelheim Problem," *Social Research* 46 (1979): 619–47.

18. André Neher, *L' Exile de la parole* (Paris: Editions du Seuil, 1970), pp. 235, 234. It is interesting to note that in Neher's article in *Evidences*, written in 1959, he focuses on the son's childlike dependency, whereas in his book he points to the son's strength in relation to the father.

19. Lawrence Langer discusses the symbolic aspect of the struggle between death and the father in his chapter on Wiesel in *The Holocaust and the Literary Imagination* (New Haven, Conn.: Yale Univ. Press, 1975). See especially pp. 86–87.

20. The *Sonderkommando* was the squad of Jewish prisoners required to take the bodies out of the gas chambers and put them in the crematoria. *Pipels* were young prisoners of about thirteen years old who were granted power over the others in exchange for favors they bestowed upon the SS.

21. Terrence Des Pres, *The Survivor: An Anatomy of Life in the Death Camps* (New York: Oxford Univ. Press, 1976), pp. 98–99.

22. Throughout *Night* there are numerous comparisons of men to animals, such as dogs, pigs, lambs, cattle, wild beasts, and even insects such as worms and ants, all used to demonstrate the reduction of man to a subhuman state in the camps.

23. A. Alvarez, in "The Literature of the Holocaust," *Commentary*, November 1964, p. 66, carries this idea to its extreme: "The process by which a child is not merely forced to witness the gradual death of his father, but is also forced to acknowledge that he is glad and relieved when the old man dies—in short when he psychically becomes his father's murderer—may fit naturally enough into the shorthand of dreams and psychosis; it is, however, beyond the conventional language of guilt and grief and suffering." Other critics refer to the son's ambivalent feelings but none go so far as to call the son "his father's murderer." See Irving Halperin, *Messengers from the Dead: Literature of the Holocaust* (Philadelphia: Westminster Press, 1970), pp. 76–77; André Neher, *Evidences*, March 1959, p. 48; and F. Lovsky, "Elie Wiesel: Compagnon des morts d'Israel," *Foi et Vie*, 1 April 1968, pp. 38–39.

24. Robert Jay Lifton, *Death in Life: Survivors of Hiroshima* (New York: Vintage Books, Random House, 1969), p. 496.

25. *Harry James Cargas in Conversation*, p. 110.

26. Lawrence Langer, *The Holocaust and the Literary Imagination*, p. 85.

27. Marc Laporte, "Elie Wiesel: D'Auschwitz à Hiroshima," *L'Express*, 6 June 1963, p. 34. Wiesel has modified his views on the death of God: "I never speak of God now. I rather speak of men who believed in God or men who denied god. How strange that the philosophy denying God came not from the survivors." "Talking and Writing and Keeping Silent," in *The German Church Struggle and the Holocaust*, ed. Franklin Littell and Hubert Locke (Detroit: Wayne State Univ. Press, 1974), p. 271.

28. Elie Wiesel, in *Harry James Cargas in Conversation*, p. 110. For a discussion of the Nietzschean death of God in terms of Jewish theology, see Emil Fackenheim, *God's Presence in History: Jewish Affirmations and Philosophical Reflections* (New York: Harper Torchbooks, 1970).

29. Alfred Kazin, *Contemporaries* (Boston: Little, Brown & Co., 1962), pp. 297–98. See also Robert Alter, *After the Tradition* (New York: Dutton, 1969), p. 152; Irving Halperin, "On Stepping into the Fiery Gates," *Judaism* 21 (1972): 405.

30. According to Sidney Finkelstein, Wiesel's novels recount his "search for something to follow or believe in, for a spiritual 'father' to replace his dead father, for a leader, a prophet, a 'Messiah', a 'new God'," "Elie Wiesel's Spiritual Journey," *Jewish Currents*, May 1967, p. 23.

31. Morton Reichek, "Elie Wiesel—Out of the Night," *Present Tense* 3 (1976): 46.

32. *Harry James Cargas in Conversation*, p. 88.

33. A. M. Dalbray, "*Les Juifs du Silence*," *Amif*, November 1967, p. 1771.

2. The Return of Lazarus

1. The three works, *Night*, *Dawn*, and *The Accident* have been published in one volume (New York: Hill & Wang, 1972). All quotations are referred to parenthetically from this edition. The theme of Lazarus links *Night* (descent into the grave) to *Dawn* and *The Accident* (emergence from the grave). It is interesting to note that the name *Lazarus* is another form of the Hebrew name *Eleazar*.

2. Hannah Arendt, *The Origins of Totalitarianism* (New York: Harcourt, Brace & World, 1951), p. 441.

3. Jean Cayrol, "Lazare parmi nous" (Paris: Editions du Seuil, 1950), and "Pour un romanesque lazaréen," in *Les Corps étrangers* (Paris: Editions du Seuil, Series 10/18, 1964). All further references to these texts appear parenthetically in the text as "LPN" and "RL," respectively.

4. Roland Barthes, "La Rature," in *Les Corps étrangers*, p. 245. See also Daniel Oyster, "Approche de Lazare," in *Jean Cayrol et son oeuvre* (Paris: Editions du Seuil, 1976); and Marc Bertrand, "Les Avatars de Lazare: le romanesque de Jean Cayrol," *French Review* 51 (1978): 674–82.

5. Theodore Adorno says of the survivor, in *Negative Dialectics* (New York: Seabury Press, 1973), p. 363: "He will be plagued by dreams such as that he is

no longer living at all, that he was sent to the ovens in 1944 and his whole existence since has been imaginary, an emanation of the insane wish of a man killed twenty years ago."

6. René Prédal, *Alain Resnais* (Paris: Minard, 1968), p. 104. See the chapter entitled "Personnages lazaréens et amours difficiles" for a discussion of *le personnage lazaréen* in the films of Resnais.

7. Maurice Blanchot, *La Part du feu* (Paris: Gallimard, 1949), p. 316.

8. Robert Jay Lifton, *Home from the War: Vietnam Veterans, Neither Victims nor Executioners* (New York: Simon & Schuster, 1973), p. 101. For a detailed analysis of survival guilt, see also Lifton's *Death in Life: Survivors of Hiroshima* (New York: Random House, 1967) and *History and Human Survival* (New York: Random House, 1970).

9. Jean Cayrol, "Nuit et Brouillard," *L'Avant-Scène*, February 1961. Elie Wiesel also asks: "If I had stayed in the camp for 15 years, would I too have become one of the oppressors?" (Victor Malka, "Face à face avec Elie Wiesel," *Réforme*, 1 April 1967, p. 11).

10. Luc Estang, "*L'Aube*," *Le Figaro Littéraire*, 1 June 1960, p. 15.

11. The reference to the resurrection of the dead at midnight occurs three times in *Dawn*, repeating the theme of Lazarus although in a different context (pp. 125, 159, 172).

12. Lothar Kahn, "What Price Jewish Bravery?" *The Reconstructionist*, 29 June 1962, p. 17. Kahn places Wiesel's novel in the context of other works glorifying the heroism of the new Jewish man of action. He feels that "this tendency toward the primitive and the brutal in the name of normalcy" is a threat to Jewish tradition and that Wiesel basically cautions against a total break with the diaspora.

13. Irving Feldman, "After the Death Camps," *Commentary*, September 1961, p. 263.

14. See *The Oath*: "Whoever kills, kills himself. . . . Just as every murder is a suicide, every suicide is a murder" (p. 55); *A Beggar in Jerusalem*: "Whoever kills, kills God. Each murder is a suicide, with the Eternal eternally the victim" (p. 208).

15. Jean-François Steiner, in *Treblinka* (Paris: Fayard, 1966), describes the difficulties of the Nazis when forced to kill their victims at close range (p. 65).

16. The absence or presence of hatred is stressed throughout the text. Elisha tries unsuccessfully to hate Dawson, believing that the inability of the Jewish people to hate ultimately resulted in their extermination. Wiesel points out in "Appointment with Hate" that only the Jew who repudiates himself is capable of hatred (LT, 131–42).

17. In the French edition, the traditional word for "executioner," *le bourreau*, is replaced by *le justicier*, which means "administrator of the necessary laws of justice."

18. Elisha is the name of the prophet of resurrection (2 Kings 13:21) and of ben Abuya, the excommunicated heretic (Hagiga 14b–15a). See Byron Sherwin, "Elie Wiesel and Jewish Theology," *Judaism* 18 (1969): 40.

19. *Death in Life: Survivors of Hiroshima* (New York: Random House, 1967), p. 490.

20. Roland Barthes, "La Rature," in *Les Corps étrangers*, p. 245.

21. The "letter" suggests a mystical link between the creator and his creation, between God and man. In *Souls on Fire*, Wiesel tells a tale about Baal Shem Tov, exiled by God because he tries to force the coming of the Messiah. The recitation of the *aleph–beith*, "the first of the sacred letters which together contain all the mysteries of the entire universe" (p. 4) grants the Rabbi the power to be redeemed and to begin again.

22. A. Alvarez, in his study of suicide, *The Savage God* (New York: Bantam Books, 1972), quotes Boris Pasternak, *An Essay in Autobiography* (trans. Manya Harari; London: Collins and Harvill Press, 1959): "A man who decides to commit suicide puts a full stop to his being, he declares himself a bankrupt and his memories to be unreal. They can no longer help or save him, he has put himself beyond their reach. The continuity of his inner life is broken, his personality is at an end" (p. 239).

23. Robert Antelme, *L'Espèce humaine* (Paris: Gallimard, 1947), p. 208.

24. Primo Levi, *Survival in Auschwitz: The Nazi Assault on Humanity*, trans. Stuart Woolf (New York: Collier Books, 1973), pp. 31–32.

25. Charlotte Delbo, *None of Us Will Return*, trans. John Githens (Boston: Beacon Press, 1968), pp. 41, 40.

26. For the survivor, crying is an important part of healing; it is "linked with hope, with the possibility of renewal," according to Lifton, in *Home from the War*, p. 276. Josephine Knopp, in *The Trial of Judaism in Contemporary Jewish Writing* (Urbana: Univ. of Illinois Press, 1975), points out that "for the first time the protagonist can cry and, in so doing, releases a bit of the pent-up horror. The physical recovery from near death now holds the promise of a spiritual recovery as well" (p. 81).

27. Heda Kovály and Erazim Kohák, *The Victors and the Vanquished* (New York: Horizon Press, 1973), p. 14. For allusions to the resurfacing of past images, see Vercors, *Les Armes de la nuit* (Paris: Editions de Minuit, 1946), p. 109, and Anna Langfus, *Bagages de sable* (Paris: Gallimard, 1962), p. 110.

28. Irving Halperin, *Messengers from the Dead: Literature of the Holocaust* (Philadelphia: Westminster Press, 1970), p. 104. The title itself of this book defines the survivor-witness.

3. The Journey Homeward

1. Albert Camus, *The Myth of Sisyphus*, (New York: Random House, 1955), p. 5.

2. Robert Jay Lifton, *Death in Life: Survivors of Hiroshima* (New York: Random House, 1969), p. 539.

3. Wiesel explains that the imagined return in *The Town Beyond the Wall*

(1962) served as a guide for his actual return in 1964 and points to their similarities ("The Last Return," I.T, 121–123).

4. Frederick Garber, "The Art of Elie Wiesel," *Judaism* 22 (1973): 305.

5. *Bulletin du Cercle Juif* (Montreal), November 1962.

6. Elie Wiesel, *From Holocaust to Rebirth* (New York: Council of Jewish Federations and Welfare Funds, 1970), p. 3.

7. Robert Jay Lifton describes the "golden age" of childhood often referred to by concentration camp survivors with regard to their early lives. This phenomenon serves to idealize the dead and allows the survivor to "reactivate within himself old and profound feelings of love, nurturance and harmony, in order to be able to apply these feelings to a new formulation of life beyond the death immersion" (*Death in Life*, p. 534).

8. The theme of the dead child is developed in *The Town*, through the story of "the little prince," Yankel (Michael's friend from the camps) and his agonizing death in Paris (pp. 87–98). See also the death of the five-year-old Mendele (110–112). The theme recurs throughout Wiesel's works. See especially *The Gates of the Forest:* "our only prophets will be dead children" (32); "the sun is but the head of a Jewish child killed and thrown to the dogs. . . . the stars are the eyes of Jewish children killed in the transparent light of dawn" (54).

9. Marcel Proust, *A la recherche du temps perdu* (Paris: Bibliothèque de la Pléiade, 1954), p. 427.

10. The theme of madness structures *The Town Beyond the Wall* as seen by Dostoevsky's quote at the beginning of the novel: "I have a plan—to go mad." Michael is angry at King Lear for fearing madness. He feels that the old man should have embraced it as a "protest against pain and injustice" (TBW, 170). Madness is also represented by Martha, the ugly creature living at the edge of town.

11. "Elie Wiesel: l'Orant," *Techniques Nouvelles*, March 1972.

12. Lothar Kahn, *Mirrors of the Jewish Mind: A Gallery of Portraits of European Jewish Writers of Our Time* (New York: Thomas Yoseloff, 1968), p. 179. Wiesel's protagonists are often characterized as wanderers who "have chosen exile in order to detach themselves from time" (GF, 12). See also *A Beggar in Jerusalem* (143–44) and *The Oath* (43).

13. While Wiesel uses the expression "the Wandering Jew" throughout his works, he distinguishes between this term and the *Na-venadnik* (beggar or wanderer), stating that the Wandering Jew is "a Christian concept, growing out of a medieval legend about a Jewish cobbler who taunted Jesus on the way to the crucifixion and was cursed to wander thereafter until Jesus' return." According to Jewish tradition, "the Jew-as-wanderer is usually symbolized by the *Lamed Vavnik*, the Just Man. . . . before the Just Man could be revealed, he had to become a *Na-venadnik*, wandering about and hiding his own identity so as to attract and help others anonymously." Lily Edelman, "A Conversation with Elie Wiesel," *Responses to Elie Wiesel*, ed. Harry James Cargas (New York: Persea Books, 1978), p. 17.

14. E. M. Cioran, *The Temptation to Exist*, trans. Richard Howard (Chicago: Quadrangle Books, 1968), p. 80.

15. It is interesting to note that the visit to the house occurs at night, suggesting as in *Dawn* an identification with the dead who rise from their tombs at midnight to lament the destruction of the synagogue. The returning survivor is dead in the eyes of the strangers who inhabit his house.

16. Wiesel describes a second return to his town in "House of Strangers" *(A Jew Today)*. This time accompanied by his wife and an American television crew, he is welcomed by town officials and is able to visit his old house. After a rapid visit, he again runs away "far from here, as far as possible" (60). See also "The Itinerary of Elie Wiesel: From Sighet to Jerusalem" (a television script written and narrated by Elie Wiesel, and presented on NBC Television's "The Eternal Light," 21 May 1972).

17. Lothar Kahn, *Chicago Jewish Forum*, Fall 1964, p. 53.

18. Kahn, *Mirrors of the Jewish Mind*, p. 182. For an analysis of the hiding of God's face, see also Norman Lamm, *"The Town Beyond the Wall* as a Key," in "Building a Moral Society: Aspects of Elie Wiesel's Work," *Face to Face: An Interreligious Bulletin*, Spring 1979, pp. 7–9.

19. Norman Friedman, "God Versus Man in the Twentieth Century," *Reconstructionist*, 28 October 1966, pp. 26–27.

20. Franz Kafka, *The Trial* (New York: Modern Library, 1937), p. 286.

21. The leitmotif of the play runs through Michael's encounter with the spectator. The deportation scene is likened to a Greek tragedy in which the characters are condemned before the curtain rises. The Jews play the role of these characters, following the instructions of an invisible director who sends them to their tragic destiny. The spectator admits that walking around the half-empty city after the deportation was like being onstage an hour after the end of the show, and Michael accuses him of having been disappointed with the performance because the actors were not convincing enough (TBW, 157).

22. *L'Herne*, No. 3 (1963), p. 215. This comment was made about Louis-Ferdinand Céline to whose works the issue is devoted.

23. Emmanuel Haymann, "Elie Wiesel: Témoin de la nuit," *Tribune Juive*, 3–9 March 1972, p. 10.

24. Thomas A. Idinopulos, "The Holocaust in the Stories of Elie Wiesel," *Responses to Elie Wiesel*, ed. Harry James Cargas (New York: Persea Books, 1978), p. 120.

25. Irving Halperin, *Messengers from the Dead: Literature of the Holocaust* (Philadelphia: Westminster Press, 1970), p. 90.

26. See Victor Brombert, *The Romantic Prison: The French Tradition* (Princeton, N.J.: Princeton Univ. Press, 1978) for a literary study of the prison metaphor and its dialectical tensions of oppression and inner freedom, concentration and expansion, suffering and security.

27. Mircea Eliade, *Myth and Reality* (New York: Harper and Row, 1963), pp. 80–81. See also Gaston Bachelard, *La Poétique d l'espace* (Paris: Presses Universitaires de France, 1958), with regard to the dynamics between the inner and outer worlds: "L'être qui se cache, l'être qui 'rentre dans sa coquille' prépare 'une sortie'. . . . en se conservant dans l'immobilité de sa coquille l'être prépare des explosions temporelles de l'être, des tourbillons d'être" (p. 110).

28. *Harry James Cargas in Conversation with Elie Wiesel* (New York: Paulist Press, 1976), p. 96, 95.

29. Abba Kovner, *A Canopy in the Desert: Selected Poems,* trans. Shirley Kaufman (Pittsburgh: Univ. of Pittsburgh Press, 1973), p. xiii.

30. *The Gates of the Forest* is the exception, where the village depicted is devoid of all Jews and retains its anonymity, playing a secondary role to that of the forest. *The Testament,* which takes place in the major countries of Europe is also an exception. Wiesel's play *The Trial of God (As it was held on February 25, 1649 in Shamgorod)* does include the name of a town in its subtitle.

31. Arnold Mandel, "Le Hassidisme, célébration ou commémoration?" *Nouveaux Cahiers,* Spring 1972, p. 70.

32. Elie Wiesel, "The Holocaust as Literary Inspiration," in *Dimensions of the Holocaust: Lectures at Northwestern University* (Evanston, Ill.: Northwestern Univ. Press, 1977), p. 8–9.

4. THE WITNESS AND HIS DOUBLE

1. Wiesel's characters are often burdened by *survivor guilt,* a phenomenon referred to by the author in such essays as "The Guilt We Share," *(LT)* and in the interview "Beyond Survival," *European Judaism* 6 (Winter 1971–72): 6. For a psychological analysis of different forms of *survivor guilt,* see Robert Jay Lifton, *Death in Life: Survivors of Hiroshima* (New York: Vintage, 1967); idem, *History and Human Survival* (New York: Vintage, 1971); idem, "The Concept of the Survivor," in *Survivors, Victims and Perpetrators: Essays on the Nazi Holocaust,* ed. Joel Dimsdale (New York: Hemisphere, 1980). Lifton distinguishes between the "numbing" and the more positive "animating" guilt, which leads to "the anxiety of responsibility." Terrence Des Pres, in *The Survivor: An Anatomy of Life in the Death Camps* (New York: Oxford Univ. Press, 1976), discusses the negative implications of *survivor guilt* and contests its importance as the motivation for bearing witness (pp. 40–45).

2. C. F. Keppler, *The Literature of the Second Self* (Tucson: Univ. of Arizona Press, 1972), pp. 18, 199. For studies on the double in literature, see Albert Guerard, "Concepts of the Double," and Claire Rosenfield, "The Shadow Within: The Conscious and Unconscious Use of the Double," both in *Stories of the Double,* ed. Albert Guerard (New York: Lippincott, 1967). See also Dostoevsky, *The Double,* trans. George Bird (Bloomington: Indiana Univ. Press, 1958), and André Gide, *Dostoevsky* (New York: New Directions, 1961).

3. Pierre Hahn, "Prix Médicis: Elie Wiesel," *Magazine Littéraire,* No. 24 (1969), p. 19. Wiesel states: "Le fils conducteur de tous mes livres . . . . Il y a toujours deux personnages qui n'en font qu'un: dans *La Ville de la chance,* Pedro et Michael; dans *Les Portes de la forêt,* Gavriel et Grégor."

4. Lily Edelman, "A Conversation with Elie Wiesel," *Responses to Elie Wiesel: Critical Essays by Major Jewish and Christian Scholars,* ed. Harry James Cargas (New York: Persea Books, 1978), p. 16.

5. George Hertz, review of *Le Mendiant de Jérusalem, Tribune Juive,* 18 October 1968, p. 19.

6. Lawrence Langer "The Divided Voice: Elie Wiesel and the Challenge of the Holocaust," in *Confronting the Holocaust: The Impact of Elie Wiesel,* ed. Alvin Rosenfeld and Irving Greenberg (Bloomington: Indiana Univ. Press, 1978), p. 40.

7. *Harry James Cargas in Conversation with Elie Wiesel* (New York: Paulist Press, 1976), p. 109.

8. See Otto Rank, "The Double as Immortal Self" in *Beyond Psychology* (New York: Dover Publications, 1941), pp. 92–96, for a discussion of the double and twin mythology: "the sacrifice of one of the twins was the condition for the survival of the other. . . . a symbolic gesture on the part of the immortal self by which it rids itself of the mortal ego" (p. 92).

9. Sigmund Freud, "The Uncanny" (1919), in *Collected Papers,* ed. Ernest Jones, trans. Joan Riviere, Vol. 4 (New York: Basic Books, 1959), p. 387.

10. Otto Rank, *Beyond Psychology,* p. 76.

11. Edelman, "Conversation," p. 16.

12. See Sidney Finkelstein, "Elie Wiesel's Spiritual Journey," *Jewish Currents,* May 1967, pp. 22–23.

13. Robert Alter, *After the Tradition: Essays on Modern Jewish Writing* (New York: Dutton, 1969), p. 155.

14. Josephine Knopp, *The Trial of Judaism in Contemporary Jewish Writing* (Urbana: Univ. of Illinois Press, 1975), pp. 6–8, 89–90.

15. Nicolas Baudy, "Elie Wiesel ou les vraies dimensions de la connaissance," *Les Nouveaux Cahiers,* Fall 1966, p. 41.

16. Gustav Davidson, *A Dictionary of Angels* (New York: Free Press, 1967), p. 117. See also *Dictionary of the Bible,* ed. James Hastings (New York: Scribner's 1963), p. 32.

17. Gavriel's recurring laugh has been linked to the theme of the absurd. Marc Saporta in "Le mur est partout," *L'Express,* 2–8 November 1964, p. 58, observes: "For Wiesel, the absurd does not lead to despair but to laughter." Joseph Sunglowsky, review of *Les Portes de la forêt, French Review* 40 (1966): 433, speaks of "the ironical laugh of Gavriel which recalls that other mysterious laugh that Jean-Baptiste Clamence hears in *The Fall.*"

18. Keppler, in *The Literature of the Second Self,* p. 11, notes that the second self "tends to be the possessor of secrets that the first self can never quite fathom and thus being the stranger is also the stronger, always tending to be in real control of the relationship." Thus the self that *knows* about the Holocaust predominates.

19. Ibid., p. 192.

20. The absence of the shadow as omen of death is discussed by Otto Rank, *Beyond Psychology,* pp. 72–74. This interpretation differs from the one held by some primitive societies who believed that catching sight of one's shadow is a sign of death. See James Frazer, *The Golden Bough,* chap. 18, sec. 3 (New York: Macmillan, 1926); and Otto Rank, *The Double,* chap. 4 (Chapel Hill: Univ. of North Carolina Press, 1971).

21. Freud, "The Uncanny," p. 387.

22. Freud, "Thoughts for the Times on War and Death" (1915), in *Collected Papers,* Vol. 4, p. 305.

23. *Harry James Cargas in Conversation*, p. 51. See also Elie Wiesel, *From Holocaust to Rebirth* (New York: Council of Jewish Federations and Welfare Funds, 1970), p. 12.

24. Albert Memmi, *La Libération du Juif* (Paris: Petite Bibliothèque Payot, 1966), p. 31

25. Wiesel states in an interview ("Entretien", *Tribune Juive*, 3–9 March 1972, p. 17): "Israel, the name of the Jewish people, contains the word 'God'. . . . The name is very important in our history and in our conscience. It is a question of God and man's struggle against God. We must therefore place the struggle against God within the tradition, within the name."

26. Thomas Idinopulos, "The Holocaust in the Stories of Elie Wiesel," *Responses to Elie Wiesel*, ed. Harry James Cargas (New York: Persea Books, 1978), p. 122.

27. *Harry James Cargas in Conversation*, p. 50.

28. Ibid.

29. Robert Alter, *After the Tradition*, p. 158.

30. Joseph Bertrand, review of *Les Portes de la forêt, Le Phare*, 28 February 1965. Other interpretations of Gavriel include Pierre-Henri Simon, *Le Monde*, 28 October 1964, pp, 10–11, who suggests he is "une présence surnaturelle, et la personnalité de Grégor qui lui a donné son propre nom, semble s'être transporté en lui." Lothar Kahn, *Mirrors of the Jewish mind: A Gallery of Portraits of European Jewish Writers of Our Time* (New York: Thomas Yoseloff, 1968), p. 183, asks if Gavriel is God, the Messiah, or "the symbol of the ghosts of the past whose power must finally be broken if they are not to be a permanently crippling force in living."

31. The voice alienated from itself is exemplified in "The Wandering Jew," where Wiesel describes his conversation with one of his masters: "I was hearing myself talk and it was someone else who was reciting a badly-learned, disjointed lesson. Everything rang false" (LT, 97).

32. *Harry James Cargas in Conversation*, p. 111.

33. Ibid., p. 110.

34. Wiesel reveals that he smuggles into every book a sentence that becomes the substance of the next book; in this case, the word "crown" (ibid., p. 91).

35. Ibid., p. 52. It is interesting to note that the author's first name begins with and last name ends with "*El*."

36. Katriel's mysterious presence has been likened to such enigmatic figures in French literature as Ménalque in André Gide's *L'Immoraliste* and Nathanaël in *Les Nourritures terrestres*. See Jack Kolbert, review of *Le Mendiant de Jérusalem, French Review* 44 (1970): 189–90.

37. In *The Gates of the Forest*, Gregor also expresses his jealousy of Leib: "I envied him his strength, his calm, his superiority. He was always the leader" (172).

38. Manès Sperber, review of *A Beggar in Jerusalem, New York Times Book Review*, 25 January 1970, pp. 1, 34.

39. Robert Misrahi, review of *Le Mendiant de Jérusalem, La Quizaine*

Littéraire, 1–15 December 1968, p. 6. He feels that, like *Night*, this novel is "le récit de la mort de Dieu dans le coeur des Juifs."

40. Dominique Baux, review of *Le Mendiant de Jérusalem, Etudes*, January 1969, p. 132

41. Keppler, *The Literature of the Second Self*, p. 18.

42. Dan Isaac, in "All My Stories are True" (*Nation*, 16 March 1970, pp. 309–10), states: "With regard to David's past, it [the parable] suggests that he had been extending his fictive imagination into the immediate sensible world around him, living out a fantasized construct rather than responding existentially to what the particular terms of time and place had to offer."

43. *Letters à un ami allemand* (Paris: Gallimard, 1948), p. 72. In *The Town Beyond the Wall*, Pedro reaffirms this philosophy: "Camus wrote somewhere that to protest against a universe of unhappiness you had to create happiness" (118). See also Wiesel's comments in "Jewish Values in the Post-Holocaust Future: A Symposium," *Judaism* 16 (1967): 291

44. Rank, *Beyond Psychology*, p. 95.

45. Paul Kleim, "Elie Wiesel devant le Mur reconquis," *Tribune de Genève*, 6 November 1968.

46. A. M. G., "Nous sommes tous des mendiants," *Terre Retrouvée*, 15 February 1969.

47. Pierre Hahn, "Prix Médicis: Elie Wiesel," *Magazine Littéraire*, No. 24 (1969), p. 20. See also Wiesel's comments in Albert Memmi, review of *Le Mendiant de Jérusalem, Le Nouvel Observateur*, 25 November–1 December 1968, p. 41.

48. Jacques de Ricaumont, "Changer le malheur: Entretien," *Le Figaro Littéraire*, 28 November 1968, p. 3.

49. *Harry James Cargas in Conversation*, p. 109

50. Terrence Des Pres, *The Survivor: An Anatomy of Life in the Death Camps* (New York: Oxford Univ. Press, 1976), pp. 29, 47–48. According to Des Pres, the survivor-witness "embodies a socio-historical process founded not upon the desire for justice . . . but upon the involvement of all human beings in common care for life and the future" (p. 47).

51. Sperber in his review of a *Beggar in Jerusalem*, p. 34, discusses the importance of the beggar as seer and messenger in Jewish tradition: "And he always carries a message, sometimes without knowing it; in fact, his unexpected arrival is in itself a message; its significance has to be interpreted like a dream."

52. Hahn, "Prix Médicis," pp. 19, 20.

5. Chronicle of Memory

1. Jewish communities in Eastern Europe kept histories of their town in the *Pinkas*, a Hebrew word meaning "book." Daniel Stern observes: "The *Pinkas*, the town's daily history, is another metaphor for the Bible, for world literature. . . ." ("The Word Testifies for the Dead," *The Nation*, 5 January 1974, p. 6).

2. Lily Edelman, "A Conversation with Elie Wiesel," *Responses to Elie Wiesel: Critical Essays by Major Jewish and Christian Scholars,* ed. Harry James Cargas (New York: Persea Books, 1978), p. 21.

3. For a discussion of the myth of Jewish ritual murder or blood libel, see George Mosse, *Toward the Final Solution: A History of European Racism* (New York: Harper Colophon Books, 1978), chap. 8.

4. Edelman, "Conversation," p. 10.

5. Wiesel states: "For me writing is a *matzeva,* an invisible tombstone, erected to the memory of the dead unburied. Each word corresponds to a face, a prayer, the one needing the other so as not to sink into oblivion" (LT, 8).

6. The town itself could be considered a significant character as indicated by the original French title of the book, *Le Serment de Kolvillàg.*

7. Elie Wiesel, in Michael Goulston and Anthony Rudolf, "Beyond Survival," *European Judaism* (Winter 1971–72): 8. See also Morton Reichek, "Elie Wiesel: Out of the Night," *Present Tense* 3 (Spring 1976): 43–44; and *A Jew Today,* where Wiesel states: "The task of the writer is, after all, not to appease, or flatter, but to disturb, to warn, to question by questioning oneself" (108).

8. Edmond Jabès, *Le Livre des ressemblances* (Paris: Gallimard, 1976), p. 89.

9. The strong identification between the father and the town corresponds to Wiesel's own father's position in Sighet. "Whatever happened in the community, they [the Jewish leaders] came immediately to him (and if I now have such a sense of community, maybe I inherited it from him)." *Harry James Cargas in Conversation with Elie Wiesel* (New York: Paulist Press, 1976), p. 70.

10. Henry Kaufman and Gene Koppel, *A Small Measure of Victory: An Interview* (Tucson: Univ. of Arizona Press, 1974), p. 25.

11. Wiesel states: "De 1945, mon arrivée à Paris jusqu'en 1955, je me suis imposé le silence. J'ai voulu comprendre ce qui s'était passé. Bien sûr, je ne comprendrai jamais." (Alain Célérier, "Elie Wiesel: Prix Rivarol," *Combat,* 6 June 1963, p. 8).

12. *Harry James Cargas in Conversation,* p. 88.

13. Primo Levi, *Survival in Auschwitz: The Nazi Assault on Humanity* (New York: Collier Books, 1973), p. 22.

14. "Why I Write," *Confronting the Holocaust: The Impact of Elie Wiesel,* ed. Alvin Rosenfeld and Irving Greenberg (Bloomington: Indiana Univ. Press, 1973), p. 201.

15. Victor Malka, "Au crépuscule du souvenir: Entretien avec Elie Wiesel," *Nouvelles Littéraires,* 11 June 1970.

16. George Steiner, *Language and Silence: Essays on Language, Literature and the Inhuman* (New York: Atheneum, 1974) p. 123. Steiner analyzes the relationship between the dissolution of humanistic values and the corruption of language under the Nazi regime.

17. Piotr Rawicz, *Blood from the Sky,* trans. Peter Wiles (New York: Harcourt Brace, 1964), p. 132.

18. See Elie Wiesel, "Trivializing the Holocaust: Semi-Fact and Semi-Fiction," *New York Times,* 16 April 1978, for a criticism of the television film,

"Holocaust," written by novelist Gerald Green. See also the *New York Times*, 23 April 1978, 30 April 1978.

19. See Paula Hyman, "New Debate on the Holocaust," *New York Times Magazine*, 14 September 1980; *SH'MA*, 2 November 1979, 16 November 1979.

20. For a detailed account of the revisionists, see Lucy Dawidowicz, "Lies About the Holocaust," *Commentary*, December 1980, pp. 31–37. Authors of these works include Paul Rassinier and Robert Faurisson (France), and Harry Barnes, David Hoggan, and Arthur Butz (United States). *The Hoax of the Twentieth Century* (Noontide Press, 1977) by Butz, a professor of electrical engineering at Northwestern University, prompted a lecture series in which Elie Wiesel and three other speakers addressed themselves to those seeking to deny the Holocaust. See Wiesel's speech "The Holocaust as Literary Imagination," in *Dimensions of the Holocaust: Lectures at Northwestern University* (Evanston: Northwestern Univ. 1977), pp. 5–19.

21. Malka, "Au crépuscule du souvenir," 11 June 1970.

22. Edelman, "Conversation," p. 19.

23. Wiesel has composed a cantata, *Ani Maamin: A Song Lost and Found Again*, trans. Marion Wiesel (New York: Random House, 1973), based on the theme of the silence of God who refused to speak out when confronted by the horrors of the Holocaust. The work was presented in November 1973 at Carnegie Hall, New York, and set to music by Darius Milhaud. See also Wiesel's *The Trial of God (As it was held on February 25, 1649 in Shamgorod)*, trans. Marion Wiesel (New York: Random House, 1979).

24. See Elie Wiesel, *The Jews of Silence: A Personal Report on Soviet Jewry* (New York: Holt, Rinehart & Winston, 1966). The title refers to the Jews of the Soviet Union immured in their fearful silence, but also to the world Jewish community that does not speak out about their repression.

25. Edelman, "Conversation," p. 14. See also Janine Launay, Judith Schwarz, and Lucienne Serrano, "In Conversation with Elie Wiesel," *Centerpoint*, Spring, 1975; pp. 63–66, where Wiesel reveals how he condensed *The Oath* from 800 to 250 pages. He says that he rewrites each book three times, until it is at the point of bursting: "J'ai là l'ideé générale d'un livre que j'espère être très condensé, très serré, si tendu qu'il semble sur le point d'éclater. Et c'est l'éclatement qui fait sa valeur" (p. 64).

26. Elie Wiesel, in Keith Runyon, "Elie Wiesel—Silence Bred from the Understanding of Jewish 'Burden,' " *Courier Journal* (Louisville), 29 November 1973, p. B23.

27. Edelman, "Conversation," p. 19.

28. André Neher, in "Le silence et l'être: Elie Wiesel," *L'Exil de la parole* (Paris: Editions du Seuil, 1970), discusses the phenomenological, scenic, and theological aspects of silence in Wiesel's work.

29. Terrence Des Pres, "The Authority of Silence in Elie Wiesel's Art," in *Confronting the Holocaust: The Impact of Elie Wiesel*, ed. Alvin Rosenfeld and Irving Greenberg (Bloomington: Indiana Univ. Press, 1978), p. 55.

30. Frederick Garber, "The Art of Elie Wiesel," *Judaism* 22 (1973): 301.

31. See Lawrence S. Cunningham, "Elie Wiesel's Anti-Exodus," in *Responses to Elie Wiesel*, pp. 23–28.

32. Elie Wiesel, *From Holocaust to Rebirth* (New York: Council of Jewish Federations and Welfare Funds, 1970), p. 3.

33. For a distinction between healthy and unhealthy silences, see *Harry James Cargas in Conversation*, pp. 45–46; *Beggar in Jerusalem*, p. 108.

34. Wiesel often evokes the image of a gathering in some secret enclave of all Holocaust survivors, assembled in a kind of mystical union and making a group decision not to speak of their experience. See *One Generation After*, p. 8, and Edelman, "Conversation," p. 19. In June 1981 such a mass meeting took place in Jerusalem, Israel, with the objective to formulate a manifesto. Elie Wiesel served as honorary chairman of this "World Gathering of Jewish Holocaust Survivors."

35. The theme of *the last witness* recurs throughout Wiesel's works. See *Legends of Our Time* (112); *A Beggar in Jerusalem* (79–80); "The Holocaust as Literary Inspiration," p. 18.

36. Edelman, "Conversation," p. 17. Wiesel reveals: "In 1945, 1946, 1947 I went through the same kind of depression, asking: 'What for? What's the use?' And today the situation is more discouraging. My young man is a special person—he is the son of a survivor, a tragic figure who feels left out, useless. I made him unclear intentionally."

37. Enid Dame, "The Vital Connection," *Congress Bi-Weekly*, 8 February 1974, p. 19.

38. Review of *Le Serment de Kolvillàg, Bulletin du Cercle Juif* (Montreal), March 1974, p. 21. See also Regina Rittel, "Le silence et la parole," *L'Arche*, May–June 1973, pp. 64–65.

39. Edelman, "Conversation," p. 20. Wiesel also notes: "Ma voix est une sorte de réceptacle. J'essaie d'y capter d'autres voix, et ensuite, je les rends mais elles retiennent quelque chose de la mienne, bien sûr, certains teints, certains tons," in Launay, Schwarz and Serrano, "In Conversation," *Centerpoint*, p. 64.

40. See Elie Wiesel, "Etre Juif, c'est quoi?" *Figaro Littéraire*, 10–16 February 1969, p. 11.

41. For a description of the role of the *Zaddik* in Hasidism, see Gershom Scholem, *Major Trends in Jewish Mysticism* (New York: Schocken, 1941), pp. 337–50. Wiesel has been likened to a *Zaddik* by Roger Berg in "Des Juifs en Europe Centrale," *Journal des Communautés*, 13 July 1973 and Arnold Mandel "Le hassidisme à la splendeur multiple," *L'Arche*, 26 January 1972.

42. Kaufman and Koppel, *A Small Measure of Victory*, p. 14.

43. "Beyond Survival," *European Judaism* 6 (Winter 1971–72): 5.

44. Edelman, "Conversation," p. 13.

45. *Harry James Cargas in Conversation*, p. 84. See also pp. 87, 67.

46. Dan Vogel, "When Silence Is Criminal," *Jerusalem Post*, 1 April 1974.

47. *Harry James Cargas in Conversation*, p. 7.

48. Ibid., p. 86. The importance of listening is stressed throughout Wiesel's work. See *A Beggar in Jerusalem:* "Do you know that it is given to us to enrich a legend simply by listening to it? It belongs as much to the listener as to

the teller. You listen to a tale, and all of a sudden it is no longer the same tale" (p. 107). See also Lia Lacombe, "Elie Wiesel: 'Les autres existent tellement que si on sait les écouter, on peut les incorporer à nous,'" *Lettres Françaises,* 16–22 May 1963.

49. Elie Wiesel, in Claudine Jardin, "Elie Wiesel: Conteur de nuit," *Figaro,* 25 March 1970. He also reveals: "Il faut parler pour pouvoir s'ouvrir, s'épanouir et rayonner. C'est sans doute pour cela que je suis écrivain" (Paul Kleim, "Elie Wiesel: une des voix les plus pures de ce temps," *Tribune de Genève,* 4 December 1968, p. 5).

50. *Harry James Cargas in Conversation,* p. 6.

51. "Jewish Values in the Post-Holocaust Future: A Symposium," *Judaism* 16 (1967): 285.

52. *Harry James Cargas in Conversation,* p. 113.

53. Elie Wiesel, in Victor Malka, "Elie Wiesel: joie et lumière," *Nouvelles Littéraires,* 31 January 1972.

54. Edmond Jabès, *Le Livre des ressemblances* (Paris: Gallimard, 1976), p. 139.

55. Ibid., p. 59.

6. My Father Is a Book

1. Czeslaw Milosz, *The Captive Mind* (New York: Alfred Knopf, 1953), p. x.

2. Arnold Ages, "Interview with Elie Wiesel on the publication of *The Testament,*" *St. Louis Jewish Light,* 4 June 1980, p. 7. Wiesel has indicated that his grandfather was a fervent follower of the Rebbe of Wisnitz. See *The Gates of the Forest,* p. 11.

3. See Nadezhda Mandelstam, *Hope Against Hope: A Memoir* (New York: Atheneum, 1980), p. 170.

4. Joseph Brodsky, "Nadezhda Mandelstam (1899–1980)," *New York Review of Books,* 5 March 1981, p. 3. See also Czeslaw Milosz, "The Nobel Lecture," ibid. pp. 11–15.

Selected Bibliography

I. Works of Elie Wiesel

Books in French

L'Aube [récit]. Paris: Editions du Seuil, 1960.
Célébration biblique [portraits et légends]. Paris: Editions du Seuil, 1975.
Célébration hassidique [portraits et légendes]. Paris: Editions du Seuil, 1972. (Prix Bordin de l'Academie Française.)
Le Chant des morts [essais et récits]. Paris: Editions du Seuil, 1966.
Contre la Mélancolie: Célébration hassidique II [Portraits et légendes]. Paris: Editions du Seuil, 1981.
Entre deux soleils [essais et récits]. Paris: Editions du Seuil, 1970.
Le Jour [roman]. Paris: Editions du Seuil, 1961.
Un Juif, aujourd'hui [récits, essais, dialogues]. Paris: Editions du Seuil, 1977.
Les Juifs du silence [témoignage]. Paris: Editions du Seuil, 1966.
Le Mendiant de Jérusalem [roman]. Paris: Editions du Seuil, 1968. (Prix Médicis, 1968.)
La Nuit [témoignage], préface de François Mauriac. Paris: Editions de Minuit, 1958.
Les Portes de la forêt [roman]. Paris: Editions du Seuil, 1964.
Le Procès de Shamgorod (tel qu'il se déroula le 25 février 1649) [théatre]. Paris: Editions du Seuil, 1979.
Le Serment de Kolvillàg [roman]. Paris: Editions du Seuil, 1973.
Le Testament d'un poète juif assassiné [roman]. Paris: Editions du Seuil, 1980. (Prix Inter, 1980.)
La Ville de la chance [roman]. Paris: Editions du Seuil, 1962. (Prix Rivarol, 1964.)
Zalmen ou la folie de Dieu [théâtre]. Paris: Editions du Seuil, 1968.

Books in English

The Accident. Translated by Anne Borchardt. New York: Hill & Wang, 1962.
Ani Maamin: A Song Lost and Found Again. Translated by Marion Wiesel. New York: Random House, 1973.

A Beggar in Jerusalem. Translated by Lily Edelman and Elie Wiesel. New York: Random House, 1970.

Dawn. Translated by Frances Frenayne. New York: Hill & Wang, 1961.

Four Hasidic Masters and Their Struggle Against Melancholy. Notre Dame, Ind.: Univ. of Notre Dame Press, 1978.

Five Biblical Portraits. Notre Dame, Ind.: University of Notre Dame Press, 1981.

The Gates of the Forest. Translated by Frances Frenayne. New York: Holt, Rinehart & Winston, 1966.

The Jews of Silence: A Personal Report on Soviet Jewry. Translated from the Hebrew by Neal Kozodoy. New York: Holt, Rinehart & Winston, 1966.

A Jew Today. Translated by Marion Wiesel. New York: Random House, 1978.

Legends of Our Time. Translated by Steven Donadio. New York: Holt, Rinehart & Winston, 1968.

Messengers of God: Biblical Portraits and Legends. Translated by Marion Wiesel. New York: Random House, 1976.

Night. Translated by Stella Rodway; foreword by François Mauriac. New York: Hill & Wang, 1960.

The Oath. Translated by Marion Wiesel. New York: Random House, 1973.

One Generation After. Translated by Lily Edelman and Elie Wiesel. New York: Random House, 1970.

Souls on Fire: Portraits and Legends of Hasidic Masters. Translated by Marion Wiesel. New York: Random House, 1972.

The Testament. Translated by Marion Wiesel. New York: Summit Books, 1981.

The Town Beyond the Wall. Translated by Stephen Becker. New York: Holt, Rinehart & Winston, 1964.

The Trial of God (As it was held on February 25, 1649 in Shamgorod). Translated by Marion Wiesel. New York: Random House, 1978.

Zalmen or the Madness of God. Translated by Nathan Edelman; adapted for the stage by Marion Wiesel. New York: Random House, 1974.

Articles, Addresses, Prefaces, Reviews

Against Despair. New York: United Jewish Appeal, 1974. Proceedings of address delivered December 8, 1973 at U.J.A. National Conference (15-page pamphlet).

"Art and Culture after the Holocaust." In *Auschwitz: Beginning of a New Era? Reflections on the Holocaust*, ed. Eva Fleischner. New York: Ktav Pub. House, 1977.

Donat, Alexander. Preface to his *Veilleur, où en est la nuit?* Paris: Editions du Seuil, 1967.

"Etre juif c'est quoi?" *Le Figaro Littéraire*, 10–16 February 1969, p. 11.

"The Fiery Shadow—Jewish Existence Out of the Holocaust." In *Jewish Existence in an Open Society: A Convocation*. Los Angeles: Jewish Centers Association, Anderson, Ritchie and Simon, 1970, pp. 39–49.

"For Some Measure of Humility." *Sh'ma*, 31 October 1975, pp. 314–15.

"Freedom of Conscience and the Jewish Holocaust." In *Religious Liberty in the Crossfire of Creeds*, ed. Franklin H. Littell. Philadelphia: Ecumenical Press, 1978.

From Holocaust to Rebirth. New York: The Council of Jewish Federations and Welfare Funds, 1970. Proceedings of address given on November 14, 1970 in Kansas City, Missouri (12-page pamphlet).

Gross, Theodore. ed. Preface to *The Literature of American Jews*, ed. by him. New York: Free Press, 1973.

"Hasidism and Man's Love of Man." *Jewish Heritage* 14 (1972): 6–12.

"The Holocaust and the Future." In *The Holocaust: Its Meaning for Christians and Jews*. St. Louis: National Conference of Christians and Jews, 1977. Introductory address delivered November 3, 1976.

"The Holocaust as Literary Inspiration." In *Dimensions of the Holocaust: Lectures at Northwestern University*. Evanston, Ill.: Northwestern Univ., 1977.

"L'Honneur d'être sioniste." *Le Figaro*, 14 November 1975.

"Une interview d'Elie Wiesel: Golda Meir ou l'art d'être grand-mère." *L'Arche*, 26 October–25 November 1971 pp. 47–51.

"The Itinerary of Elie Wiesel: From Sighet to Jerusalem." *The Eternal Light*. National Broadcasting Co. TV script written and narrated by Elie Wiesel, broadcast 21 May 1972.

"Jewish Values in the Post-Holocaust Future: A Symposium." *Judaism* 16 (1967): 266–99.

"Ominous Signs and Unspeakable Thoughts." Editorial, *New York Times*, 28 December 1974, p. 23.

"On Being a Jew." *Jewish Heritage* 10 (1967): 51–55. Proceedings of address delivered at commencement exercises of the Jewish Theological Seminary of America, 4 June 1967.

"On Revolutions in Culture and the Arts." In *Revolutionary Directions in Intellectual and Cultural Production: Their Consequences for the Higher Learning*. New York: Research Foundation of City University of New York, 1975. Address delivered May 4, 1973 at Tenth Anniversary Convocation of Graduate School of City University of New York.

Our Jewish Solitude. New York: United Jewish Appeal, 1976. Address delivered December 11, 1975 on receiving First David Ben Gurion Award (12-page pamphlet).

"Out of the Ashes." *Jewish Heritage* (1970): 19–30. Proceedings of symposium on "Jewish Writers in the Soviet Union," 22 February 1970.

"A Personal Response." *Face to Face: An Interreligious Bulletin*, Spring 1979, pp. 35–37.

"Pilgrimage to the Country of Night." *New York Times Magazine*, 4 November 1979, p. 36.

Review of *Blood from the Sky* by Piotr Rawicz. *Hadassah Magazine*, March 1964, p. 13.

Review of *The House of Ashes* by Oscar Pinkus. *The New York Times Book Review*, 6 September 1964, p. 4.

Review of *Idiots First* by Bernard Malamud and *Herod's Children* by Ilse Aichinger. *Hadassah Magazine*, November 1963, pp. 18–19.

Review of *Incident at Vichy* by Arthur Miller. *Hadassah Magazine*, March 1965, pp. 11–12.

Review of *The Liberation of the Jew* by Albert Memmi. *The New York Times Book Review*, 26 March 1967, p. 6.

Review of *The Painted Bird* by Jerzy Kosinski. *The New York Times Book Review*, 31 October, 1965, p. 5.

Review of *The Terezin Requiem* by Josef Bor, *The New York Times Book Review*, 27 October 1963, p. 4.

Review of *While Six Million Died: A Chronicle of American Apathy* by Arthur D. Morse; and *The Holocaust: The Destruction of European Jewry* by Nora Levin. *Hadassah Magazine*, March 1968, 16–17.

Roth, John. Prologue to his *A Consuming Fire: Encounters with Elie Wiesel and the Holocaust*. Atlanta; John Knox Press, 1979.

"Survivors' Children Relive the Holocaust." *The New York Times*, 16 November 1975.

"Talking and Writing and Keeping Silent." In *The German Church Struggle and the Holocaust*, eds. Franklin H. Littell and Hubert G. Locke. Detroit: Wayne State University Press, 1974, pp. 269–277.

"Telling the Tale." *Dimensions of American Judaism* 2 (1968): 9 12; 3 (1968): 35

"Le Témoin et sa vérité." *L'Arche*, April 1967.

"Then and Now: the Experiences of a Teacher," *Social Education*, April 1948, pp. 10–15.

"Trivializing the Holocaust: Semi-Fact and Semi-Fiction." *The New York Times*, 16 April 1978, Section D, pp. 1, 29.

Two Images, One Destiny. New York: United Jewish Appeal, 1974. Address delivered June 1974 at Jewish Agency Assembly in Jerusalem (14-page pamphlet).

"Why I Write." In *Confronting the Holocaust: The Impact of Elie Wiesel*, eds. Alvin H. Rosenfeld and Irving Greenberg. Bloomington: Indiana University Press, 1978, pp. 200–206.

"Words from a Witness." *Conservative Judaism* 21 (1967): 40–48.

II. Works about Elie Wiesel*

Books

Abramowitz, Molly. *Elie Wiesel: A Bibliography*. The Scarecrow Author Bibliographies, No. 22. Metuchen, N.J.: Scarecrow Press, 1974.

Alexander, Edward. *The Resonance of Dust: Essays on Holocaust Literature and Jewish Fate*. Columbus: Ohio State Univ. Press, 1979.

*All the works listed do not treat Wiesel's texts uniquely but do contain information pertinent to a study of his work.

Alter, Robert. "Elie Wiesel: Between Hangman and Victim." In his *After the Tradition*, pp. 151–60. New York: E.P. Dutton, 1969.

Berenbaum, Michael G. *The Vision of the Void: Theological Reflections on the Works of Elie Wiesel*. Middletown, Conn.: Wesleyan Univ. Press, 1979.

Bosmajian, Hamida. *Metaphors of Evil: Contemporary German Literature and the Shadow of Nazism*. Iowa City: Univ. of Iowa Press, 1979.

Cargas, Harry James. *Harry James Cargas in Conversation with Elie Wiesel*. New York: Paulist Press, 1976.

————, ed. *Responses to Elie Wiesel: Critical Essays by Major Jewish and Christian Scholars*. New York: Persea Books, 1978.

Chouraqui, Bernard. "La tentative." In his *Le Scandale Juif ou la subversion de la mort*, pp. 160–173. Paris: Editions Libres Hallier, 1979.

Des Pres, Terrence. *The Survivor: An Anatomy of Life in the Death Camps*. New York: Oxford Univ. Press, 1976.

Estess, Ted L. *Elie Wiesel*. New York: Frederick Ungar Pub. Co., 1980.

Ezrahi, Sidra DeKoven. *By Words Alone: The Holocaust in Literature*. Chicago: Univ. of Chicago Press, 1980.

Friedman, Maurice. "The Dialogue with the Absurd: The Later Camus and Franz Kafka; Elie Wiesel and the Modern Job." In his *To Deny Our Nothingness: Contemporary Images of Man*, pp. 335–54. New York: Dell Pub. Co., 1967.

————. "Elie Wiesel: The Job of Auschwitz." In his *The Hidden Human Image*, pp. 106–34. New York: Dell Pub. Co., 1974.

Haft, Cynthia. *The Theme of Nazi Concentration Camps in French Literature*. The Hague, Netherlands: Mouton, 1973.

Halperin, Irving. "From *Night* to the *Gates of the Forest*: The Novels of Elie Wiesel." In his *Messengers from the Dead: Literature of the Holocaust*, pp. 65–106. Philadelphia: Westminster Press, 1970.

Kahn, Lothar. "Elie Wiesel: Neo-Hasidism." In his *Mirrors of the Jewish Mind: A Gallery of Portraits of European Jewish Writers of Our Time*, pp. 176–93. New York: Thomas Yoseloff, 1968.

Kazin, Alfred. "The Least of These." In his *Contemporaries*. pp. 296–300. Boston: Little, Brown, 1962.

Knopp, Josephine Z. "The Holocaust: Elie Wiesel." In her *The Trial of Judaism in Contemporary Jewish Writing*, pp. 70–102. Urbana: Univ. of Illinois Press, 1975.

Langer, Lawrence L. "The Dominion of Death." In his *The Holocaust and the Literary Imagination*, pp. 74–123. New Haven, Conn.: Yale Univ. Press, 1975.

————. *The Age of Atrocity*. Boston: Beacon Press, 1978.

Neher, André. "Le silence et l'être: Elie Wiesel." In his *L'Exil de la parole: Du silence biblique au silence d'Auschwitz*, pp. 228–45. Paris: Editions du Seuil, 1970.

Rosenfeld, Alvin H. *A Double Dying: Reflections on Holocaust Literature*. Bloomington: Indiana Univ. Press, 1980.

Rosenfeld, Alvin H., and Greenberg, Irving, eds. *Confronting the Holocaust: The Impact of Elie Wiesel*. Bloomington: Indiana Univ. Press, 1978.

Roth, John K. *A Consuming Fire: Encounters with Elie Wiesel and the Holocaust.* Prologue by Elie Wiesel. Atlanta, Ga.: John Knox Press, 1979.

Schneersohn, Isaac, ed. *D'Auschwitz à Israel: Vingt ans après la liberation.* Paris: Centre de Documentation Juive Contemporaine, 1968.

Sherwin, Byron L., and Ament, Susan G., eds. *Encountering the Holocaust: An Interdisciplinary Survey.* Chicago: Impact Press, 1979.

Simon, Pierre-Henri. "Elie Wiesel, Prix Rivarol, 1963." In his *Diagnostic des lettres françaises contemporaines,* pp. 287–91. Paris: Renaissance du Livre, 1966.

Steiner, George. *Language and Silence: Essays on Language, Literature and the Inhuman.* New York: Atheneum, 1967.

Periodicals

The following bibliography of published interviews and articles on Elie Wiesel derives principally from French sources. For bibliographies of works on Wiesel in English, see Molly Abramowitz, *Elie Wiesel: A Bibliography* (Metuchen, N.J.: Scarecrow Press, 1974); and Irving Abrahamson, "Elie Wiesel: A Selected Bibliography" in *Confronting the Holocaust: The Impact of Elie Wiesel,* eds. Alvin H. Rosenfeld and Irving Greenberg (Bloomington: Indiana University Press, 1978). Articles of special interest will be indicated by an asterisk.

General

Baudy, Nicholas. "Elie Wiesel ou les vraies dimensions de la connaissance." *Les Nouveaux Cahiers,* Fall 1966, pp. 39–45.

"Building a Moral Society: Aspects of Elie Wiesel's Work." *Face to Face: An Interreligious Bulletin,* Spring 1979 (entire issue devoted to Wiesel).

Derczanski, Alex. "Comprendre Wiesel." *Esprit,* September 1980, pp. 93–94.

"Entretien avec Elie Wiesel." *Tribune Juive* (Strasbourg), 3–9 March 1972, 16–19.

Fine, Ellen. "Dialogue with Elie Wiesel." *Centerpoint: A Journal of Interdisciplinary Studies,* (New York) Fall 1980, pp. 19–25.

Finkelstein, Sidney. "Elie Wiesel's Spiritual Journey: The Jeremiah of the Holocaust seen as in Jewish Isolation." *Jewish Currents,* May 1967, pp. 22–28.

Fiske, Edward B. "Elie Wiesel: Archivist with a Mission." *New York Times,* 31 January 1973, pp. 34, 64.

Friedman, Maurice. "Witness and Rebellion: The Unresolved Tension in the Works of Elie Wiesel." *Judaism* 28 (1979): 484–91.

Garber, Frederick. "The Art of Elie Wiesel." *Judaism* 22 (1973): 301–8.

Goulston, Michael and Anthony Rudolf. "Beyond Survival." (Interview with Elie Wiesel and Eugene Heimler.) *European Judaism* 6 (Winter 1971–72): 4–10.

Green, Mary Jean. "Witness to the Absurd: Elie Wiesel and the French Existentialists." *Renascence* 29 (1977): 170–184.

Halperin, Jean. "Un messager du passé et de l'avenir." *Tribune Juive*, 3–9 March 1972, p. 12.

Haymann, Emmanuel. "Elie Wiesel: Témoin de la nuit." *Tribune Juive*, 3–9 March 1972, 10–11.

Hyams, Barry. "Witness and Messenger." *The Reconstructionist*, 28 October 1966, 15–20.

Idinopulous, Thomas A. "The Holocaust in the Stories of Elie Wiesel." *Soundings* 60, (1972): 200–215.

Kahn, Lothar. "French-Jewish Writers: An Overview." *Jewish Book Annual* 25 (1967–68): 60–69.

Kaufmann, Henry and Gene Koppel. *Elie Wiesel: A Small Measure of Victory, An Interview*. Tucson: Univ. of Arizona, 1974 (28–page pamphlet).

Laporte, Marc. "Elie Wiesel: D'Auschwitz à Hiroshima." *L'Express*, 6 June 1963, p. 34.

Lovsky, F. "Elie Wiesel, compagnon des morts d'Israël." *Foi et Vie*, 68 (1968): 36–58.

Rabi, Wladmir. "Elie Wiesel: Un homme, une oeuvre, un public." *Esprit*, September 1980, pp. 79–92.

Reichek, Morton. "Elie Wiesel: Out of the Night." *Present* Tense, Spring 1976, pp. 41–47.

Sherwin, Byron. "Elie Wiesel and Jewish Theology." *Judaism* 18 (1969): 39–52.

———"Elie Wiesel on Madness." *Central Conference* of American Rabbis, 19 (1972): 24–32.

"Le Témoignage d'Elie Wicsel: Un dossier." *Tribune Juive*, 3–9 March 1972, pp. 9–19 (entire issue devoted to Wiesel).

L'Aube

L'Action Laïque, February 1961.

Bercher, Marie-Louise. "Chronique littéraire." *L'Alsace*, 30 June 1960.

Berthier, Pierre. "Une Oeuvre grande et tragique." *La Cité* (Brussels), 16 June 1960.

La Boucherie Française, 1 March 1961.

"Bourreau de soi-même." *La Gazette de Lausanne*, 2 June 1960.

Brierre, Annie. "*L'Aube* par Elie Wiesel." *Nouvelles Littéraires*, 7 July 1960.

Bulletin Bibliographique de l'Institut Pédagogique National, January 1961.

Bulletin Critique du Livre Français, 16 (1961): 191.

Bulletin des Lettres, 15 November 1960.

Bulletin du Cercle Juif (Montreal), June-July 1960, p. 3.

Cassou, Jean. "Le Pèse-Lettres—*L'Aube*." *Le Peuple* (Brussels), 21 June 1960.

*Castelnau, Marie-Pierre. "Les Lettres: *L'Aube*." *L'Information d'Israel*, 26 May 1960.

Chavardès, Maurice. "La Fin de l'illusion lyrique." *L'Observateur littéraire*, 7 July 1960.

Croix de l'Est, 9 October 1960.

Daoust, René. *"L'Aube."* *Relations* (Montreal), March 1961.

De Coninck, Marie-Claire. "La Tragédie du peuple juif." *Le Courrier,* 9 September 1960.

Demeuse, Pierre, *"L'Aube."* *Le Peuple* (Brussels), 21 June 1960.

Dizon, Vincent. *"L'Aube."* *Le Crestois,* 3 September 1960.

Documentation, November 1960.

*Estang, Luc. *"L'Aube."* *Le Figaro Littéraire,* 18 June 1960, p. 15.

*Feldman, Irving. "After the Death Camps." *Commentary,* September 1961, pp. 262–64.

Fransen, A. M. *"L'Aube."* *La Revue Nouvelle,* 15 February 1961.

Garzouzi, Calypso. *"L'Aube."* *Journal d'Alexandrie,* 9 September 1962.

La Gazette de Libre Belgique, 10 June 1960.

Hamelin, Jean. "La Vie littéraire." *La Presse* (Montreal), 10 September 1960.

Hertz, Henri. "Les Lettres." *Vie Juive,* October 1960, pp. 22–24.

*Kahn, Lothar. "What Price Jewish Bravery?" *The Reconstructionist,* 29 June, 1962, pp. 14–18.

Kiesel, Frédéric. "Du conte au 'roman' de poète." *Métropole,* 5 June 1960.

Lalou, René. *"L'Aube."* *Les Annales,* September 1960.

———. "Le Goût des livres." Radio-Diffusion, France III, 22 June 1960.

La Libre Belgique, 2 June 1960.

"Les livres: *L'Aube."* *Revue Université Laval,* June 1961.

*Mitgang, Herbert. "An Eye for an Eye." *New York Times Book Review,* 16 July 1961, p. 23.

Naguère, Madeleine. *"L'Aube."* *Le Petit Matin,* 18 June 1960.

Petit, Henri. "Elie Wiesel, *L'Aube:* Deux hommes devant la mort." *Le Parisien Libéré,* 7 June 1960, p. 6.

Philippon, Henri. "Une histoire émouvante." *Paris-Jour,* 8 June 1960, p. 14.

"Pour Elie Wiesel une 'Aube' sanglante succède à la 'Nuit.' " *Tribune de Genève,* 9 December 1960.

"Un Roman de la lucidité: *L'Aube* d'Elie Wiesel (peut-on tuer?)" *Oise-Matin,* 19 July 1960.

*Rudel, Yves-Marie. *"L'Aube."* *Ouest-France,* 22 July 1960.

Saulnier, Adam. *"L'Aube,* un beau livre d'homme." *Force Ouvrière,* 1 June 1960.

Schepmans, Jacques. "Valeur de l'Homme." *La Cité* (Brussels), 9 June 1960.

Trait d'Union, September–October 1960.

*Van Gerdinge, René. "Le Crépuscule de l'aube." *Témoin de la Vie,* 7 June 1960.

Varonnes, Jean-Charles. "L'Aveuglante vérité de l'homme." *Centre-Matin,* 6 January 1960, p. 8.

———. "Ce monde où nous vivons." *Centre-Matin,* 1 June 1960.

"Vient de paraître." *La Croix,* 5–6 June 1960.

Voici Pourquoi, 4 July 1960.

"La Vraie réalité." *Lettres-Françaises,* No. 837, 1960.

Wintzen, René. *"L'Aube* d'Elie Wiesel." *Témoignage Chrétien,* 17 June 1960.

*Ziegler, Jean. "Les Nouveaux 'Justes': Un roman, *L'Aube,* décrit l'organisation secrète des ravisseurs d'Eichmann." *La Gazette de Lausanne,* 9 July 1960.

Célébration biblique

Adler, Daniel. "Démons et merveilles." *Presse Nouvelle Hebdo*, 30 January 1977.

Alys, Marc. "Entrez dans la Bible." *Le Figaro*, 15 December 1975.

Ami d'Israel, March 1976.

"Au Hasard des lectures: *Célébration biblique*." *Amitiés France-Israel*, June 1976.

Berg, Roger. "*Célébration biblique*." *Le Journal des Communautés*, December 1975.

"La Bible au coeur." *Cahiers du Livre Chrétien*, January 1976.

Le Bibliothécaire, April 1976.

Bibliothèque pour Tous, January 1976.

Boly, Joseph. "*Célébration biblique*." *Quatre Millions Quatre*, 4 December 1975.

Bulletin des Lettres, January 1976.

Butheau, R. "Dieu et les chrétiens dans le monde contemporain." *Le Progrès de Lyon*, January 1976.

Cahiers Bernard Lazare, January–February 1976.

Camby-Darmon, Judith. "Le Juif du XXème siècle." *Cahiers du Centre Communautaire Laïc Juif*, April 1976.

Centre National des Vocations, March 1976.

Choulet, Antoine. "*Célébration biblique*." *Vie Chrétienne*, July 1976.

Christianisme au XXème siècle, 5 January 1976.

"Conversation avec Elie Wiesel." *Panorama d'Aujourd'hui*, February 1976.

Dossiers Documentaires, No. 49, 1976 (Ref. 18135).

Franck, B. "La Bible pour notre temps." *La Tribune Juive* (Strasbourg), 5 March 1976.

Guichard, A. "Vive émotion après le vote du 16ème Colloque des Intellectuels juifs de langue française." *Le Monde*, 13 November 1975.

Horald, Patrice. "Les démences." *L'Alsace*, 18 March 1977.

"Image de l'Ancien Testament." *Témoignage Chrétien*, 25 December 1975.

Keller, J. P. "Moeurs d'aujourd'hui." *Les Dernières Nouvelles*, 28 December 1975.

*Kleim, Paul. "La Bible, vous connaissez?" *La Tribune de Genève*, 22 February 1977.

Le Clec'h, Guy. "Les Juifs du commencement." *La Terre Retrouvée*, 1 January 1976.

"Lu pour vous . . . *Célébration biblique*." *Le Républicain Lorrain*, 7 December 1975.

Lys, Daniel. "*Célébration biblique*." *Elle*, 24 November 1975.

*Malka, Victor. "Job ou la mémoire juive." *Nouvelles Littéraires*, 15 December 1975.

Marissel, André. "Chronique: *Célébration biblique*." *Paix et Liberté Hebdo* (Brussels), 16 January 1976.

"Misdrah Elie," *L'Arche*, January 1976.

Notre Communauté, March-April 1976.

Nouailhac, A. M. "*Célébration biblique*." *SIDIC*, [Société Internationale pour le Developpement Industrial et Commercial], 1 (1976).

"Nous avons reçu . . ." *La Revue de la Wiso*, January 1976.

Perchenet, Annie. "*Célébration biblique*." *Sens*, April 1976.

Potin, Jacques. "Un rendez-vous avec les grandes figures de la Bible." *La Croix,* 11 January 1976.

"Pour le Judaîsme, un misdrah d'Elie Wiesel." *Le Monde,* 28 May 1976.

Renaissance de Fleury, Pâques [Easter] 1976.

Revue Encyclopédique Juive, March 1976.

"Rubrique des livres." *SIDIC,* 1975.

Simon, U. E. "*Célébration biblique.*" *Society for Old Testament Study,* 1977.

"Spiritualité: *Célébration biblique* d'Elie Wiesel." *Lire,* February 1976.

La Suisse (Geneva), 24 December 1975.

La Terre Retrouvée, 20 July 1976.

"Vient de paraître: *Célébration biblique* d'Elie Wiesel." Nouvelles Littéraires, 24 November 1975.

Célébration hassidique

Allouche, Jean-Luc. "*Célébration hassidique.*" *Le Rayol,* April, 1972.

Ami d'Israël, 2 November 1972, p. 29.

Arnothy, Christine. "Le passé, composé de chagrins." *Le Parisien Libéré,* 22 February 1972.

Bandler, Michael. "A Nostalgic Glimpse at Hasidism." *Commonweal,* 28 April 1972, pp. 194–96.

Berthier, Pierre. "Un vivant et un mort." *La Cité* (Brussels), 16 January 1972.

Bulletin Critique du Livre Français, January 1973.

Cahiers Bernard Lazare, August 1972, p. 38.

"*Célébration hassidique:* Un livre et une conférence d'Elie Wiesel." *Méridional,* 25 January 1972.

Choisir (Geneva), November 1972.

Le Christianisme du XXe Siècle, 2 March 1972.

*Clairet, Joseph-Pierre, "Aux Sources d'Eugène Ionesco." *Le Phare,* 13 August 1972.

Coopération (Basel), September 1972.

Cousty, Paulette, "Un livre singulier." *Le Populaire du Centre,* 8 February 1972.

Derville, Anne. "L'Ardente quête de Dieu d'un juif déporté à quinze ans." (Interview.) *La Vie Catholique Illustrée,* 22 March 1972, pp. 33–34.

"Elie Wiesel à Toulouse." *Aviv* (Toulouse), February 1972, p. 20.

"Elie Wiesel à Toulouse: 'Le hassidisme, c'est la dimension esthétique du judaïsme.' " *La Dépêche du Midi,* 27 January 1972.

*"Elie Wiesel, l'orant." *Techniques Nouvelles,* March 1972.

*Ertel, Rachel. "Dans la tradition yiddish." *La Quinzaine Littéraire,* 16–31 March 1972, pp. 6–8.

Grandjean, Michèle. "Elie Wiesel au Centre Edmond-Fleg," *Provençal,* 26 January 1972.

Guye, Simone. "Le Livre dont on parle." *Vie Protestante,* 18 February 1972.

Halperin, Jean. "Le Chant de la mémoire." *Information Juive,* March 1972.

Hruby, K. *"Célébration hassidique."* SIDIC [Société Internationale pour le Développement Industriel et Commercial], March 1972, pp. 41–42.

Information Catholiques Internationales, 15 April 1972.

Juin, Hubert. "Puissance de la légende." *Les Lettres Françaises,* 2 February 1972.

*Kaufmann, Francine. "Actualité du hassidisme: Mais comment peut-on être hassid?" *La Terre Retrouvée,* 15 May 1972.

———. "Deux écrivains de la colère." (James Baldwin and Elie Wiesel), *L'Arche,* August 1972, pp. 19–20.

Kiehl, Roger. "Hier à Strasbourg, Elie Wiesel a évoqué pour les étudiants juifs le hassidisme tel qu'il l'a connu." *Dernières Nouvelles d'Alsace,* 28 January 1972.

Kleim, Paul. "Célébration hassidique." *La Tribune de Genève,* 23 January 1973.

*Kolbert, Jack. *"Célébration hassidique."* The French Review,* 66 (1973): 673–674.

Kollender, Yves. "Elie Wiesel ou le buisson ardent." *Tribune Juive* (Strasbourg), 28 January 1972, pp. 19–20.

Lapouge, Gilles. "Retour à la joie." *France-Soir,* 20 January 1972.

Lascault, Gilbert. "La Prose de Chagall." *Art Vivant,* May 1972.

*Le Clec'h, Guy. *"Célébration hassidique* d'Elie Wiesel." *La Terre Retrouvée,* 1 February 1972.

La Libre Belgique, 16 November 1972.

*Malka, Victor. "Elie Wiesel: Joie et lumière." (Interview.) *Nouvelles Littéraires,* 31 January 1972.

*Mandel, Arnold. "Le Hassidisme à la splendeur multiple." *L'Arche,* January 1972, pp. 70–71.

———. "Le Hassidisme, célébration ou commémoration?" *Les Nouveaux Cahiers,* Spring 1972, pp. 68–70.

———. "Le Hassidisme dit par Elie Wiesel." *Le Monde,* 11 February 1972.

Marissel, André. "Célébration hassidique." *Esprit,* June 1972, pp. 1092–93.

*Martin-Chauffier, Louis. "Avec Elie Wiesel l'écriture se fait prière." *Le Figaro Littéraire,* 21 January 1972, p. 17.

Meyer, Heinrich. *"Célébration hassidique."* Books Abroad.* April 1973.

Parole et Pain, January–February 1973.

Pasquier, Camille. *"Célébration hassidique."* Témoignage Chrétien,* 23 March 1972.

"Pensée Juive: *Célébration hassidique."* L'Amitié Judéo-Chrétienne de France,* July 1972, p. 156.

Perchenet, Annie. *"Célébration hassidique."* Cahiers Universitaires Catholiques,* February 1973.

Petitdemange, G. *"Célébration hassidique."* Etudes,* March 1972.

"Philosophie." *Informations Industrielles et Commerciales,* 9 October 1972.

Plazy, Gilles. "Pour Elie Wiesel l'amour de Dieu a besoin du rêve et du rire." *Télérama,* 22 July 1972.

Potin, Jacques. "Aux sources de la foi juive." *Croix,* 6 February 1972.

"Récit: *Célébration hassidique."* Christianisme,* 2 March 1972.

La Revue Encyclopédique Juive, December 1971.

Révue Générale (Brussels), No. 3 (1972).

Rondeau, M. J. *"Célébration hassidique."* Bibliographie,* January 1973, pp. 66–67.

Salomon, Jacques. "La Chaîne de transmission." *Israelitische Wochenblatt* (Zurich), 4 February 1972, p. 34.

Scarabbe (Brussels), No. 4, 1972.

*Silberman, Charles E. "How To Live Joyously When There Are No Answers." *New York Times Book Review*, March 5, 1972, pp. 1, 26.

Stéphane, Nelly. "*Célébration hassidique*." *Europe*, April 1972.

Susini, Marie. "Les Fous de Dieu." *Le Nouvel Observateur*, 21 February 1972, pp. 47–48.

"Le Témoignage d'Elie Wiesel." *Liaison*, 3 March 1972, pp. 11–19.

Waynbaum, Maurice. "*Célébration hassidique*." *Les Fiches Bibliographiques*, 1972.

Le Chant des morts

*Alain, Jean-Claude. "Les poids des morts." *Réforme*, 17 September 1966, p. 10.

Allouche, Felix. "Un livre qui est un 'Kaddich.' " *L'Information d'Israël*, August 1966.

Ariel, No. 15 (1967), p. 93.

Arnothy, Christine. "Les lettres: *le Chant des morts*." *Le Parisien Libéré*, 12 July 1966.

Aymon, Jean Paul. "Elie Wiesel, rescapé des camps ou le plaidoyer des morts." *Le Droit de Vivre*, July 1966.

Berg, Roger. "*Le Chant des morts*." *Journal des Communautés*, 22 June 1966.

Berthier, Pierre. "Des nouvelles qui hurlent la misère et la solitude de l'homme: *Le Chant des morts*." *La Cité*, (Brussels), 13–15 August 1966, p. 13.

Buenzod, Emmanuel. "Moments littéraires." *Gazette de Lausanne*, 6–7 August 1966.

Bulletin Critique du Livre Français 12 (1967): 815–16.

Bulletin du Cercle Juif (Montreal), August–September 1966, p. 3.

Burncoa, Charles. "Récits: *Le Chant des morts* par Elie Wiesel." *Nouvelles Littéraires*, 21 July 1966, 4.

Chase, Kathleen. *Books Abroad*, 42 (1968): 76.

"Chronique littéraire." *Paix et Liberté*, 12 June 1966.

Cotta, Michèle. "Entre les lignes: Oui à non et non à oui." *L'Express*, 13–19 June 1966, p. 124.

Dubois, Louis. "Elie Wiesel: *Le Chant des morts*." *Vers l'Avenir*, 26 June 1966.

Fabre, A. "*Le Chant des morts*." *L'Education Nationale*, 15 December 1966, p. 30.

French News, 3 July 1969.

Gentily, A. M. "La Chronique: Le tutoiement." *La Terre Retrouvée*, 1 October 1966, p. 7.

*Haedens, Kleber. "Les Pas et les cris étouffés des amis perdus." *Paris Presse L'Intransigeante*, 18 June 1966.

"In memoriam." *Panorama chrétien*, August 1966.

*Jardin, Claudine. "Pour Elie Wiesel l'homme est devenu juif." *Le Figaro*, 9 June 1966, p. 23.

Kattan, Naim. "Elie Wiesel: Légendes et prières." *Le Devoir* (Montreal), 6 August 1966, Sec. 2, p. 10.

Kieffer, Rosemarie. "Notes de Lecture: *Le Chant des morts*." *Luxemburger Wort*. 9 July 1966.

*Le Clec'h, Guy. "Elie Wiesel entre la mort des siens et la vie des autres." (Interview.) *Le Figaro Littéraire*, 9 June 1966, p. 4.

La Libre Belgique, July 1966.

"Lire ou ne pas lire: *Le Chant des morts*." *La Voix de la Résistance*, 6 July 1966.

"Un Livre par Jour: Perdre la foi?" *La Gazette de Lausanne*, 8 June 1966.

"Livres." *Elle*, 21 July 1966.

Livres et Lectures, November 1966.

Mandel, Arnold. "*Le Chant des morts*." *Information Juive*, October 1966, p. 6.

Notes Bibliographiques, November 1966.

Rabi. W. "Lettres: Elie Wiesel, témoin." *L'Arche*, October 1966, p. 51.

*Ramoni, James. "La Tragédie de Job: Un climat de profonde culpabilité." *La Tribune de Genève*, 30 October 1966.

"Résponse à 'Tréblinka': *Le Chant des morts*." *Le Républicain Lorrain*, 12 July 1966.

*Saporta, Marc. "Entre Auschwitz et Hiroshima." *La Quinzaine Littéraire*, 15 July 1966, p. 7.

Van Gerdinge, René. "La Rançon des morts." *Témoin de la Vie*, 7 September 1966.

"Vient de paraître." *Le Monde*, 4 June 1966, p. 10.

Willy, Renée. "*Le Chant des morts*." *Maroc du Main*, 5 November 1966.

Entre deux soleils

Bulletin Critique du Livre Français, January 1971.

Bulletin du Livre, May 1970.

Cahiers Bernard Lazare, July 1970, p. 47.

La Croix, 18 May 1970.

Dalmais, I. H. "Les Juifs: Histoire et mystère." *Livres et Lectures*, No. 260, pp. 577–78.

La Dépêche du Midi, 18 August 1970.

Dominique. "Elie Wiesel, le droit de vivre et les Juifs du silence." *Le Droit de Vivre*, July 1970.

Fabre, A. "*Entre deux soleils*." *Les Livres*, February 1971.

Hamlin, Colette. "Elie Wiesel: *Entre deux soleils*." *Tout Rouen*, 19 April 1971.

Hermone, Jacques. "Elie Wiesel: *Entre deux soleils*." *Information Juive*, July 1970.

Ikor, Roger. "J'ai peur pour Israël." *Le Figaro Littéraire*, 30 March–5 April 1970, p. 10.

Indications (Brussels) 28, 1971.

* Jardin, Claudine. "Elie Wiesel: Conteur de nuit." *Le Figaro*, 25 May 1970.

Kahn, Lothar. "*Entre deux soleils*." *Books Abroad* (Norman, Okla.), April 1971.

Kleim, Paul. "*Entre deux soleils*." *Coopération* (Basel); 2 March 1972.

*Lapouge, Gilles. "Elie Wiesel, le témoin: Entretien." *La Quinzaine Littéraire*, 16–31 July 1970, 14–15.

La Libre Belgique, 10 July 1970, p. 7.

"La ligne mélodique." *L'Arche*, May 1970, p. 57.

*Malka, Victor. "Au crépuscule du souvenir: Entretien avec Elie Wiesel." *Nouvelles Littéraires*, 11 June 1970.

Méridional, 23 August 1970.

Mespouille, José. "Entre deux soleils." *Vers l'Avenir*, 24 July 1970.

Notre Communauté, June 1970.

*Poliakov, Léon. "Les Interrogations d'Elie Wiesel." *Le Monde*, 22 August 1970, p. 11.

"Prélude à la rentrée littéraire." *Cri du Monde*, September 1970.

Reflet, Michel. *"Entre deux soleils."* *L'Amitié Judeo-Chrétienne*, July–September 1971, p. 36.

La Tribune de Genève, 19 November 1971.

Tribune Juive (Strasbourg), 11 June 1970, p. 23.

Wintzen, René. *"Entre deux soleils."* *Témoignage Chrétien*, 15 May 1970.

Le Jour

Actualité Littéraire, No. 78–79, p. 17.

*Albérès, R. M. "Présence de l'âme." *Nouvelles Littéraires*, 23 March 1961.

Angoff, Charles. "Speaking of Books—*The Accident*." *Jewish Exponent*, 27 April 1962, p. 21.

L'Arche, March 1961, pp. 46–51.

Bercher, Marie-Louise. "Chronique littéraire." *L'Alsace*, 4 May 1961.

Berthier, Pierre. "Un message profond." *Le Cité*, 23 March 1961.

Bulletin Bibliographique de l'Institut Pédagogique, October 1961.

Bulletin Critique du Livre Français, 16 (1961): 363.

Bulletin des Lettres, 15 April 1861.

Bulletin du Cercle Juif, (Montreal), June–July 1961, p. 2.

Centre-Matin, 31 May 1961.

Champomier, Jean. *"Le Jour."* *Dépêche-Eclair*, 7 March 1961.

Dalmas, André. "Six Romanciers." *Combat*, 2 March 1961, p. 7.

*Daoust, René. *"Le Jour."* *Relations* (Montreal), January 1962, p. 26.

Doubinsky, Nadi. *"Le Jour."* *Vie Juive*, May 1961.

Feuille d'Avis-Neuchâtel, 10 March 1961.

*Fontaine, André. *"Le Jour* d'Elie Wiesel." *Le Monde*, 27 May 1961, p. 9.

Gagnon, Laure. "Notes de lecture: Elie Wiesel, *Le Jour."* *Lettres Françaises*, 23 March 1961, p. 3.

Garzouzi, Calypso. "Livres nouveaux: *Le Jour* par Elie Wiesel." *Journal d'Alexandrie*, 25 July 1961.

Guillet, H. "Littérature: *Le Jour."* *Livres et Lectures*, April 1961.

Kiesel, Fréderic. "Trois livres du martyre juif." *Métrople*, 4 March 1961.

Leenhardt, A. "*Le Jour.*" *Bulletin du Centre Protestant d'Etudes et Documentation*, July 1961.

*Meyskah, Line. "Leur passé nous fait peur." *Tribune Juive* (Strasbourg), 3–9 March 1972, pp. 14–15.

Notes Bibliographiques, June 1961, pp. 545–46.

Pontramier, Pierre. "*Le Jour.*" *Les Fiches Bibliographiques*, 1961.

*Rabi. "La Fin d'un traumatisme." *La Terre Retrouvée*. 15 May 1961, p. 6.

*———. *Information Juive*, January 1962.

*Ramoni, James. "Le Jour s'est levé pour Elie Wiesel: Une étude clinique du désespoir." *Tribune de Genève*, 18 March 1961.

Selection des Libraires de France, May 1961.

Signes du Temps, August–September 1961, p. 27.

Le Soir de Bruxelles, 6 July 1967.

Van Dooren, J. J. "*Le Jour.*" *Le Soir*, 15 September 1961.

*Van Gerdinge, René. "La Résurrection des vaincus." *Témoin de la Vie*, 7 April 1961.

Wintzen, René. "Du crépuscule des dieux à la lumière du jour." *Témoignage Chrétien*, 2 June 1961.

Un Juif, aujourd'hui

Actuel Livres, 15 May 1977.

Ages, Arnold. "We Did Not Even Have the Strength To Cry." *Le Bulletin*, 29 September 1977.

"A la recherche de Jérusalem." *Brèche*, Summer 1977.

Ami d'Israël. January–February 1978.

Amitiés France-Israel, May 1977.

Arnaud-Matech, A. "*Un Juif, aujourd'hui.*" *La Raison Présente*, No. 44.

*Berg, Roger. "*Un Juif, aujourd'hui.*" *Le Journal des Communautés*, April 1977.

Berthier, Pierre. "L'Europe d'hier." *La Cité* (Brussels), 22 May 1977.

Le Bibliothècaire, No. 4, 1977.

Boly, Joseph. "*Un Juif, aujourd'hui.*" *Quatre Millions Quatre* (Brussels), 28 April 1977.

Bonhomme, Maya. "*Un Juif, aujourd'hui.*" *L'Atélier du Gué*, No. 5, 1977.

"Connaissance du Judaïsme." *Les Cahiers du Livre*, May 1977.

Eléments de Bibliographie, No. 112 (Ref. 892).

"Elie Wiesel croit." *Tribune Juive Hebdomadaire*, 23 June 1977.

*"Elie Wiesel, directeur de conscience." *Le Monde*, 6 May 1977.

Esprit, July–August 1977.

"Et que vous lisiez . . ." *Notes de Lectures de l'Alsace* 3 August 1978.

"Etre Juif, aujourd'hui, dans l'affirmative ou l'interrogation." *La Libre Belgique*, 10 August 1977.

Freneuil, Martine. "Réflexion sur la question juive." *Le Quotidien du Médecin*, 22 April 1977.

Fuchs, Eric. "*Un Juif, aujourd'hui.*" *Le Journal de Genève*, 19 July 1977.

Gonzales, M. "Interview d'Elie Wiesel." *Télérama*, 4 November 1977.

Guguenheim, M. G. "Réflexion sur le dernier livre d'Elie Wiesel: *Un Juif, aujourd'hui*." *Notre Communauté*, September–October 1977.

Halperin, Jean, "Die Grösste Judische Stimme." *La Revue Juive*, July 1977.

La Haute Marne Libérée, 4 June 1977.

Information Juive, April 1977.

*Kattan, Naïm. "La mystique juive d'hier et d'aujourd'hui." *Le Devoir* (Montreal), 8 August 1977.

La Liberté de l'Est, 24 June 1977.

Lire, June 1977.

*Lovsky, F. "*Un Juif, aujourd'hui*." *Bulletin du Centre Protestant d'Etudes et de Documentation*, July–August 1977.

Lure, Daisy de. "Le Pont d'Elie Wiesel." *Réforme*, 5 January 1977.

Marcon, Léa. "Nouveau chez votre libraire." *Tribune Juive* (Strasbourg), 24 April 1977.

Mutualité, June 1977.

Nemo, Philippe. "Réflexion sur la mémoire juive." *Nouvelles Littéraires*, 5 May 1977.

"New York ou Jérusalem." *L'Arche*, May 1977.

Notes Bibliographiques de Culture et Bibliothèques pour Tous, June 1977.

Nouaihac, A. M. "Elie Wiesel: *Un Juif, aujourd'hui*" *Service International de Documentation Judéo Chrétienne*, No 9 (1977).

Office Chrétien du Livre, May 1977.

Ouvrard, P. "*Un Juif, aujourd'hui*." *Impact*, No. 2 (1977).

Panaorama Aujourd'hui, June 1977.

"Le peuple Elu." *La Revue du Liban*, 30 July 1977.

Plazy, Gilles. "Elie Wiesel, une célébration de la mémoire." *Le Quotidien de Paris*, 1977.

"Le Point de vue du libraire sur *Un Juif, aujourd'hui*." *Tribune Juive* (Strasbourg), 9 June 1977.

Potin, Jacques. "La Condition Juive et Jérusalem." *La Croix*, 9 May 1977.

———. "Elie Wiesel" *Un Juif, aujourd'hui*." *Le Monde de la Bible*, November–December 1977.

La Quinzaine Littéraire, 16 April 1977.

"Une Rencontre avec François Mauriac." *Le Figaro*, 2 April 1977.

"Rencontres bibliques avec Elie Wiesel." (Enregistrées sur cassettes d'après les émissions sur France-Inter), *Nouvelles Littéraires*, 26 May 1977.

Renaud, Jacques. "Tout est mysticisme." *Le Devoir* (Montreal), 26 November 1977.

La Revue de la Wizo, April–June 1977.

"Rubrique religions." *Bibliographies de France*, January 1978.

"Sans haine ni revanche." *Elle*, 27 June 1977.

SIDIC Information [Société Internationale pour le Développement Industriel et Commercial], May 1977.

Techniques Nouvelles, September 1977.

"Témoignage: *Un Juif, aujourd'hui*, récits, essais et dialogues d'Elie Wiesel."
Informations catholiques et internationales, 15 July 1977.
Valeurs Actuelles, 23 May 1977.

Les Juifs du silence

Allouche, Félix. "Nouveaux ouvrages: *Les Juifs du silence.*" *L'Information d'Israël*,
14 December 1966.
"Antisémitisme en U.R.S.S.: *Les Juifs du silence.*" *Avenir du Luxembourg*, 1
November 1966.
Le Berry (Bourges), 5 October 1966.
*Bertrand, Joseph. "Elie Wiesel et les Juifs de Russie." *Le Phare Dimanche*, 4
December 1966.
Bulletin du Cercle Juif, (Montreal), November 1966, p. 3.
Cahiers Bernard Lazare, 10 December 1966.
Chavannes, B. P. "*Les Juifs du silence.*" *L'Ami d'Israël*, No. 3 (1967), pp. 59–62.
Chédel, André. "*Les Juifs du silence.*" *Coopération* (Basel), 12 December 1966.
———. "*Les Juifs du silence.*" *Journal Israëlite Suisse*, 25 November 1966, p. 69.
———. "Ces 'ombres,' les Juifs d'U.R.S.S." *Gazette de Lausanne*, 17–18 Decem-
ber 1966, p. 3.
Chrestien, Michel, "David roi d'Israël vit et vivra." *La Nation Française*, 19
January 1967.
Le Cri du Monde, November 1966.
*Dalbray, A. M. "*Les Juifs du silence.*" *AMIF*, November 1967, pp. 1769–72.
Dardel, Eric. "Les Juifs du silence." *Justificatif*, July–September 1967, pp.
75–76.
Doughi. "Chronique: *Les Juifs du silence.*" *L'Appel* (Supplément à *Parole
Ouvrière*), 16 December 1966.
Les Echos, 23 December 1966.
L'Ecole Menagère Française, 12 January 1967.
Eléments de Bibliographie, No. 25, p. 186.
"Est-il possible d'être Juif et Soviétique? Le romancier Elie Wiesel répond à
cette question." *Tribune de Lausanne*, 6 November 1966.
Les Fiches Bibliographiques, 1967.
*Fontaine, André. "Elie Wiesel: *Les Juifs du silence.*" *Le Monde*, 25 October 1966,
p. 5.
Forces Nouvelles, 13 August 1967.
Fournier, Eva. "*Les Juifs du silence*: Le premier témoignage sur les 2,200,000
israélites d'U.R.S.S." *France Soir*, 22 November 1966.
Gaspard, Armand. "Enquête et témoignage de l'écrivain Elie Wiesel pour les
'Juifs du silence' en Union Soviétique." *Tribune de Genève*, 17–18 December
1966.
Germain, F. "*Les Juifs du silence.*" *Etudes*, December 1966.
Hecht, Yvon. "Les Juifs du silence sont-ils condamnées par le silence des
Juifs?" *L'Express*, 28 October 1966.

Houriet, J. B. "Les Murailles du silence et de la foi." *Journal de Genève*, 24 May 1968.

Illustré Protestant, January 1967.

Jicey. "U.R.S.S.: Cri de détresse." *L'Observateur du Moyen-Orient et de l'Afrique*, 11 November 1966, p. 23.

Juvenal, 18 November 1966.

*Kahn, Lothar. "*The Jews of Silence*." *American Zionist* 57 (1967): 25.

La Libre Belgique, 2 December 1966.

"Le Livre du Jour: Les Juifs du silence." *Gazette de Lausanne*, 23 January 1967.

"Livres: Entre les lignes." *L'Express*, 19 June 1966.

Lovsky, F. "*Les Juifs du silence*. *"Bulletin du Centre Protestant d'Etudes et de Documentation*, May 1967.

Magazine Littéraire, 2 November 1966.

*Malka, Victor. "Face à face avec Elie Wiesel: Poète de la souffrance juive." (Interview.) *Réforme*, 1 April 1967, p. 11.

*Mandel, Arnold. "La Vie Littéraire: *Les Juifs du silence*." *Information Juive*, November 1966.

Marissel, André. "*Les Juifs du silence*." *Nouvelles Littéraires*, 10 November 1966.

*Martin-Chauffier, Louis. "Elie Wiesel et le mystère juif." *Le Figaro Littéraire*, 17 November 1966.

Maurice, Jack. "*Jews of Silence*." *The Jerusalem Post*, 30 December 1966

Neuveglise, Paule. "Un document sur la vie des juifs en U.R.S.S." *France-Soir*, 3 September 1960.

Nicol, Jean. "*Les Juifs du silence*." *Choisir*, January 1967, p. 17.

Notes Bibliographiques, February 1967.

Notre Communauté, December 1966.

"Nous ne ferons pas silence." *Bulletin de Nos Communautés*, 2 December 1966, p. 3.

Pétard, Jean-Claude. "*Les Juifs du silence*." *Jeunesse Information*, March 1967.

*Pulzer, P.G.J. "Western Europe." *International Affairs*, April 1968.

La Quinzaine Littéraire, 1–15 November 1966.

Roche, Emile. "L'An prochain à Jérusalem." *Combat*, 12 December 1966.

Salomon, Michel. "Un combat solitaire." *L'Arche*, October 1966, p. 21.

Schnir, M. R. "Cette année à Jérusalem." *Le Déporté*, November 1966.

Schwarz, Jean. "Causerie: *Les Juifs du silence*." *Trait d'Union*, December 1966.

*Singer, I. B. "A State of Fear: *The Jews of Silence*." *New York Times Book Review*, 8 January 1967, Sec. 7, p. 16.

Stern, Daniel. "*The Jews of Silence*." *Commonweal*, 12 May 1967, pp. 232–34.

Toulat, Jean. "De l'U.R.S.S. aux U.S.A., de l'Argentine à l'Angleterre, 13 millions de Juifs." *Informations Catholiques Internationales*, 15 January 1968, pp. 4–5.

Valeurs Actuelles, 29 December 1966.

Le Mendiant de Jérusalem

Albères, R. M. "Du côté de l'Orient." *Nouvelles Littéraires*, 24 October 1968.

Amer, Henri. "Elie Wiesel: *Le Mendiant de Jérusalem*, un conte plutôt qu'un roman." *Dépêche du Midi*, 11 December 1968.

Anex, Georges. "Le Fémina à Marguérite Yourcenar, le Médecis à Elie Wiesel." *Journal de Genève*, 26 October 1968.

Arnothy, Christine. "Elie Wiesel obtient le Prix Médicis." *Oise-Matin*, 26 November 1968.

"Avec son *Mendiant de Jérusalem* Elie Wiesel a évoqué la guerre des 'Six Jours.' " *Le Progrès*, 18 December 1968.

*Bandler, Michael J. "At the Jerusalem Wall; I Shout, and So I Am." *Christian Science Monitor*, 19 February 1970, Sec. B, p. 11.

*Baudy, Nicolas. "Deux écrivains devant le mur." *Les Nouveaux Cahiers*, Spring 1969, pp. 55–58.

*Baux, Dominique. "*Le Mendiant de Jérusalem*." *Etudes*, January 1969, pp. 130–32.

Beaupère, R. "*Le Mendiant de Jérusalem*." *Lumière*, July–October 1969, p. 123.

Berg, Roger. "*Le Mendiant de Jérusalem*." *Journal des Communautés*, 6 December 1968, p. 5.

Berthier, Pierre. "Après les prix." *La Cité* (Brussels), 14–15 December 1968, p. 13.

*Blot, Jean. "Elie Wiesel: *Le Mendiant de Jérusalem*." *Nouvelle Revue Française*, No. 33 (1969), pp. 617–19.

Bonnier, Henri. "Un monde de violence." *La Dépêche du Midi*, 18 October 1968.

Bournin, André. "Feminia et Médicis sans surprise. *La Nouvelle République de Centre-Ouest*, 26 November 1968.

Bouvier, Emile. "Chronique Littéraire." *Midi Libre*, 3 December 1968.

*Breton, Jean. "Interview: Elie Wiesel." *Micro-Caméra* January 1969, pp. 31–32.

Bulletin Bibliographique de l'Institut Pédagogique, May 1969.

Bulletin Critique du Livre Français, February 1969.

Le Bulletin des Lettres, 15 January 1969, p. 18.

Bulletin du Cercle Juif, (Montreal), November–December 1968, p. 5.

Cahiers Bernard Lazare, November 1968, p. 23

Cenni, René. "Elie Wiesel: 'Les histoires comme les êtres ont tous le même commencement . . .' " *Nice-Matin*, 4 January 1969.

*Chalon, Jean. "La Kabbale a joué en faveur d'Elie Wiesel." (Interview.) *Le Figaro Littéraire*, 2–8 December 1968, pp. 20–21.

Champury, E. "*Le Mendiant de Jérusalem*." *Couturier*, 26 February 1969.

*Cheigam, Rachel. "Il y a deux peuples admirables: le Tchèque et le Juif." (Interview.) *La Terre Retrouvé*, 1 November 1968, p. 12.

Colin-Simard, Annette. "Une légende qui a traversé les siècles." *Le Journal du Dimanche*, 1 December 1968.

Le Cri du Monde, January 1969.

La Croix, 27 November 1968.

Deman, Colette. "*Le Mendiant de Jérusalem.*" *Le Courrier* (Geneva), 13 December 1968.

Descargues, Pierre. "*Le Mendiant de Jérusalem.*" *Feuille d'Avis de Lausanne*, 26 November 1968.

"Deux votes bloquées au Médicis." *L'Eclair*, 26 November 1968.

"Devant le mur." *Tribune Juive*, 18 October 1968, p. 21.

"D'origine roumaine Elie Wiesel s'est fixé à New York après des études à la Sorbonne." *Le Télégramme de Brest et de l'Ouest*, 26 November 1968.

*Duranteau, Josane. "Les Contes de la sagesse." *Les Lettres Françaises*, 4–10 December 1968, p. 11.

———. "Le Femina et le Médicis ou une certaine distance." *Les Lettres Françaises*, 27 November 1968, p. 20.

Dutoit, Ernest. "Le Prix Médicis à Elie Wiesel pour *Le Mendiant de Jérusalem.*" *La Liberté* (Fribourg), 18 January 1969.

Les Echos, 29 November 1968.

Ecole, April 1969.

Elbaz, André. "Les Romanciers juifs français d'aujourd'hui." *Liberté*. November 1970.

"Elie Wiesel à la maison communautaire." *La Dépêche de Midi*, 12 December 1968.

"Elie Wiesel a parle de son livre, *Le Mendiant de Jérusalem.*" *Nice-Matin*, 19 December 1968.

"Elie Wiesel: l'obsession de transmettre." *Le Populaire du Centre*, 11 December 1968.

Fabre, M. "*Le Mendiant de Jérusalem.*" *Le Courrier*, 13 December 1968.

"Femina et Médicis sans surprise." *Combat*, 26 November 1968.

Femme d'Aujourd'hui, 5 February 1969.

France-Dufaux, Paule. "La Confrontation au pied du mur." *Le Soleil*, 14 January 1969.

Giron, Roger. "Elie Wiesel a écrit le roman de la guerre des Six Jours." *France-Soir*, 26 November 1968, p. 2.

*Hahn, Pierre. "Prix Médicis: Elie Wiesel." *Magazine Littéraire*, No. 24 (1969), pp. 19–20.

Halperin, Jean. "Elie Wiesel, Prix Médicis 1968." *Journal Israélite Suisse* (Zurich), 6 December 1968.

———. "Jérusalem, où tout homme devient pèlerin." *Journal de Genève*, 15 June 1968.

*Hertz, George. "*Le Mendiant de Jérusalem.*" *Tribune Juive*, 18 October 1968, p. 19.

Hisssel, J. "Elie Wiesel: *Le Mendiant de Jérusalem.*" *Eglise Vivante*, No. 1 (1969), p. 79.

Humanisme, 9 December 1968.

"Impressions de Conférence. Elie Wiesel: Son oeuvre est celle d'un poéte." *Centre-Presse*, 11 December 1968.

Industrie-Flash (Brussels), January 1969.

Information Juive, January 1968.

*Isaac, Dan. "All My Stories are True." *The Nation*, 16 March 1970, pp. 309–10.

Itinéraire, June 1969, pp. 215–216.

Jan, Yrènc. "Médicis: Devant le mur." *L'Aurore*, 26 November 1968.

Jardin, Claudine. " 'Chaque meurtre est un suicide.' " *Le Figaro*, 28 October 1968.

Jeunesse, December 1968.

*Jordan, Clive. "Bearing Witness." *New Statesman* 75 (1970): 95–96.

Jourdan, Bernard. "*Le Mendiant de Jérusalem*." *L'Ecole et la Vie*, February 1969, p. 39.

Kahn, Lothar. "*Le Mendiant de Jérusalem*." *Books Abroad*, July 1969.

Kattan, Naïm. "Ce mur où se recueillent bafoués et dépossédés de la terre." *Le Devoir*, 4 December 1968.

Kieffer, Rosemarie. "*Le Mendiant de Jérusalem*." *Luxembourger Wort*, 3 October 1968.

*Kleim, Paul. "Elie Wiesel devant le Mur reconquis." *Tribune de Genève*. 6 November 1968.

*———."Elie Wiesel: Une des voix les plus pures de ce temps." (Interview.) *Tribune de Genève*, 4 December 1968, p. 5.

*Kolbert, Jack. "Elie Wiesel: *Le Mendiant de Jérusalem*." *The French Review* 44 (1970): 189–190.

*Langer, Lawrence. "*A Beggar in Jerusalem*." *Woman's American Ort Reporter*, March–April 1970, p. 4.

Leonardini, Jean-Pierre. "Le Médicis à Elie Wiesel." *L'Humanité*, 26 November 1968.

*Leviant, Curt. "Elie Wiesel: A Soul on Fire." *Saturday Review*, 31 January 1970, pp. 25–28.

"La Littérature juive." *Objectif Midi* (Provence) 1er trimestre, 1969, p. 80.

Lovsky, F. "*Le Mendiant de Jérusalem*, *Bulletin du Centre Protestant d'Etudes et de Documentation*, February 1969.

Malka, Victor. "Elie Wiesel et le destin juif." *Réforme*, 26 October 1968.

Mandel, Arnold. "Les Lettres: *Le Mendiant de Jérusalem*." *Information Juive*, February 1969.

Martin-Chauffier, Jean. "Elie Wiesel est devenu américain de droit sans cesser d'être un écrivain français." *Le Figaro Littéraire*, 18–24 November 1968, pp. 22–23.

Mattei, Claude. "Actualité israélienne: Eternité israélite." *Le Provencal*, 1 December 1968.

"Le Médicis à Elie Wiesel." *Le Courrier de la Saone-et-Loire*, 26 November 1968.

*Memmi, Albert. "*Le Mendiant de Jérusalem*." *Le Nouvel Observateur*, 25 November–1 December 1968, p. 41.

"*Le Mendiant de Jérusalem* d'Elie Wiesel: un 'petit médicis' au style haché et au récit manquant d'unité." *La Lanterne* (Brussels), 26 November 1968, p. 10.

Mespouille, José. "*Le prochain Renaudot? Le Mendiant de Jérusalem*." *Le Courrier de l'Escaut*, 22 October 1968.

Michel, Pierre-Gérard." *Le Mendiant de Jérusalem*." *Le Berry Républicain*, 28 November 1968.

*Misrahi, Robert. "*Le Mendiant de Jérusalem.*" *La Quinzaine Littéraire*, 1–15 December 1968, pp. 4–6.

*Moeykens, D. "*Le Mendiant de Jérusalem*, Prix Médicis." *La Revue Nouvelle*, January 1969, pp. 104–5.

Le Mois Médical et Littéraire, No. 2 (1969): 48–50.

Monnoyer, Maurice. 'La Guerre et la paix en Israël." *Nord-Eclair*, 11 December 1968.

Neuveglise, Paule. "Elie Wiesel (Prix Médicis) a appris le français à 15 ans en sortant des bagnes nazis." *France-Soir*, 27 November 1968.

Notices Bibliographiques, No. 1 (1969): 14–16.

*"Nous sommes tous des mendiants." *La Terre Retrouvée*, 15 February 1969.

*Onimus, Jean. "Chroniques des romans." *La Table Ronde*, February 1969, pp. 136–37.

Pas à Pas, December 1968.

Politi, Maurice. "La Vie des livres: *Le Mendiant de Jérusalem.*" *L'Information d'Israël*, 29 November 1968.

Le Populaire du Centre, 26 November 1968.

"Pour assumer l'Histoire." *Pourquoi Pas?* (Brussels), 26 December 1968.

Poy, J. du. "Le Prix Médicis à Elie Wiesel." *Journal de Corse*, December 1968.

"Les Prix littéraires." *La République du Centre*, 26 November 1968.

*Rabi. "Elie Wiesel, le témoin." *L'Arche*, November 1968, p. 68.

———. "Le dur métier de juger." *L'Arche*, January 1968, pp. 56–57.

*Rawicz, Piotr. "Médicis: Elie Wiesel, un enfant de genocide." *Le Monde*, 26 November 1968, p. 28.

Le Républicain Lorrain, 26 November 1968.

"Rescapé d'Auschwitz." *Le Figaro*, 26 November 1968.

La Revue Encyclopédique Juive, November 1968.

Reynaud, S. "*Le Mendiant de Jérusalem.*" *La France Agricole*, 10 October 1969.

* Ricaumont, Jacques de. "Le Prix Médicis à Elie Wiesel: Changer le malheur." (Interview.) *Nouvelles Littéraires*, 28 November 1968, p. 3.

Rolin, Gabrielle, "Femina et Médicis: Accord parfait." *Les Nouvelles Littéraires*, 28 November 1968.

"La Saison des prix." *La République des Pyrénées*, 26 November 1968.

"La Saison des prix littéraires." *La Dordogne Libre*, 26 November 1968.

Saporta, Marc. "Pourquoi être américain?" *Communiqué de Presse, Services Américains d'Information et de Relations Culturelles*, No. 159.

Secrétaires d'Aujourd'hui, February 1969.

Shavey, Pierre. "Lu pour vous." *Lion*, March 1969, p. 18.

Simon, Pierre-Henri. "*Le Mendiant de Jérusalem.*" *Le Monde*, 23 November 1968.

———. "La Méditation des mendiants." *Le Devoir* (Montreal), 30 November 1968.

Le Soir, 24 November 1968.

*Sperber, Manès. "*A Beggar in Jerusalem.*" *New York Times Book Review*, 25 January 1970, pp. 1, 34.

Stiglauer, H. "*Le Mendiant de Jérusalem.*" *Les Fiches Bibliographiques*, 1968.

La Table Ronde, February 1969.

Tauxe, Henri-Charles. "Moments littéraires." *La Gazette de Lausanne*, 30 November 1968.

Thiriet,Yolande. "Le passé conjugé au présent." *Le Comptois*, 26 November 1968.

"Trois romanciers et un théme: Israël." *La Croix*, 29 September 1968.

La Voix de la Résistance, January 1969, p. 5.

La Nuit

*Alvarez, A., "The Literature of the Holocaust." *Commentary*, November 1964, pp. 65–69.

Bulletin (International Writers Association for the UN), June/July 1959, p. 17.

Deford, Miriam Allen. "His God Was Found Wanting." *The Humanist*, 21: (1961): 122–23.

Feigelson, Ralph. *"La Nuit."* Paris *La Presse Nouvelle*, 31 October–1 November 1959, p. 1.

Finn, James. "Terribly Alone in a World without God." *Commonweal*, 6 January 1961, pp. 391–92.

Heimler, Eugene. "Funeral of Faith." *London Jewish Chronical*, 16 September 1960, p. 17.

Grusd, Edward. "Two Views of Auschwitz." *National Jewish Monthly* 75 (1961): 43.

*Lerner, May. "The Guilty." *New York Post*, 24 June 1963, p. 27.

*Mauriac, François. "Un enfant juif." *Le Figaro Littéraire*, 7 June 1958, pp. 1, 4.

*Neher, André. "Elie Wiesel: *La Nuit*." *Evidences*, March 1959, p. 48.

*Paull, Irene. "The Night of Nazism." *Jewish Currents*, April 1961, pp. 39–40.

Samuels, Gertrude. "When Evil Closed In." *New York Times Book Review*, 13 November 1960, p. 20.

Les Portes de la forêt

Berg, Roger. *"Les Portes de la forêt." Journal des Communautés*, 26 February 1965.

*Bertrand, Joseph. "Elie Wiesel: *Les Portes de le forêt*." *Le Phare*, 28 February 1965.

Bulletin Critique du Livre Français XIX (November 1964), 1105.

Bulletin du Cercle Juif (Montreal), November 1964, p. 3.

Bulletin de l'Institut Pédagogique National, 1964.

Cahiers Bernard Lazare, November–December 1964.

*Daiches, David. "After Such Knowledge." *Commentary*, December 1965, pp. 105–10.

*Descargues,Pierre. "Dieu inculpé de meurtre par quatre talmudistes dans un camp de concentration." *Tribune de Lausanne*, 13 September 1964.

Elman, Richard. "Betrayed into Living." *New York Times Book Review*, 12 June 1966, p. 5.

Feuille d'Avis de Neuchâtel, 17 November 1964.

Le Figaro Littéraire, 1 October 1964.

*Fremont-Smith, Eliot. "The Song and the Dagger." *New York Times*, May 23, 1966, p. 39.

Guissard, Lucien. "La Rentrée dans le roman, esclaves, guerriers et proscrits." *La Croix de Belgique*, 27 September 1964.

*Halperin,Irving. "Suffering and Fervor in Wiesel's *Gates* of the Forest" *Jewish Book Annual*, 27 (1969): 55–61.

Halperin,Jean. "*Les Portes de la forêt.*" *L'Information Juive*, November 1964.

*Kattan, Naïm. "Les Lettres étrangères: *Les Portes de la forêt* d'Elie Wiesel." *Le Devoir* (Montreal), 31 December 1964.

Kleim, Paul. "Invitation á un voyage sans confort." *Tribune de Genève*, 27 November 1964.

*Lacombe, Lia. "Rire pour les enfants." *Les Lettres Françaises*, 18 November 1964, p. 3.

Lectures pour Tous, November 1964.

Le Hurle, Louis. "Romans divers." *Echo de Lauvion*, 1 November 1964.

La Libre Belgique, 18 September 1964.

Marissel, André. "Visionnaires et accusateurs." *Réforme*, 2 November 1964, p. 12.

Mazellier, O. "*Les Portes de la forêt.*" *Bulletin du Centre Protestant d'Etudes et de Documentation*, March 1965.

Notes Bibliographiques, January 1964.

Notices Bibliographiques, 1 February 1965, p. 9.

Politi, Maurice. "Elie Wiesel poursuit sa quête de l'absolu." *L'Information d'Israël*, November 1969, p. 6.

———. "La Quête d'Elie Wiesel." *La Terre Retrouvée*, 15 November 1964, p. 8.

*"A propos des *Portes de la forêt*—Elie Wiesel: 'Nous sommes des déracinés dans le temps et dans l'espace." n.d., October 1964, pp. 12–18. (Document available in archives of Les Editions du Seuil, Paris.)

"Proscrit et prophète." *Gazette de Lausanne*, 13 October 1964.

Roberge, Henri. "*Les Portes de la Forêt.*" *Lectures*. April 1966, pp. 214–15.

*Saporta, Marc. "Le Mur est partout." *L'Express*, 2–8 November 1964, p. 58.

*Simon, Pierre-Henri. "La Vie littéraire: Lyrisme, prophétisme, simplicité." *Le Monde*, 28 October 1964.

*Sungolowsky, Joseph. "*Les Portes de la forêt.*" *The French Review*, 11 (1966): 432–33.

Van Gerdinge, René. "*Les Portes de la forêt.*" *Lumières*, 7 November 1964.

*Wain, John. "The Insulted and the Injured." *The New York Review of Books*, 28 July 1966, pp. 22–23.

Willy, Renée. "Vos meilleurs amis, les livres." *L'Action Mutualiste*, 3 ᵉᵐᵉ trimestre, 1964.

Le Serment de Kolvillág

Ami d'Israël, No. 4 (1973).

Berg, Roger. "Les Livres des Juifs en Europe Centrale." *Journal des Communautés*, 13 July 1973.

Berthier,Pierre. "Anvers 1809, Kolvillàg." *La Cité* (Brussels), 27 May 1973.

Boly, Joseph. "Elie Wiesel: La littérature juive d'expression française." *Rénovation* (Brussels), 1 November 1973, p. 15.

Bulletin du Cercle Juif (Montreal), March 1974, pp. 20–21.

Butheau, Robert. "Revue des livres." *Le Progrès.* 12 August 1973.

Cahiers Bernard Lazare, November 1973, p. 46.

Cahiers du Livre Chrétien, August–September 1973.

Christianisme, 28 June 1973.

La Croix, 12 December 1973.

*Dame, Enid. "The Vital Connection." *Congress Bi-Weekly*, 8 February 1974, pp. 18–19.

*Edelman, Lily. "A Conversation with Elie Wiesel." (Interview.) *National Jewish Monthly*, November 1973, pp. 5–15.

Eléments de Bibliographie, November 1973.

"Elie Wiesel: C'est pour oublier qu'on parle.'" *Techniques Nouvelles* (Brussels), November 1973, p. 29.

Fiske, Edward. "Avenging Gods,Human Wolves." *New York Times*, 16 January 1974, p. 37.

France-Soir, 8 August 1973.

Haymann, Emmanuel. "Kolvillàg ne témoigne plus." *Tribune Juive* (Strasbourg), 5 July 1973.

Hruby, K. "*Le Serment de Kolvillàg.*" *SIDIC* [Société Internationale pour le Développement Industriel el Commercial] 6 No. 3 (1973).

Information Juive, September 1973.

Kahn, Lothar, "*Le Serment de Kolvillàg.*" *Books Abroad* (Norman, Okla.), 19 May 1974.

*Kleim, Paul. "Histoire d'un pogrom." *La Tribune de Genève*, 25 August 1974.

*Launay, Janine, Schwarcz, Judith and Serrano, Lucienne. "In Conversation with Elie Wiesel." (Interview.) *Centerpoint* (New York), Spring 1975, pp. 63–66.

Le Clec'h, Guy. "Le Livre du silence." *La Terre Retrouvée*, 1 June 1973.

Lectures pour tous, September 1973.

Lovsky, F. "*Le Serment de Kolvillàg.*" *Bulletin du Centre Protestant d'Etudes et de Documentation*, December 1973.

*Malka, Victor. "Entretien avec Elie Wiesel: 'Nous sommes tous des survivants.'" *Le Monde*, 14 June 1973.

———. "*Le Serment de Kolvillàg* d'Elie Wiesel." *Nouvelles Littéraires*, 25 June 1973.

Mandel, Arnold. "Livres: Clôture et ouverture." *L'Arche*, 2 November 1973, p. 28.

*Martin-Chauffier, Jean. "L'Impossible loi du silence." *Le Figaro*, 12 May 1973, p. 16.

Le Méridional-La France, 19 August 1973.

Montalbetti, Jean. "Et si Dieu était coupable?" *Le Point*, September 1973.

Notre Communauté, June 1973.

Le Nouvel Observateur, 13 August 1973.

Panorama Aujourd'hui, September 1973.

Pasquier, Camille. "Dans la nuit contre la nuit." *Témoignage Chrétien*, 2 August 1973.

Petitdemange, G. "*Le Serment de Kolvillàg.*" *Etudes*, October 1973.

Le Républicain Lorrain, 3 June 1973.

La Révue Encyclopédique Juive, April-May 1974.

*Rittel Regina. "Du medium à l'écrivain." *Les Nouveaux Cahiers*, Fall 1973, pp. 64–66.

———. "Le Silence et la parole." *L'Arche*, May 1973, pp. 64–65.

*Stern, Daniel. "The Word Testifies for the Dead." *The Nation*, 218 (1974): 24–26.

Télérama, 16 June 1973.

Tribune de Lausanne, 17 June 1973.

"La Ville ravagée par le pogrom, Elie Wiesel: *Le Serment de Kolvillàg.*" *La Croix*, 3 June 1973.

*Vogel, Dan. "When Silence Is Criminal." *Jerusalem Post*, 1 April 1974.

*Ziegler, Marie-Claire. " 'Ne sommes-nous pas le peuple de la mémoire?' " *Journal de Genève*, 22 July 1973.

Trilogy: La Nuit, L'Aube, Le Jour

L'Arche, January 1961, p. 46.

Le Bulletin du Livre, November 1969, p. 36.

Halperin, Irving. "Postscript to Death." *Commonweal*, 13 March 1964, pp. 713–15.

Homme et Techniques, June 1970.

Levy, Henry W. "Elie Wiesel: The Man and the Writer." *Pioneer Woman*, January 1973, pp. 6–7.

*Monnoyer, Maurice. "La Mort à sa porte." *Nord-Eclair*, 9 January 1970.

"*La Nuit, L'Aube, Le Jour.*" La Croix de Belgique, 8 March 1970.

La Quinzaine Littéraire, 16-30 November 1969, p. 30.

"Une Trilogie: *La Nuit, L'Aube, Le Jour.*" *Dialogue* (Montreal) 1 (1962): 4.

*Weinberg, Henry. "Elie Wiesel: *La Nuit, L'Aube, Le Jour.*" *The French Review*, 44 (1971): 975–76.

La Ville de la chance

*Aubery, Pierre. "Elie Wiesel: *La Ville de la chance.*" *The French Review*, XXXVII, No. 6 (May 1964), 703–704.

Berthier, Pierre. "Un roman Juif." *La Cité*, (Brussels), 6 October 1962.

Bliven, Naomi. Review of *The Town Beyond the Wall*. *New Yorker Magazine*, 9 January 1965, pp. 115–16.

*Bortoli, Georges. "Elie Wiesel a vu Dieu mourir à Buchenwald." *Le Figaro Littéraire*, 15 June 1965.

Bulletin Critique du Livre Français. 18 (1963): 212–13.

Bulletin du Centre Protestant d'Etudes et de Documentation, January 1963.

Bulletin du Cercle Juif (Montreal), November 1962.

*Célerier, Alain. "Elie Wiesel: Prix Rivarol." *Combat*, 6 June 1963, p. 8.

Christian-Yves. "Notes: *La Ville de la chance*." *Arts*, 2 January 1963.

"Dans la tête des autres." *Libération*, 6 November 1962.

Defossez, M. P. "Plaisir de lire." *La Croix de l'Est*, 20 January 1963.

Delaunay, Janine. "Elie Wiesel: Prix Rivarol, 1963: 'Il y a des choses qu'on ne peut écrire qu'en français.' " *Libération*, 2 June 1963.

*Denhaive, Jean. "Dans le sillage de Camus: *La Ville de la chance*." *Vers l'Avenir*, 6–9 October 1962.

*Descargues, Pierre. "Elie Wiesel le polyglotte: Pourquoi écrit-il en français?" *Tribune de Lausanne*, 9 June 1963.

Doubinski, Nadi. "*La Ville de la chance*." *La Vie Juive*, February–March 1964, pp. 28–29.

Drouvet, Jacques-Paul. "Cinq minutes avec Elie Wiesel, laureat du Prix Rivarol." *Semaine Provence*, 7 June 1963.

Fabre, A. "*La Ville de la chance*." *L'Education Nationale*, 28 February 1963.

Friedman, Joseph. "The Shame of Survival." *Saturday Review*, 25 July 1964, p. 26.

Friedman, Norman. "God versus Man in the Twentieth Century." *The Reconstructionist*, 28 October 1966, pp. 21–28.

Ginsbourg, M. "Lectures: *La Ville de la chance*." *AMIF*, January 1963, 105–12.

Halperin, Jean. "*La Ville de la chance*." *Trait d'Union*, February 1963, pp. 39–40.

L'Information d'Israël, 5 July 1963.

Journal de Jura, 25–26 January 1964.

Kalda, A. "Trois bon prix." *Arts*, 5–11 June 1963.

*Lacombe, Lia. "Elie Wiesel: 'Les autres existent tellement que si on sait les écouter, on peut les incorporer à nous. . .' " *Les Lettres Françaises*, 16–22 May 1963.

*Laporte, Marc. "Elie Wiesel: D'Auschwitz à Hiroshima." *L'Express*, 6 June 1963, p. 34.

Malrieux, Jean. "*La Ville de la chance*." *Cahiers du Sud*, April 1964.

Mandel, Arnold. "*Livres d'amis*." *L'Arche*, October 1962, pp. 53–54.

*Mauriac, François. "Le Bloc-Notes de François Mauriac." *Le Figaro Littéraire*, 8 June 1963, p. 20.

Notes Bibliographiques, December 1962.

Notices Bibliographiques, 7 August 1963.

Nouvelles Littéraires, 27 September 1962.

Politi, Maurice. "*La Ville de la chance*: Le nouveau roman d'Elie Wiesel." *L'Information d'Israël*, 2 November 1962.

Rabi. "Volante mémoire." *La Terre Retrouvée*, 1 November 1962.

Ramoni, James. "*La Ville de la chance*." *Tribune de Genéve*, 23 December 1962.

Reichman, Edgar. "L'Impossible retour." *Democratie*, 14 March 1962.

Sénart, Philippe. "Retour aux sources." *Combat*, 6 December 1962.

*Simon, Pierre-Henri. "L'Oeuvre d'Elie Wiesel, prix Rivarol." *Le Monde*, 19 June 1963, p. 11.

Smet, Michel de. "Géographie sentimentale." *Le Soir*, 17 January 1963.

"Un Témoin couronné." *Nouvelles Littéraires*, 6 June 1963.

Vandorme, Mona. "*La Ville de la chance.*" *Le Peuple* (Brussels), 9 October 1962.

Wintzen, René. "*La Ville de la chance.*" *Témoignage Chrétien*, 12 October 1962.

Ziegler, Jean. "Elie Wiesel, qui fut cet enfant juif." *Journal de Genève*, 20 July 1963.

Zalmen ou la folie de Dieu

"Bibliographie: Les Juifs en U.R.S.S." *L'Ami d'Israël*, No. 3 (1969), pp. 61–62.

Bulletin Critique du Livre Français, 23 (1968): 606.

Bulletin de l'Institut Pédagogique, February 1969.

Coin, Marianne. "Vient de paraître." *La Terre Retrouvée*, 1 December 1968, p. 5.

Combat, 17 March 1968.

Delfosse, Louis. "Chez les Juifs du silence: Zalmen." *Le Courier de l'Escaut* (Tournai), 30 May 1968.

"Elie Wiesel abord le théâtre." *Tribune de Lausanne*, 7 April 1968.

"Elie Wiesel parle de la souffrance d'Israël." *Journal des Communautés* (Entretien.) 28 June 1968, pp. 1–2.

"Elie Wiesel: Une grande voix juive contemporaine.", *L'Alsace*, 22 February 1966.

Ellenberger, Michel. "*Zalmen.*" *Les Fiches Bibliographiques*, 1968.

Le Figaro, 13 March 1968.

Ganter, Edmond. " 'Suis-je le gardien de mon frère?' " *Le Courrier* (Geneva), 25 October 1968.

Gazette de Lausanne, 6–7 April 1968.

Gussow, Mel. "Wiesel Play gives Voice to Soviet Jews." *New York Times*, 10 May, 1974.

Information Juive, October 1968.

*Isaac, Dan. "Turning Wine into Grape Juice." *Village Voice* (New York), 13 June 1974.

Justificatif Cahier-Théâtre Louvain, No. 6 (1968–1969), pp. 36–37.

*Kerr, Walter. "In Russia He Heard No One Cry Out." *New York Times*, May 26, 1974.

*Leviant, Curt. "A Voice from the Silence." *Midstream*, August–September 1974, pp. 91–93.

La Libre Belgique, 26 April 1968.

Livres et Lectures, November 1968.

Mandel, Arnold. "Elie Wiesel, Dramaturge." *L'Arche*, April 1968.

*————. "Elie Wiesel: *Zalmen ou la folie de Dieu.*" *Information Juive*, April 1968, p. 8.

Mercoeur, Antoine. "Les Ondes inspirées." *Nouvelles Littéraires*, 18 April 1968, p. 2.

*Michel, Marcelle. "France-Culture: *Zalmen ou la folie de Dieu.*" *Le Monde*, 8 March 1968, p. 5.

*————. "Drame: *Zalmen ou la folie de Dieu.*" *Le Monde*, 2 April 1968, p. 16.

Sainer, Arthur. "The Jews Cry for Help But There Is No Help." *Village Voice* (New York), 29 March 1976, p. 107.

*Saporta, Marc. "Vertu de la folie." *La Quinzaine Littéraire*, 1–15 May 1968, pp. 12–13.

Tribune Juive, (Strasbourg), 26 April 1968.

Zendel, José. "Zalmen: Est-ce pour rien?" *Les Cahiers Littéraires*, 10–23 March 1968, pp. 18–19.

*Ziegler, Marie-Claire. "Elie Wiesel: Un témoin de l'horreur." *La Gazette Littéraire*, 6–7 July 1968.

Index